D1117348

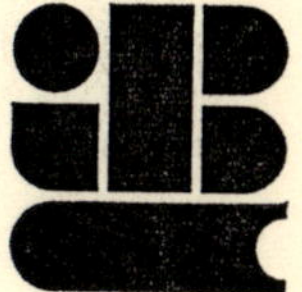

PROBLEM DRINKERS

A National Survey

Don Cahalan

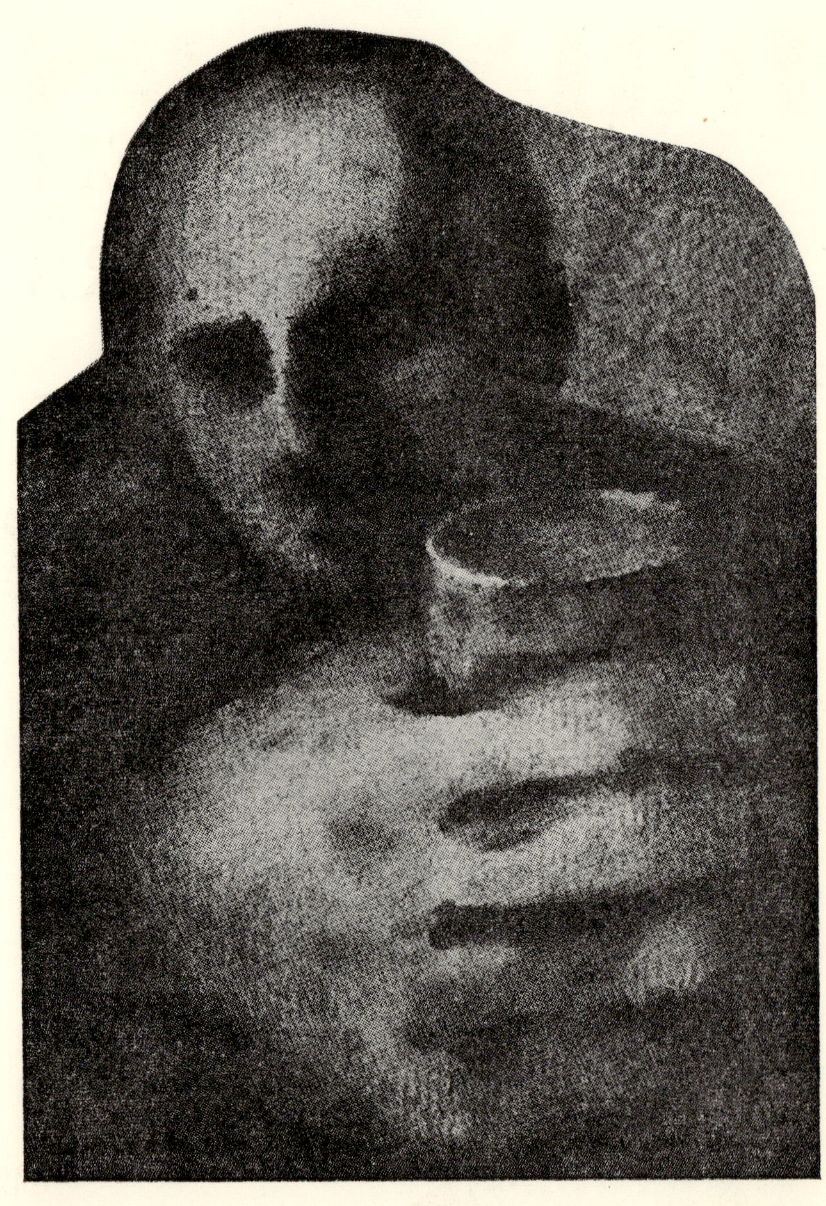

PROBLEM DRINKERS

Jossey-Bass Inc., Publishers
615 Montgomery Street • San Francisco • 1970

PROBLEM DRINKERS
A National Survey
by Don Cahalan

Jossey-Bass, Inc., Publishers
615 Montgomery Street
San Francisco, California 94111

Library of Congress Catalog Card Number 73-133617

International Standard Book Number ISBN 0-87589-080-6

Manufactured in the United States of America
Composed and printed by York Composition Company, Inc.
Bound by Chas. H. Bohn & Co., Inc.

JACKET DESIGN BY WILLI BAUM, SAN FRANCISCO

FIRST EDITION

Code 7028

THE JOSSEY-BASS BEHAVIORAL SCIENCE SERIES

General Editors

WILLIAM E. HENRY, *University of Chicago*

NEVITT SANFORD, *Wright Institute, Berkeley*

Preface

Problem Drinkers is about people's drinking problems and does not use alcoholism as a central concept. It presents an analysis of the various types of problems in relation to alcohol which develop in the lives of Americans, describing which subgroups are most susceptible to problems associated with drinking. The data are drawn from a new national survey—the first national probability sample ever conducted on the prevalence of alcohol-connected problems—and a review of prior studies bearing on the subject.

The national survey on which *Problem Drinkers* is based was conducted in 1967 through intensive personal interviews with 1,359 adults representative of the total population of the United States, exclusive of Alaska and Hawaii. This survey was the second stage in a longitudinal series of studies conducted by the Social Research Group, The George Washington University, and supported by a series of grants from the National Institute of Mental Health. A prior stage, in which a national sample including the same respondents was interviewed in 1964–1965, served as the basis of a descriptive monograph (Cahalan, Cisin, and Crossley, 1969) on detailed patterns of drinking behavior among the many subgroups within the adult population. A final stage, projected for about 1975, will permit a more detailed analysis of changes in drinking behavior and problems over a ten-year time span.

The research program was begun in 1960 under the direction of Ira H. Cisin and Wendell Lipscomb in the Department of Public Health, State of California, as a San Francisco area series of studies which were continued under the direction of Genevieve Knupfer in 1962, when Cisin initiated a series of community and national surveys under the aegis of The George Washington University. The two series of studies were rejoined under my direction in 1968. Appendix B lists the studies conducted and the publications which have emerged to date from the two series of studies.

Recent surveys in this same series (Cahalan, Cisin, and Crossley, 1969) have shown that the vast majority of adult Americans drink at least occasionally, and that most of them appear to encounter little in the way of problems as a consequence. However, this analysis indeed bears out the actuarial prediction that a substantial number of Americans should be found to have at least short-lived problems connected with drinking at some time during their lives, since so very many drink at least occasionally and since it appears so very many people in our mobile society have problems at least occasionally—thus yielding a fairly high probability that many will encounter problems related to drinking.

For further perspective on the findings in *Problem Drinkers,* the reader is referred to the related Cahalan, Cisin, and Crossley (1969) monograph, for that work underscores the conclusion that drinking per se and problem drinking are not necessarily closely related. That monograph bears out the indications of earlier studies that there are a number of subgroups in America in which most members drink fairly often but in which relatively few drink heavily, and that there are other groups with high rates of heavy drinkers in relation to the proportion of those drinking at all. While in the aggregate the number of problem drinkers is large enough to be of considerable public health and social concern, it must be remembered that at present problem drinking is distinctly a minority phenomenon.

Problem Drinkers does not pretend to provide any sweeping solutions to the many perplexing and controversial issues concerning ways of reducing the rather considerable numbers of persons who misuse alcohol to the disservice of themselves, their families and friends and co-workers, and society in general. However, it is hoped that the analysis may help to clear away some of the mythology and other underbrush which have cluttered the field of alcoholism for many a generation. This research was planned more to raise questions than to provide answers; but it is hoped that future pursuit of answers may contribute to better programs for preventive public health and for the treatment of people with drinking problems.

Special appreciation is due the following persons, as well as the many other staff members in the Washington and Berkeley offices of the Social Research Group who made contributions to the study: Ira H. Cisin, professor of Sociology and director of the Social Research Group, lent professional encouragement and statistical counsel throughout, as well as helpful editorial suggestions.

Robin Room had a primary role in shaping the definitions of drinking problems, as well as in the review of past alcohol studies and in the analysis of the data from the new national survey. Helen M. Crossley made many contributions to the planning of the national survey on which this study is based. A significant legacy to the present study was contributed by my predecessor as project director for the Drinking Practices Study in Berkeley, Genevieve Knupfer, and by her colleagues Walter Clark and Robin Room, whose prior San Francisco area studies provided many of the underpinnings for the national survey. Nathan Rosenberg, research psychologist in the National Center for Prevention and Control of Alcoholism, NIMH, provided helpful suggestions on research content and analytic procedures. Richard Jessor, Institute of Behavioral Science, University of Colorado, furnished information that made it possible to replicate some of the principal features of his tri-ethnic Colorado community study (Jessor *et al.*, 1968) of alcohol-related problems.

I dedicate the book to Ellen Cahalan—prodder, listener, sympathizer, quibbler, critic, naysayer, agent provocateur, meal-fixer, copyreader, devil's advocate, encourager, tea-fixer, general fixer, and always partner.

Berkeley, California
September 1970

DON CAHALAN

Note on Supplementary Materials

The following additional documentary information, "Supplementary Tables and Scoring Procedures," totaling approximately sixty pages, are available from the author upon reimbursement for cost of reproduction: Procedures for development of problem drinking scores (in detail); development of major social-psychological variables (details on exact content of items); development of reduced inventories of items for application in later surveys (through use of multiple correlation measures, applied to both problem-drinking categories and items in social-psychological variables); approximately fifteen pages of miscellaneous tables of primarily technical interest, as cited in the text of this book.

Contents

PROBLEM DRINKERS

A National Survey

I Problem Drinking vs. Alcoholism

There is little debate on whether the misuse of alcohol constitutes a serious problem in most Western countries, but there is much confusion and uncertainty on what to do about it. In Puritan times, the drunkard was considered a moral leper, to be confined to the stocks and publicly ridiculed to serve as an example to the passerby. During the industrial revolution, the forces of temperance banded together to combat the evils of demon rum through prayer and the Anti-Saloon Lobby (Gusfield, 1962), with their activities culminating in that "noble experiment," the Prohibition era. Since the repeal of Prohibition, the attempts to reduce drunkenness and the economic, social, and physical effects of excessive use of alcohol have taken a more scientific and humanitarian (as opposed to moralistic) turn. As a result, research and writing on all aspects of alcohol, from its effects on fruit flies and mice to its effects on men and society, have grown apace; the number of professional writings on alcohol has grown to the more than seventy thousand items in the master catalog at the Rutgers Center of

Alcohol Studies (Keller, 1968). Yet the genuine progress in mitigating problems related to alcohol of recent years does not seem to be at all in proportion to the efforts expended upon alcohol programs by the medical profession, the other healing arts, social agencies, and legal institutions. Thus a stock-taking is in order, to see whether a redirection of effort in the field of alcohol problems may be helpful.

In such an emotion-laden and important social area as the abuse of alcohol, there are bound to be differences of opinion on which methods of treatment are best. The current rather popular conception of alcoholism as a "disease" has led to certain improvements in the lot of the derelict drunk, who is less frequently thrown in jail to sober up. But alcoholics labeled as such under the disease concept are still considered poor risks as patients by many in the medical fraternity; thus it appears that the disease approach to alcohol problems has not as yet made material inroads on solving the problems. Hence many in the medical profession, as well as others in public health and the other healing arts, readily concede that a new or supplementary approach to drinking problems is in order.

Drinking itself is statistically normal behavior in the United States: the 1964–1965 George Washington University survey found 68 per cent of the adult population saying they drink at least once a year, and only 22 per cent saying they had never drunk alcoholic beverages. Seventy-seven per cent of the men and 60 per cent of the women drank at least once a year; and among the men, a majority in each age group from twenty-one to sixty-five drank at least once a month (Cahalan, Cisin, and Crossley, 1969, p. 22). However, the same study found that "heavy drinking" (somewhat arbitrarily defined) is indulged in by a relatively small minority. Thus we should expect that the attitude of the general public in the United States is favorable or at least permissive toward drinking in moderation, but unfavorable toward persistent heavy drinking or loss of control in drinking, "problem drinking," or "alcoholism."

The number of "alcoholics" in the United States has been estimated by Keller (1962, p. 326) as totaling about 4.5 million. The proportion of "problem drinkers" according to one rather arbitrary (but statistically useful) definition later in this book was found to be about 9 per cent (although plausible alternative definitions yielded a range of from about 3 per cent to 30 per cent). Thus the prevalence of alcoholism and problem drinking can be interpreted as being rather closely congruent or as being in wide disagreement, depending upon the necessarily arbitrary definitions which one prefers to use. However, comparing estimates of alcoholics and problem drinkers is a rather futile exercise, because the concepts of alcoholism and problem drinking are not very similar, do not necessarily apply to the same sufferers, and may have quite different implications for etiology and preventive public health measures and treatment.

One official definition of alcoholism is that of the World Health Organization (1952): "Alcoholics are those excessive drinkers whose dependence upon alcohol has attained such a degree that it shows a noticeable mental disturbance or an interference with their bodily and mental health, their interpersonal relations, and their smooth social and economic functioning; or who show the prodromal signs of such developments." Seeley (1959) has criticized this definition on the grounds of vagueness, lack of rigor, and lack of operational significance. Perhaps the greatest limitation of this definition is that it has lent itself too readily to a rigid and narrow definition of alcoholism as a disease. It is true that some authorities (notably Jellinek, 1952 and 1960a, and Keller, 1962) have distinguished between specific types of alcoholism. However, the net effect of well-intentioned efforts to establish some specific types of alcoholism as constituting a disease has led to popularization of the concept of alcoholism as constituting an either-or, all-or-nothing, disease entity—with adverse inhibiting effects upon openness of inquiry into research or treatment.

A review of the writings of some of the leading authorities of the recent past demonstrates that some of them have tried mightily to qualify their concepts and definitions of alcoholism, in keeping with the real complexity of the subject. Thus Jellinek, in one of his fairly early formulations (1952), very carefully made a distinction between two categories of alcoholics, namely alcohol addicts and habitual symptomatic excessive drinkers, referring to the latter as nonaddictive alcoholics, and saying that "strictly speaking, the disease conception attaches to the alcohol addicts only, and not to the habitual symptomatic excessive drinkers" (p. 674). He pointed out that "the disease conception of alcohol addiction does not apply to the excessive drinking, but solely to the 'loss of control' which occurs in only one group of alcoholics and then only after many years of excessive drinking" (p. 674), adding that "the fact that many excessive drinkers drink as much as or more than the addict for thirty or forty years without developing loss of control indicates that in the group of 'alcohol addicts' a superimposed process must occur" (p. 674). While Jellinek went on to qualify his distinction between the alcohol addict and the habitual symptomatic excessive drinker by saying that it cannot be stated with assurance whether the superimposed process of addiction is psychopathological or physiological, his concept of the addictive alcoholic has been seized upon by many in the medical profession (and others who are physiologically oriented) to maintain a wide conceptual gap between the alcoholic and the allegedly nonaddictive problem drinker—a gap which a growing number of public health workers believe is detrimental to a better understanding and control of problem drinking.

Despite Jellinek's regard for the rights of the individual drinker, his conceptions appear to have been subtly influenced by the Protestant ethic. His phases of alcohol addiction, with its orderly—and, inferentially, irreversible—progression of malign symptoms, through the prealcoholic phase, the prodromal phase, the crucial phase, and finally the chronic phase is of a piece with Hogarth's famous illustration of a drunkard's progress on the downward path to perdition. While Jellinek does not say that the phases of alcohol addiction always occur in the same order, his vivid descriptions of the progress of alcoholism are so well attuned to the values of the middle-class Western physician and welfare worker that his cautions are largely overlooked by those who apply his concepts and by the many writers who repeat his early concepts. However, a number of writers, including Hoff (1968) and Room (1970), have shown that the classical Jellinekian progression of symptoms does not apply to the real world often enough to have much operational significance.[1]

Keller, the editor of *Quarterly Journal of Studies on Alcohol* and an associate of Jellinek's, departs somewhat from the classical Jellinek concepts in his definition of alcoholism as "a chronic disease manifested by repeated implicative drinking so as to cause injury to the drinker's health or to his social or economic functioning" (1962, p. 316), although Keller continues to refer to alcoholism as a disease. Keller's constancy in this view is evident in the following observations:

[1] Room (1970) summarizes the merits of the Jellinek ordered phases of symptoms of alcoholism by concluding that the available research "does not support an assumption of universality in the prevalence of drinking history items in samples of alcoholics" (p. 8). In the same paper, he notes that the model of unilinear evolution of alcoholism is a Darwinian assumption that changes always take place in the same order and that change is irreversible.

> But is alcoholism a disease? I think it is (and well named alcoholism, and I wouldn't attach the label alcoholism to anything that isn't a disease). I think it is a disease because the alcoholic can't consistently choose whether or not he shall engage in a self-injurious behavior—that is, any of the alcoholismic drinking patterns. I think of it as a psychological disablement. And I don't think physical dependence or tolerance or altered cell metabolism (in which I can't believe on the basis of the evidence up to now) have anything to do with the case. At least, I am convinced they are not essential. Nor does it bother me that there are stages in alcoholism, or a variety of developmental courses, or various degrees of severity, or different orders and combinations of manifestations, or that the symptoms (including loss of control) don't operate twenty-four hours a day 365 days a year. There are lots of diseases with such inconstant characteristics, and not only psychological diseases—for example, tuberculosis and diabetes. . . . Disease has been the province of medicine (doctors) in recent times; under the movement toward "comprehensive medicine" which seems to be under way, other professions are to have a part in determining what shall be recognized as disease. Some doctors resent this development, and some are frightened, but others welcome it. In some forthcoming comments which will appear in the *Journal* . . . in response to an article which argues that alcoholism is not a disease, you will find some physicians literally hooting at a standard medical dictionary definition of disease.[2]

It seems clear that the concept of alcoholism as a physical disease entity has survived despite its limitations not only because it fits into the Zeitgeist of the Protestant ethic and into the microbe-hunters' age of medicine (which has shown such signal success in dealing with infectious and degenerative diseases), but also because of a well-intentioned motive to use the prestige of the medical profession in attempting to bring about better treatment of those with alcohol problems. As Jellinek himself put it, in discussing the expediencies involved in getting alcoholism to be accepted as a disease: "The official acceptance by the medical profession of the disease conception of 'alcoholism' is required not only for the continued life of its propagation through citizens' groups but also to encourage a much larger number of physicians to acquire experience in the treatment of acute intoxication, alcohol addiction itself, and the various organic and mental complications" (1960a, p. 160). He goes on to say that medical acceptance of the dis-

[2] Letter to Robin Room, October 20, 1969.

ease concept is also needed in order to induce hospitals to accept alcoholics for treatment, and that medical acceptance of the concept also is fundamental to a policy of supporting clinical activities and research work by the large foundations.

But though the concept that alcoholism is a disease may be expedient in attempting to get the problem drinker better treatment, research findings suggest that the concept may be needlessly confusing the general public. Thus, in an Iowa survey, Mulford and Miller found their respondents about evenly divided as to whether the alcoholic is best described as sick (65 per cent) or morally weak (75 per cent), with many agreeing to both propositions (1961, p. 320); and while Haberman and Sheinberg (1969) found that roughly two-thirds of a sample of New York City adults considered alcoholism an illness (p. 1210), fewer than half agreed with the illness concept of alcoholism in connection with symptomatic drinking (p. 1212) or thought that a physician could best help correct the behavioral manifestations of alcoholism (p. 1214).

Reinert (1968a) has pointed to the adverse effects of the concept of alcoholism as a disease upon the problem drinker by noting that the "once an alcoholic, always an alcoholic" dictum "frightens early alcoholics away from recognizing their problem and from seeking treatment" (p. 23), and that a large group of patients who are unable to stop drinking after treatment or the ministrations of Alcoholics Anonymous withdraw from help because of a feeling of shame and a sense of failure: "The concept of alcoholism as an irreversible disease has built into it a way of perpetuating itself. . . . One result is that we see the kind of alcoholics that we predict we will see. Another result is that attempts to teach moderation to early alcoholics are discouraged since they are doomed to fail by definition" (p. 25). Roman and Trice (1967) and Roman (1968) also contend that the sick role has made alcoholics worse, not better.

The limitations of the concept of alcoholism as a disease are summed up by Scott (1968, p. 221) as follows:

> To assert that alcoholism itself is a disease runs the risk of obscuring the probable truth that it may be a symptom of a number of quite separate conditions; it also tends to direct the problem to medical practitioners who, with their tradition of requiring the patient to be the passive recipient of treatment, may perpetuate errors. Thus it is possible that some forms of alcoholism are not

diseases of individuals but of society; some may drown themselves in alcohol as lemmings drown themselves in the sea, and both may be responding to social rather than personal cues. Epidemiological studies, for example, of the notable differences in hospital admissions for English and Scottish alcoholics, may be the appropriate corrective. Some forms of alcoholism should properly be grouped with other killing conditions such as obesity, smoking, possession of a high-powered motor bicycle. Looked at in this way it may be bad psychology to call these persons "sick" and to be squeamish about such terms as "immaturity," "lack of wisdom," and "self-indulgence" where they are manifestly justified. Such terms as "self-indulgent" or "unreliable" may be objective descriptions, to be sharply distinguished from moral judgments such as "shameful," "wicked," etc. Addicts need someone who will call a spade a spade in a realistic fashion without adopting a punitive, moralistic, or superior attitude. They know their weaknesses only too well and do not regard them as an illness, though they may secondarily bring illness. Certainly excesses of every sort may lead to illness or even to death, but we should guard against labeling everything which may shorten life as a disease, and the person who deliberately incurs risk as necessarily sick.

As Wexberg (1951) points out, "The emotional impact of the statement 'alcoholism is a sickness' is such that very few people care to stop to think what it actually means. . . . It derives its dynamics from the strong need to contend with the antitherapeutic effects of a viewpoint, represented mainly by puritans, drys, and temperance unions, which considers drinking as nothing but a vice" (p. 217).[3] Szasz expresses a viewpoint in keeping with this, in which he says that the disease concept of alcoholism is well intentioned but "none the less morally and socially disastrous" because "the upshot is deprivation of personal liberties in the name of medical help" (1967, p. 259). He concludes that "if our ultimate aim is a society where individuals are self-disciplined, rather than controlled by external authority, we cannot expect to advance toward that goal by proliferating laws for the coercive medical control of an ever-increasing variety of behaviors, among them the proper use of alcoholic beverages" (1967, p. 267).

[3] Witness the recent attempts on the part of lawyers to get the courts to accept alcoholism as a disease, with the implication that the individual's personal responsibility for public drunkenness is thereby diminished; to this attempt the courts in some instances have responded that they are reluctant to rule that alcoholism is clearly a disease in the absence of unequivocal evidence in support of this view (U.S. Supreme Court, *Powell* v. *Texas,* 1968).

Even some of those who have been sympathetic with the motives involved in calling alcoholism a disease are having serious misgivings about the effectiveness of such a course, as evidenced by Mulford's comments (1970):

> The factor having greatest influence on community reaction to alcohol abuse in recent years is the increasing acceptance of the concept that alcoholics suffer the disease of "alcoholism." Replacing yesterday's idea that "drunkards" are possessed by "demon rum" with today's idea that "alcoholics" are possessed by "alcoholism" means more humanitarian treatment of the alcohol abuser. However, medically oriented clinicians have not shown that they are any better prepared to exorcise "alcoholism" than the morally oriented clergy and courts were to exorcise the "demon." Jellinek (1960, pp. 35–41) has noted that neither alcoholics nor their presumed disease has been fitted into the medical model. "Alcoholism" has not been defined in terms that tell a physician what to do about it [p. 5]. . . . Acceptance of the disease concept has led to social action which has served the cause of the alcohol abuser in many ways, but it is not an unmixed blessing. Its acceptance has aroused public interest and sympathy to the point of funding programs of education, research, and treatment. This disease concept also has meant the establishment of detoxification and treatment centers for problem drinkers. Such special institutions are defensible on humanitarian grounds. . . . Special treatment facilities are also justified to the extent that they contribute to research. However, such institutions are *not* defensible as adequate instruments for attacking the problems of alcohol abuse. Treatment centers can be expected to reach about one-tenth of all problem drinkers. The 5 per cent who come before the courts can be committed for treatment and another 5 per cent may volunteer for treatment. But, the fact that Alcoholics Anonymous with its open-door invitation to all problem drinkers reaches less than 10 per cent of them suggests the need for something more than welcome signs [p. 5]. . . . The disease "alcoholism" has not been defined and there is no specific treatment for it. Physicians can hardly be expected to apply a nonexistent treatment to an undefined disease in a population that denies the disease and rejects the treatment [p. 6].

Jellinek himself recognized that the "alcoholism is a disease" stance could be subject to misinterpretation and misuse, as witness the following, from his later writings: "Research, treatment, and prevention of the various species of alcoholism are affected not only by the acceptance or rejection of the disease conception, but also by the formulation of the nature of such an illness. If the formulation rigidly claims that alcohol addiction or any other species of alcoholism is purely a medical problem, any preventive attempt may be seriously impaired. The usefulness of the idea that alcoholism is a medical and public health problem depends, to a large extent, upon the recognition of social and economic factors in the etiology of all species of alcoholism" (1960a, p. 158).

Other writers have attacked the viability and the usefulness of the disease concept itself in connection with alcohol-related problems. As Chafetz (1966) says: "We . . . must conclude that alcoholic excesses, alcoholic problems, alcoholism, or any other label you care to affix is produced by complex, multidimensional factors, and that, in fact, there is no such thing as an alcoholic. . . . For too long we have been impaled upon the stereotype of 'the alcoholic,' and we have not dared to look below the surface" (p. 810). Associates of Chafetz demonstrated the warping effect of the alcoholic concept upon medical thinking by a controlled experiment which demonstrated that when physicians were asked to select alcoholics from an alcoholic clinic's clients for treatment in a special project, their selections were dependent upon the physicians' modal conception of the alcoholic as being the typical revolving-door derelict; and physicians tend to be biased toward a medical (and primarily neurophysiological) diagnosis rather than one which takes cognizance of social and psychological malfunction of the clinic patient (Blane, Overton, and Chafetz, 1963; Blane, 1966).

The growing number of other writers who have voiced their uneasiness about disease concepts of alcoholism includes Williams (1966) and Mendelson and Stein (1966), who conclude that "an adequate and well-accepted definition of alcoholism has yet to be developed" (p. 3). Hoff (1968) prefers the term *problem drinking* to that of *alcoholism,* citing Plaut's report of the Cooperative Commission on the Study of Alcoholism (1967) as taking the position that distinctions between types of problem drinkers are unfortunate when certain classes thereby may be accorded less help and understanding than others. Finally, Seeley (1962, p. 592) summarizes his misgivings about the usefulness of the "alcoholism is a disease" concept as follows:

> We have now come close to saying, I believe, that in the domain of well-marked, evitable, undesirable behavior sequences, the

> question of what is to be designated as a disease and what otherwise is a matter of social policy is to be decided in terms of its consequences for (primarily) the continuation or sequel of the behavior process itself. Such a view clearly opens the door to more humane, physicianlike "treatment" of many sequences of conditions, but it opens also a veritable lawyer's nightmare of a door to far more than we might wish. What is to prevent, on this view, a gradual process of apostasy from the Church or the Communist Party—or, per contra, the increasing conservatism that accompanies maturation in many—from being defined as a disease, and the exhibitor of the behavior from being consigned to a compulsory "treatment" more dangerous than persecution?

Seeley goes on to conclude that while we may call alcoholism a disease if we so desire, the issue is whether we *should;* and that in any case we should make it clear to the public that this labeling is adopted for policy reasons, with the labeling to be withdrawn "if it seemed wise at a later date" (1962, p. 593).

Thus, to summarize, it would appear that the concept of alcoholism as a disease may have had the undesirable consequences of driving a wedge between the alcoholic and society, of providing the problem drinker with an alibi for failure to change his behavior, and of creating an atmosphere in which alcoholism becomes a stubborn disease to cure because it is perceived as possessing only the derelict or semiderelict or the incompetent who is incapable of control over his own behavior. But if these limitations of the "alcoholism is a disease" concept are granted, what concepts are more likely to bring about better understanding and control of misuse of alcohol?

Habits of thought in the Western world make it all too easy for the labeling process to operate to constrict or to freeze concepts prematurely in a rigid, value-laden mold. As Lewin (1936) has pointed out, our culture is steeped in Aristotelian either-or thinking so that we have a tendency to define things and people in absolutist terms. Thus the youth who gets involved in some escapade is swiftly labeled a juvenile delinquent, and the man who continues to get into trouble because of his drinking is readily labeled an alcoholic; such facile labeling helps to relieve the tensions and to reinforce the rectitude of the labeler, but it seldom contributes to efficiency in diagnosis or treatment of social ills. Our cultural tendencies toward binary either-or judgments are further reinforced by the moralistic absolutisms of the Puritan heritage and of the temperance era (Gusfield, 1962). A further pressure toward use of such labels as alcoholic is occasioned by the success or popularity, in the recent past, of the process of either-or differential diagnosis in medicine and psychiatry and public health, so that even the experienced professional researcher or public health worker may be led astray by the pressures to apply simplistic labels. The net effect of such pressures toward labeling has been unfortunate for both the advancement of the behavioral sciences and the well-being of the persons who are the victims of the labeling process.

Achieving a better understanding of the relationship of alcohol to human problems becomes doubly important when it is recognized that the old perspectives involved in the concept of alcoholism simply have not been very effective in coping with the fact that, generation after generation, a substantial minority of the vast majority who drink manage repeatedly to get themselves into serious troubles over their drinking. This study of problem drinking was begun with the conviction that there is more to be gained by analyzing the prevalence of a range of specific, operationally defined problems related to alcohol than by conducting a nose count of alcoholics. The view is here advanced that a too-literal acceptance of traditional concepts of alcoholism in research or in public health or in the treatment of people with drinking problems is no more likely to be fruitful in the future than it has been in the past.

One essential criterion for useful definitions related to alcohol problems is that any labels should be as free as possible of adverse side effects, such as serving as barriers to thinking on the part of physicians, social workers, special-interest groups, and the general public. Further, the terms used to describe drinking problems should be such as to encourage (rather than discourage) research and debate about the etiology of abuse of alcohol and other drugs. It would appear that the modest term *drinking problem* could qualify on all counts, because it puts the emphasis upon the behavior rather than on the person (and thus serves less readily as a permanent label for the person with drinking problems), and because it permits inquiry into whether there may be many different types of drinking problems and problem drinkers.

For a number of reasons, it is believed that the concept of problem drinking—always to be accompanied by a statement of what kind of problem—is much to be preferred to that of alcoholism. One reason is that the requirement of specifying what kind of problem is both an encouragement and a challenge to investigate and to help to mitigate the wide range of actual problems or potential problems in which alcohol may play a part. Another reason is that problem drinking as yet has not become overloaded with the emotional and demonic connotations which have collected around the concept of alcoholism. Problem drinking can be positioned as the responsibility of a wide range of preventive public health and treatment agencies (including the sufferer's family and work associates, in addition to social agencies), whereas alcoholism has been too narrowly fixed as the exclusive domain for the medical profession or such specialized agencies as Alcoholics Anonymous. Perhaps most important of all, a shift to general acceptance of the concept of problem drinking from that of alcoholism can help pin the responsibility on both the problem drinker and society to bring about some solution to problems related to excessive drinking at an early stage, rather than after the sufferer hits bottom. An additional advantage of the problem drinking concept is that it implies that a legitimate distinction can be made between the problem drinker and the great majority of nonproblem drinkers, whereas alcoholism may imply that the root of the difficulty lies exclusively in the alcohol rather than involving also individual and environmental factors.

For all these reasons, problem drinking or drinking problems are the concepts used in this study, rather than alcoholism. Wherever it is necessary, the terms are used in connection with a specification of what kind of problem is being discussed. Often the general terms *problem drinking* and *drinking problems* will be used as a form of shorthand, in the interest of simplicity, when their meaning should be clear. However, it always should be kept in mind that the more precise terms *problems associated with use of alcohol* or *problem-related drinking* would be more appropriate, for they emphasize that the focus is upon the problems *associated with* drinking of certain kinds under certain circumstances, rather than implying that drinking per se necessarily constitutes the problem.

A useful and uncomplicated definition of problem drinking is provided in the report by Plaut (1967) of the findings of the Cooperative Commission on the Study of Alcoholism: "Problem drinking is a *repetitive use of beverage alcohol causing physical, psychological, or social harm to the drinker or to others.* This definition stresses interference with functioning rather than any specific drinking behavior" (pp. 37–38). This definition is compatible with the more general definition that "a problem—any problem—connected fairly closely with drinking constitutes a drinking problem" (Knupfer, 1967, p. 974), which appears to enjoy the concurrence of most researchers who have published the results of sample surveys which measured some aspects of problems associated with alcohol (Bailey, Haberman, and Alksne, 1965; Clark, 1966; Mulford and Miller, 1960b).

One catch to Plaut's definition of problem drinking as "causing physical, psychological, or social harm to the drinker or to others" is the difficulty of establishing causality in relation to problems. In any studies done at single points in time, when an association (or connection or correlation) is found between a problem and drinking, it is not a simple matter to determine which came first, the problem or the drinking. As will be discussed in detail later, in many instances it is very hard to determine whether a maladjustment in interpersonal relations stemmed from someone's excessive drinking, or whether the drinking was a reaction to (and perhaps even an attempted solution for) an intolerable situation.

Terms such as *problems associated with drinking* are of legitimate use only if it is clearly understood that the measurement of a correlation is an important, but only an interim, step in the process of scientific research. It is necessary first to establish the extent to which certain types of drinking are correlated with certain types of problems, in order to determine which correlations are high enough to indicate there may be a high ultimate payoff (in terms of mitigating human problems) in a more intensive investigation. Most of the research to date appropriately has been of this preliminary correlation-hunting variety; and the chief emphasis of this study necessarily is upon establishing the correlates of problems rather than their causes.

This study, therefore, represents an early stage in the investigation of problem drinking, focusing as it does primarily upon the correlations between certain types of drinking and specific types of problems. In order to establish more clearly whether the drinking caused the problem or the problem caused the drinking, two subsequent stages will be needed. The first will be the completion of longitudinal surveys or observational studies in which changes in people's environments between time A and time B are related to subsequent changes in drinking behavior or health or interpersonal relations. (This study is able to yield a few preliminary short-term findings of a longitudinal variety, because it is based on data from two interviews with the same set of respondents, conducted about three years apart.) The final stage of scientific investigation should be the conducting of controlled experimental studies in which alternative remedial measures are put into effect (paralleled with observation of appropriate control groups) over a period of time, and ultimate results are measured in terms of the extent to which specific remedial programs are followed by measurable lessening in problems related to drinking.

It is easy to summarize the findings of past studies of problem drinking because the useful ones are so very few. Most studies of the characteristics of the institutionalized alcoholic are of little value because they have been poorly done (with unscientific samplings, for example), or because it is impossible to determine whether the characteristics of the alcoholic are connected primarily to his drinking or the fact that he is institutionalized (and thus more likely to come from the ranks of the poor, the unemployed, and the incompetent). However, one exception is Malzberg's statistical study of admission rates to hospitals for alcoholic psychosis (1960), which yielded the following findings with a bearing on the variables to be reported on in our national survey:

> Alcoholic psychoses in 1949–1951 had a geographic pattern very similar to patterns for heavy drinking as measured in the 1964–1965 national survey reported in *American Drinking Practices* (Cahalan, Cisin, and Crossley, 1969), with the coastal (rather highly urbanized) areas having relatively high rates and the South having relatively low rates. Malzberg found higher alcoholic psychosis rates in urban areas than in rural, among the unmarried, among those of lower-status occupations, and among native whites compared to the foreign-born. The 1964–1965 national survey by George Washington University found the same pattern for heavy drinking.

Relatively few detailed studies of problem drinking within the general population were conducted prior to the national probability sampling reported in this book. However, several prior community or national studies, summarized below, yielded findings which were very helpful in the planning of the detailed national survey.

A national survey conducted by Mulford (1964) included questions on whether respondents had ever had any of the following types of troubles because of their drinking: threatened or actual loss of a job, threatened or actual loss of a spouse, complaints from family members about money spent on alcohol, arrests for misuse of alcohol, and having a physician tell them that drinking was injuring their health. Higher rates were found for men, younger persons, the less-educated, and the highly urbanized, and among those who were single or divorced, than among the women, the well-educated, the rural residents, and married persons. In another study, confined to Iowa, Mulford and Miller (1960b) found that the personal-effects drinkers (those who rely on alcohol to alleviate stress, rather than drinking merely for sociability) sought a greater number of goals through the use of alcohol and drank often in situations where there was a relative absence of restrictive group norms—such as in taverns and bars. Similar findings were obtained in the national survey reported on below.

Another survey including some questions on problems related to drinking, reported by Bailey, Haberman, and Alksne (1965), was applied on a sample of residents of the Washington Heights Health District in New York City. Respondents were classified as probable alcoholics on the basis of responses regarding difficulties due to drinking, or liver trouble and other health problems, as reported by either the person or some member of his family. This study yielded findings which were generally congruent with the national survey reported on below, particularly with respect to higher rates of problems related to drinking on the part of men, the unmarried, and those of lower education. While the findings were dissimilar in that a high rate of probable alcoholics was found among persons sixty-five to seventy-four, the authors attributed this finding to the number of elderly widowers with drinking problems who were included in this specific urban area (p. 29).

The first community survey which was designed primarily for the purpose of measuring the prevalence of specific problems associated with drinking was conducted in 1964 in San Francisco under the direction of Knupfer and her associates in the Drinking Practices Study group of the California State Department of Public Health. The national survey reported on in this book closely paralleled this San Francisco study in its methods, and both surveys were conducted with probability samples (random sampling) of the adult household population. Despite the difference in this urban sample and the national sample, both as to composition of the population and in the methods used, the findings were closely parallel in the prevalence of "serious" social consequences as regards the higher rates found for men, for those of lower socioeconomic status, those divorced or separated, and those of Irish descent. (In both studies, Jews were found to have extremely low rates of problems related to drinking.)

Helpful insights into potentially fruitful areas of exploration for a study of problem drinking also emerged from the first phase of the George Washington University national survey, conducted in 1964–1965 (Cahalan, Cisin, and Crossley, 1969). This survey had the primary purpose of describing drinking practices rather than drinking problems. However, it included several measures which tapped certain components of problem drinking, notably the (rather arbitrary) measure of heavy drinking (pp. 10–17) and a measure of heavy escape drinking to avoid problems of living (pp. 166–179). Some of the findings relevant to the present inquiry were as follows:

> Seventy-seven per cent of the men and 60 per cent of the women drank at least once a year; and 21 per cent of the men and 5 per cent of the women were classified as "heavy" drinkers [p. 185]. . . . There was no exact correspondence between the correlates of merely drinking and being a "heavy drinker," as the following enumeration will demonstrate [1969, primarily from Chart 3, p. 189].
>
> *Most likely to be drinkers:* (1) Men under fifty-five. (2) Men and women of higher social status. (3) Professional people; semiprofessionals; technical workers; sales workers; managers; officials. (4) College graduates. (5) Single men. (6) Residents of suburban cities, towns. (7) Those whose fathers were foreign-born, especially of Italian origin. (8) Jews, Episcopalians.
>
> *Among drinkers, most likely to be heavy drinkers:* (1) Men aged forty-five to forty-nine. (2) Men of lower social status. (3) Operatives; service workers. (4) Men who completed high school but did not finish college. (5) Single, divorced, or separated men and women. (6) Residents of largest cities. (7) Those whose fathers were Latin American or Caribbean, Italian, or British in origin (Irish, when standardized for age levels). (8) Protestants of no specific denomination; Catholics; those without religious affiliation.

From many standpoints, the 1964–1965 national survey demonstrated that the misuse of alcohol represents more of a threat to those of lower social status than to others (1969, p. 196). While it was found that a higher proportion of higher-status respondents drank and drank frequently, a higher proportion of the lower-status respondents who did drink were classified as "heavy" and "escape" drinkers (in the sense that they drank to escape from the problems of living). The finding that individuals of different social-psychological characteristics had different ways of coping with stress led to the hypothesis that there may be three basic types of dependency which bear upon susceptibility to alcohol and other drugs: people dependency, thing dependency, and self-dependency (1969, p. 206). While this hypothesis has not been fully tested, the findings of the follow-up survey on problem drinking yield further evidence bearing on the issue of susceptibility. That problem drinking is usually the outcome of a long chain of events and many years of drinking is evidenced by the finding that 70 per cent of the male heavy drinkers and 50 per cent of the female heavy drinkers began drinking before the age of twenty-one (1969, p. 102).

Thus while no two of the earlier studies of drinking were designed to yield parallel information, and while only the Knupfer study was planned as a detailed analysis of the prevalence of a range of specific types of problems related to drinking, it was possible to draw a few basic conclusions for the purpose of planning the national survey. One conclusion was that even within the noninstitutionalized household population of the United States, there should be vastly different rates of problem drinking by such common cultural or demographic variables as sex, age, socioeconomic status, urbanization, and religious and ethnic background; and thus these should be planned as the independent variables for study of the prevalence of the dependent variables of the various types of problem drinking. Another conclusion was that various social-psychological factors—such as differences in perceptions or attitudes concerning the appropriate function of alcohol—and various personality measures (such as neurotic tendencies, alienation from society, and impulsivity or weak ego control) could interact as intervening or contingent variables with the demographic-cultural independent variables to affect the rates of problem drinking (1969, pp. 154–164).

The national survey on drinking problems reported upon in this book was conducted through reinterviews in 1967 with a subsample of 1,359 persons who were initially interviewed in 1964–1965. Detailed questions about drinking problems were asked only in the 1967 survey, and correlated against independent and intervening variables constructed from items asked at either the first or the second stage. The ways in which these variables are linked together in theory and in practice are discussed in detail in Chapter Three. But first, it is in order to define the dependent variables—the specific types of problems associated with drinking—and to describe how these variables were measured.

II Defining Drinking Problems

This study had as its primary objectives the measurement of the prevalence of various types of problem drinking, an analysis of their correlates, and a preliminary examination of the extent of changes in problem drinking over a three-year period. The research strategy which was adopted was to measure the prevalence of as wide a range of actual or potential problems associated with the use of alcohol as was practicable within the limitations of the survey interview instrument in a national sample of adults, building particularly upon the foundations laid down by Knupfer (1967) and Clark (1966) and their associates in their recent San Francisco studies of problem drinking. In order to clarify the context of the total research program within which the present study represents an intermediate stage, a brief inventory of the various surveys in the series is in order.

First, a series of exploratory and problem-defining community studies were conducted, in Berkley and Oakland (Cisin, 1963; Fink, 1965; Knupfer *et al.,* 1963), and in Richmond, Virginia (Kirsch, Newcomb, and Cisin, 1965) and Hartford (Cahalan *et al.,* 1965).[1]

[1] The California studies were conducted under the auspices of the Cali-

These studies helped to establish which survey techniques were most appropriate to measurement of drinking behavior, and to establish, in a preliminary way, the correlates of various kinds of drinking behavior. Second, large-scale descriptive surveys of drinking behavior were conducted in San Francisco (Knupfer and Room, 1964) and in the country as a whole (Cahalan, Cisin, and Crossley, 1969). These surveys have served as the basis for many articles and reports on drinking behavior, most of which have concentrated on describing the quantity, frequency, circumstances, and style of people's drinking, rather than focusing primarily on problems related to drinking. Third, quantitative surveys emphasizing measurement of correlates of various types of problems associated with drinking were conducted, in San Francisco (Clark, 1966; Knupfer, 1967), Hartford (Cahalan, 1968), and the United States as a whole. The national survey provided the data for this book.[2] All three of these surveys entailed follow-up interviews with respondents whose drinking habits had been measured two or three years earlier; these surveys provided a greater quantity and variety of information because two interviews were conducted with each respondent and because the two-stage design permitted analysis of short-term changes in drinking during the time between the two interviews. Finally, a longer-term measurement of change, on a national scale, is projected for approximately 1975–1978, at which time it is hoped that a final follow-up will be conducted of those initially interviewed in 1964–1965 and 1967, so as to measure longer-term changes in many specific aspects of problem drinking and their correlates.

RESEARCH STRATEGY AND STANDARDS

The first stage of interviewing was conducted in 1964–1965, when a probability sample of 2,746 respondents was initially interviewed in a descriptive survey of drinking practices (Cahalan, Cisin, and Crossley, 1969). The second stage was conducted in 1967, when

---

fornia Department of Public Health and the Mental Research Institute (see references above). The Richmond and Hartford studies and the national surveys were conducted by the Social Research Group, The George Washington University. These two research programs were merged in 1968 under the aegis of the Social Research Group.

[2] A San Francisco survey of 786 men between twenty-one and fifty-nine years of age (those of above-average risk of having drinking problems) was conducted in 1967–1968, and a similar national sampling of 978 men was completed in 1969. The results of these two studies will appear in a later monograph.

a subsample of 1,359 respondents was interviewed; at that time the primary focus was upon problems associated with drinking.[3] Data from both sets of interviews have been combined in certain instances in which the passage of about three years would be considered unlikely to bring about much change, thus providing a richer fund of background information on the respondent than could have been covered in a single interview.

The sample of the household population of adults ruled out persons under twenty-one and those not currently resident in households. Thus the problem drinking of juveniles and of transients, institutionalized persons, and military personnel not living in household quarters was not measured in this national survey. A key decision in the planning of this series of longitudinal surveys was to follow up an essentially "normal" (or at least noninstitutionalized) population over a period of years (Cisin, 1963), so as to chart the development and change in drinking behaviors as they occur. This research design will make it possible to study the correlates of problems related to drinking as they develop or diminish over time, without relying upon findings of questionable validity from gathering retrospective case histories of institutionalized or otherwise publicly identified alcoholics.

The survey, conducted as it was through use of trained interviewers who were laymen, was not planned to measure such physiological or psychological symptoms as appropriately would be measured by physical examinations or intensive questioning in which the insights of the physician, psychiatrist, or clinical psychologist would be required. Thus while many questions, including self-administered checklists of symptoms, were asked to measure physical or psychological symptoms of types which could be reported in an interview, no attempt was made to measure latent physical or psychological damage attributable to misuse of alcohol beyond those symptoms of which the respondent himself could be aware and could be induced to report. Such degenerative conditions could—and should—be assessed in other studies, through professional physical and psychiatric examinations

[3] See Appendix A for a discussion of the sampling procedures and completion rates. In brief, 90 per cent of the eligible respondents in the initial survey were interviewed. From those 2,746 persons, a subsample of 1,810 respondents was selected for reinterview, of whom 81 per cent of living eligible respondents wre reinterviewed. Thus 90 per cent of 81 per cent, or 72 per cent of the selected eligible respondents, were represented in the final two-stage interviewing of 1,359 persons.

applied to subsamples of persons who have been interviewed on their drinking behavior in surveys of this type; for only through such a combination of research methods can the most thoroughgoing analysis of the correlates of problem drinking be ensured.

Preliminary studies brought into focus a number of cautions and requirements to be taken into account in measuring drinking problems on a national scale. First, specific problems should be covered as intensively as possible consistent with the limitations of the survey method. One would hardly consider jeopardizing the whole interview by inquiring about certain kinds of proscribed behavior, such as sex offenses committed while intoxicated. However, it has been found that most common or garden varieties of drinking problems can be covered with candor in a survey: witness the fact that separate validation studies by Robins (1966) and Knupfer and Monsky (1966) found the ostensibly sensitive issue of "trouble with the law" associated with drinking was fairly accurately reported, as measured against independent checks against police records for the same individuals.

Second, the decision was made to cover not only actual problems but potential problems as well. The study aimed to cast as broad a net as possible, so as not to miss any significant problems. In a longitudinal study, it is important to get some measurement on what are conceded to be extremely mild forms of potential problems at the time of first measurement, in order to be able to trace the growth or diminution of the intensity or breadth of problems with the passage of time and the occurrence of marked life stresses. This strategy of using a wide net with fine mesh provides some insurance against overlooking any ultimately significant events which may appear inconsequential at the time they are first noted. The wide-net approach results in focusing some attention on behavior which later may be found to be unimportant in terms of the individual's and society's long-term well-being; some possible instances of this are enumerated below. However, this approach appears to be the soundest one to use until there have been a sufficient number of longitudinal studies of drinking problems to refine the specific types of problems down to a list of almost universally consequential ones for future research application.

Third, in any ultimate determination of which types of drinking problems are "consequential" in the long run, care must be taken to avoid any sweeping assumptions that there exists a single basic underlying causal chain (akin to Jellinek's progression of symptoms of alcoholism) in which certain specific symptoms of problems usually precede the development of other, more "serious," problems. However, while future research should not be hampered by too many assumptions concerning the process of change in problem drinking, it is possible to make a few tentative predictions about the usual order in which certain types of problems or symptoms develop. For example, it seems only reasonable to expect that problems regarding drinking are not likely to develop unless the individual has first developed a tendency toward fairly often drinking amounts of alcohol sufficient to affect his behavior or his subjective or physical functioning. Put in broader terms, a plausible hypothesis is that increases in the quantity drunk and the frequency of drinking, and the development of indications of loss of control over one's drinking, would be more likely to precede the development of interpersonal problems related to alcohol. However, longitudinal studies of the evolution of drinking-related behavior should be designed so as to test the existence of all possible types of interactions among the various types of potential problems.

The present national study had the benefit of the experiences of others who have conducted preliminary studies of problem drinking, including the observations of Bailey growing out of the Washington Heights (New York City) study mentioned earlier. Thus she pointed to the continued usefulness of some of the Jellinek concepts regarding preserving distinctions among types of alcoholism (such as purely psychological dependence on alcohol, as distinct from very heavy drinking coupled with poor nutritional habits resulting in deficiency disease; and loss of control over the amount of drinking, as distinct from inability to abstain but without loss of control over the amount drunk on any given occasion). Bailey also mentioned the need to define the degree of severity of drinking problems, the amount of deviance observed, and the recency with which an alcohol problem has been manifested (1966, pp. 2–3).

In somewhat similar terms, Knupfer pointed out that "an operational definition [of problem drinking] must take into account type, intensity, and recency of problem" (1967, p. 976). Measurement of intensity is necessary in order to have some conception of whether the problem is consequential; and (as will be seen) the establishment of levels in intensity at the present state of the art has to rely primarily on subjective judgment. Measurement of recency not only indicates whether the problem is current and whether the behavior may have been subject to recent change but also can be used to infer frequency of the behavior—under the rationale that the best estimate of the frequency of a behavior is a function of its recency.

This list of definitional requirements for problem drinking is analogous to a list prepared by Kvaraceus and Miller (1959) in the field of juvenile delinquency: they define juvenile delinquency as constituting "norm violations which possess the following characteristics: severity, form, frequency, and relationship of act to prior behavior and individual personality" (p. 43). It should be noted that most definitions of problem drinking (including Plaut's, cited above), alcoholism, and any other form of delinquent or deviant behavior lay great emphasis upon the factor of frequency or repetitiveness: it is as though one hallmark of the mores is that many forms of behavior are condonable if they happen infrequently (except for events with lasting consequences, such as homicide), but are judged as "serious" if they happen repeatedly. It would seem that the mores take into account the actuarial likelihood of some nuisance being committed repeatedly; society's standards for conduct involve the inference that if undesirable behavior happens repeatedly, it must be because the culprit is deliberately flouting society's rules or is not competent to conform.

The general application of the criterion of repetitiveness or chronicity, through refraining from labeling a heavy drinker as an "alcoholic" until he has exhibited repeated deviance from norms of social drinking for a lengthy period, is in keeping with public tolerance in allowing young men to "sow their wild oats," and in holding off in declaring someone a delinquent until he has been involved in repeated transgressions. It is also congruent with the medical profession's distinction between acute and chronic disease, and with the mental health distinction between temporary and chronic neuroses and psychoses.

One important limitation alluded to earlier of any survey conducted at a single point of time is that single surveys cannot pin down with any precision whether a problem associated with drinking is the result, or the cause, of drinking. Problems associated with drinking can be a function of many prior "causes": emergency stress and strain which may induce the individual (sometimes perhaps quite sensibly) to drink as a means of escape; upward or downward mobility which changes the person's social contacts or accustomed behaviors; and other aspects of his objective and subjective environment—including his values, attitudes, outlook, and level of aspiration. Much problem drinking may reflect mere incompetence in interpersonal relations on the part of the drinker or the people who are significant in his life; and other influences include early training and supervision and the life style within the person's subgroup. As we will see, while it is possible rather readily to predict who will have drinking problems, all of these factors may interact in peculiar ways to make it very difficult to predict whether a person will (or will not) be one of the small minority who will continue to have stubborn problems related to drinking over a considerable period of time.

Again, no measurement of cause and effect in assessing the relationship of drinking and problems is possible unless one can determine which came first, the drinking or the problem: and even if this difficult task is achieved, both the drinking and the problem may be attributable to additional factors. Establishing a temporal sequence may be done in two ways: either through asking the persons involved questions at one point of time concerning the sequence of events which may have occurred in the remote past—a course vulnerable to forgetfulness or distortions of memory; or through several measurements of current behavior and circumstances over a period of time. Only the longitudinal approach is unobjectionable in principle, since it avoids the biases of retrospection. However, in a preliminary survey of this type, which is one stage in a series of longitudinal studies, the investigator has a responsibility to try to gather such information as he can, so as to make some interim progress in understanding the correlates of problem drinking. Thus the decision was made to cover as many actual or potential problems related to drinking as might conceivably later be found to be of importance in tracing the course of people's drinking and problem experiences in later stages of the longitudinal study. As a consequence, the list of problems which are measured in this present stage of the study, while broad in scope, is rather ad hoc and represents a mixture of problems, potential problems, potential solutions to problems, and effects of problems. The research strategy which was adopted was to leave to a later stage the sorting out of causes and effects, but to concentrate upon trying not to miss covering potentially important problems just because of difficulty in establishing cause and effect at this stage.

CRITERIA FOR SPECIFIC PROBLEMS

If we accept for the time being Plaut's definition of problem drinking as "a repetitive use of beverage alcohol causing physical, psychological, or social harm to the drinker or to others" (1967, pp. 37–38), the task becomes one of defining and measuring the specific types of problems of interest. For perspectives on selecting for measurement the "physical" and "psychological" aspects of problems related to drinking, it seems prudent to examine the concepts of established authorities in the field of alcohol, even though we may prefer to focus our concern on problem drinking rather than on alcoholism. Jellinek distinguished these types of alcoholism fitting into either the physical or psychological realms of problems related to drinking (1960a, pp. 36–39):

> *Alpha alcoholism* represents a . . . *purely* psychological *continual* dependence or reliance upon the effect of alcohol to relieve bodily or emotional pain. The drinking is "undisciplined" in the sense that it contravenes such rules as society tacitly agrees upon —such as time, occasion, locale, amount and effect of drinking —but does not lead to *"loss of control"* or *"inability to abstain. . . ."* *Beta alcoholism* is that species of alcoholism in which such alcoholic complications as polyneuropathy, gastritis, and cirrhosis of the liver may occur without either physical or psychological dependence upon alcohol. . . . Withdrawal symptoms . . . do not emerge. Beta alcoholism too may develop into gamma or delta alcoholism, but such a transition is less likely than in the instance of alpha alcoholism. *Gamma alcoholism* means that species of alcoholism in which (1) acquired increased tissue tolerance to alcohol, (2) adaptive cell metabolism . . . , (3) withdrawal symptoms and "craving," i.e., physical dependence, and (4) loss of control are involved. In gamma alcoholism there is a definite progression from psychological to physical dependence and marked behavior changes. . . . Alpha and beta alcoholism . . . may develop under given conditions into gamma alcoholism. This species produces the greatest and most serious kinds of damage. The loss of control, of course, impairs interpersonal relations to the highest degree. The damage to health in general and to financial and social standing is also more prominent than in other species of alcoholism. Gamma alcoholism is apparently (but not with certainty) the *predominating* species of alcoholism in the United States and Canada, as well as in other Anglo-Saxon countries. It is what members of Alcoholics Anonymous recognize as alcoholism to the exclusion of all other species. . . . *Delta alcoholism* shows the first three characteristics of gamma alcoholism as well as a less marked form of the fourth characteristic—that is, instead of loss of control there is inability to abstain. . . . This species of alcoholism and its underlying drinking pattern have been . . . described in [Jelli-

> nek's] Chapter II in connection with the *predominant* species of alcoholism ("inveterate drinking") in France and some other countries with a large wine consumption. . . . There are . . . many other species of alcoholism—if it is defined as any drinking that causes any damage. . . . Among these other species is periodic alcoholism, which in Europe and Latin America is still designated as dipsomania. . . . We may denote it as *Epsilon alcoholism.*

The national survey tapped some, but not all, of the types of symptoms covered by Jellinek under Alpha alcoholism (psychological dependence upon alcohol) and of Gamma alcoholism (that portion having to do with withdrawal symptoms and loss of control but not the issues of increased tissue tolerance or adaptive cell metabolism, which are medical questions considered to be inappropriate for application in surveys at the present state of the art). Beta alcoholism was hardly tapped at all in the survey because it is too specialized a medical issue. Delta alcoholism (inability to abstain) was not covered because (as Jellinek says) it appears to be uncommon in the American culture; but Epsilon alcoholism was covered insofar as inquiring into whether the respondent had gone on binges of more than a day in length.

From the hypotheses of Jellinek and Keller, Plaut's definition of problem drinking, and the types of drinking problems measured in past surveys as described earlier, eleven specific types of problems were singled out for analysis in the data from the national survey: (1) frequent intoxication, or exceeding what was defined as a moderate level in a combined frequency and amount-per-occasion measure, or getting intoxicated fairly often; (2) binge drinking—being intoxicated for more than one day at a time; (3) symptomatic drinking behavior (symptomatic dependence upon alcohol), as inferred from finding it difficult to stop drinking once started, blackouts or memory lapses after drinking, sneaking drinks, and so on; (4) psychological dependence on alcohol; (5) problems with current spouse or with relatives related to one's drinking; (6) problems with friends or neighbors over one's drinking; (7) problems concerned with one's work or employment occurring in relation to one's drinking; (8) problems with the police, or accidents in which someone was hurt or property damage occurred, in relation to one's drinking; (9) health (for example, physician advised respondent to cut down on drinking); (10) financial problems connected with one's drinking; (11) belligerence or fighting associated with one's drinking.

The first four types of potential problems are seen to be concerned with drinking behavior itself or with reasons for drinking. The next four types of problems are connected with interpersonal relations. The last three are miscellaneous problems, or potential problems, not conclusively classifiable into either drinking behavior or interpersonal relations. Thus the classifications permit the use of a typology which takes into account the interactions of drinking behavior and interpersonal problems. The findings of such a typology are presented below. But first, some more details about the eleven specific types of problems are explored.

The data for scoring each respondent on each of the eleven types of problems were obtained from approximately seventy-five items applied at the time of the second stage of interviewing in 1967.[4] The specific types of problems are based primarily upon the types utilized in the San Francisco study reported by Knupfer (1967) and Clark (1966), with some differences in the details.[5]

The approximately seventy-five questionnaire items on heavy drinking or potential drinking problems asked in the Stage II survey were combined into the eleven specific problem areas summarized below. The rationales for including each of the types of drinking problems (or potential problems) in this analysis of the data for this national survey are discussed, along with some details on the way in which each problem area was scored.

[4] In addition, a limited number of questions related to potential drinking problems were asked during the first stage (1964–1965), thus permitting a limited analysis of change in behavior correlated with drinking problems. This analysis of short-term change is presented in Chapter Six.

[5] The time period utilized in the national study for "current" problems was the last three years (approximately the time between the two stages of interviews), while the "current" time span for the San Francisco survey was the preceding twelve months. Methods of questioning differed somewhat, with the national survey utilizing a combination of interview questions and a self-administered "inventory of experiences related to drinking," while the San Francisco survey utilized intensive interview questions alone. The specific types varied slightly, with the national survey and Clark's analysis of the San Francisco study including aggressiveness and Knupfer's analysis omitting it; and the San Francisco study reported problems with spouse alone, while the national study lumped together problems with spouse and relatives. The specific questions also differed. Readers interested in complete details are invited to compare the procedures used in the national survey to the details provided in Appendices to the Knupfer and Clark articles; tables available from the author upon request.

Frequent intoxication. It seems reasonable to assume that frequency of intoxication is a legitimate index of potential problems because people are more likely to get into trouble with others or to jeopardize their own health and security if they get drunk often. Frequency of intoxication was estimated in this survey by considering the amount respondents reported they usually drank per occasion or upon specific occasions, the frequency with which they drank fairly large amounts, and the frequency with which they reported getting high or tight.[6] In order to get a high score on this potential drinking problem (score of two or three) one would have to be drinking a minimum of five or more drinks at least once a week, or eight or more drinks on one of the most recent two drinking occasions and twice in the last two months, or twelve or more drinks on one of the last two occasions and twice in the last year; or currently be getting high or tight at least once a week. It is believed that the minimum number of drinks per occasion necessary to qualify the respondent as having a potential problem of frequent intoxication was set high enough to include only those who were running considerable risk of frequent impairment of their health, safety and well-being, or interpersonal relations. As will be shown later, a fairly high proportion of men in their twenties had a relatively high score on this index of potential problem drinking. While persons of superior physique and drive (such as a Churchill or a Grant) may be able to handle these quantities of alcohol with aplomb, it is unlikely that many could do so without running into complications.

Binge drinking. The criterion for qualifying on this potential problem was being intoxicated for at least several days at one time or for two days on more than one occasion. It will be seen that relatively few persons qualified as being binge drinkers. This measure is subject to some unreliability because of differences in individuals' definitions of staying intoxicated for several days at a time. Binge drinking is one manifestation of Jellinek's loss of control (1960a, p. 41) and is characterized as Epsilon alcoholism (p. 39).

Symptomatic drinking. This includes behavior symptomatic of Jellinek's Gamma alcoholism (1960a, p. 37) insofar as the exhibiting of signs of physical dependence and loss of control. Measures were

[6] The frequent intoxication potential problem area, as with the psychological dependency area (see below), is based on present behavior ("Do you . . . ?") and not on the time period of three years otherwise used in the current Problems scores.

based on those used in the California study of Knupfer (1967), which in turn were adapted from the Mulford and Miller studies in Iowa (1960b). These included the seven items of drinking to get rid of a hangover, having difficulty in stopping drinking, having blackouts or lapses of memory, skipping meals while on a drinking bout, tossing down drinks for a quicker effect, sneaking drinks, and taking quick drinks in advance of a party to make sure that one gets enough. On individual items, it is possible that the same behavior might have variable meanings in different contexts, as in the instance of an exuberant (and healthy) youth who sneaks drinks or takes quick drinks in advance of a party or skips meals while drinking—as contrasted to similar behavior on the part of the mother of several small children, or on the part of a locomotive engineer. However, it is believed that the level of behavior necessary to qualify with a high score in this category of "symptomatic drinking behavior" was set high enough (positive responses to three or more of the seven items) to include primarily those at risk of being (or becoming) addicted to, or unduly dependent upon, alcohol.

Psychological dependence. Like Jellinek's Alpha alcoholism, this includes items on drinking to alleviate depression or nervousness or to escape from the problems of everyday living.[7] The items here are similar in content to those described by Riley, Marden, and Lifschiz (1948) as personal reasons and by Cahalan, Cisin, and Crossley as escape reasons (1969, p. 166); they include saying: a drink is helpful when depressed or nervous; an important reason for drinking is to forget everything, to help forget one's worries, to cheer one up when in a bad mood, or a drink is needed when one is tense or nervous. The significance of drinking in order to obtain relief from one's personal problems may mean quite one thing if done infrequently (such as in a man's drowning his sorrow upon the loss of a favorite relative or friend) and quite another if heavy drinking is indulged in regularly for mood changing or relief of tensions. Again, a fairly high number of responses in this category were required (at least one out of five mentions of psychological effects of alcohol being very helpful or im-

[7] Unlike the other problem areas, except frequent intoxication, the psychological dependence measure is based on present behavior ("Do you . . . ?") without reference to the time period of three years generally used in the "current" scoring. Also the respondent qualifying for a higher score on this variable has to have been drinking at least four drinks on some occasions within the last three years.

portant, plus two others rated fairly helpful or important) to qualify a person as psychologically dependent on alcohol.

Problems with spouse or relatives. Items included the spouse's leaving or threatening to leave the respondent or becoming angry or concerned over the respondent's drinking, the spouse's or a relative's asking the respondent to cut down on his drinking, or the respondent himself feeling his drinking had had a harmful effect on his home life. (Respondents were considered as having higher scores on this problem if the spouse was reported as getting angry or threatening to leave the respondent over his drinking, or any two of the following: spouse concerned over drinking, spouse or relative said respondent should cut down, or respondent felt drinking had had a harmful effect on his marriage or home life.)

Since the family role is a significant part of most people's lives, trouble in the family over one's drinking is assumed to have a serious potential in most cases. Sometimes the implications of the problem may be contingent upon (a) whether the spouse has unreasonable or arbitrary standards for behavior, such as objecting if the respondent has a single drink under any circumstances; (b) the circumstances under which the drinking occurs; and (c) the quality of the relationship between the respondent and the spouse—for example, is the drinking an excuse for the spouse to harass the respondent, or is the drinking an overt or covert means on the part of the respondent to vent his spleen on his spouse. But while the exact implications of the context of the "problems with spouse or relatives" may be unavailable in the interview record, at minimum this sort of potential or actual problem *does* signify that alcohol is perceived as playing *a* role in an interpersonal problem, even if not necessarily a causal role. Findings in this survey will show later (Table 2) that reports of troubles with spouse or relatives about one's drinking were usually accompanied by other potential problems related to drinking: those persons with a high score on spouse-or-relative troubles had an average of 2.4 *additional* problems or potential problems related to drinking, and only 23 per cent of persons with a high score on spouse-or-relative problems did not report having a high score on one or more other problems related to drinking.

Problems with friends or neighbors. Includes the respondent's report that friends or neighbors had suggested he cut down on his drinking, or that he himself felt his drinking had been harmful to his friendships and social life. This set of potential problems is subject to the same variability in implications and consequences as "problems with spouse or relatives." In addition, it is likely that heavy drinkers will gravitate toward a different set of persons who will drink with them or condone their heavy drinking. Thus this index of problem drinking is a conservative indicator of the extent of disaffection of friends or neighbors related to drinking. (Higher scores on this type of problem included instances in which two or more of the following applied: friends indicated the respondent should cut down on drinking, neighbors so indicated, or respondent felt his drinking had had a harmful effect on his friendships and social life.)

Job problems. This set of problems includes the respondent's having lost or nearly lost a job because of drinking, having had people at work suggest that he cut down on drinking, or having reported himself that his drinking had been harmful to his work and employment opportunities. Whether drinking affects one's job performance and working relationships is of course contingent upon whether the job practically "requires" drinking and whether the individual can organize his work and life style so as not to interfere too much with his drinking, and is subject to further variations in consequences depending upon whether the individual may be retired or otherwise outside the labor force (including those unemployable because of their drinking). To some, jeopardy of a job because of drinking will have serious consequences; to others it will be a trifling matter. Further, as demonstrated by Trice (1962) in a study of Alcoholics Anonymous members, job changes and unemployment can be as much a function of occupational type and socioeconomic status as it is of the drinking behavior: that "alcoholism is not a process developing apart from social organization but is deeply embedded therein" (p. 509). However, the level of responses on job problems was set high enough so that relatively few qualified on this index; and thus it is believed that this index is also a conservative indicator of the prevalence of job problems related to drinking. (A respondent was given a higher score on this problem if he said he had lost a job, or nearly lost one, from his drinking; or if people at work said he should cut down; or if he felt his drinking had a harmful effect on his work or employment opportunities.)

Problems with law, police, accidents. A person was scored as having a problem of this type if he reported trouble with the law over driving after drinking, or over-drinking, or that his drinking contributed to an accident in which there was personal injury.[8] The findings may reflect differences by ethnic minority group, age, sex, and socioeconomic status, since police are reputed to be more severe with members of minorities, young men, and those who are poor and thus less resourceful about doing their heavy drinking in private. However, those who have problems with the law or police are therefore more likely to be disadvantaged in their future interpersonal relationships, regardless of whether their drinking actually warranted the attention of the police.

Health. A high score on this index was based on the respondent's reporting both that he felt drinking had been harmful to his health and that a physician had advised him to cut down on his drinking. Some of these instances may reflect not so much a problem as a potential solution, if the physician's suggestion causes an awakening to the potential detrimental effects of excessive drinking; and in other instances the report that a physician suggested cutting down might have stemmed either from the respondent's hypochondria in seeking out the physician or reporting his advice, or from having an overzealous physician. Therefore, such instances of reported physician's advice to cut down on drinking should be followed by more detailed knowledge of the person's circumstances or his subsequent behavior, if we are to be able to assess whether the reported health problem is primarily a problem or a solution. That a health problem related to drinking often may not be a long-term problem is implied in the finding that 53 per cent of those with a high score on the health problem did not achieve high scores on any other potential problem.

Financial problems. This category included instances where the respondent reported he felt drinking had had a harmful effect on his financial position. Responses may have been affected in a few instances by free-floating anxiety rather than by objective experience with spending for drink beyond one's means; however, relatively few persons admitted to having had a drink-related financial problem, and most of them had high scores on other problems.

Belligerence. In these cases the respondent felt aggressive or cross after drinking, or got into a fight or a heated argument. This is

[8] This category included a very few persons who reported getting into an accident; these individuals were lumped with the problems with law or police group because legal implications were involved in most instances.

included as a potential problem, although the belligerence must be expressed in order to do damage to one's interpersonal relationships. Further, in some cultural contexts the expression of belligerence in relation to drinking may represent a relatively healthy and socially accepted outlet (MacAndrew and Edgerton, 1969, Chapter Five). Belligerence was retained as a potential problem in order later to test the hypothesis that a covert reaction of belligerence may often be followed by later increase in interpersonal problems.

A crucial question to be answered in relation to this study of problem drinking is the issue of validity: to what extent can people be relied upon to tell the interviewer the "truth" about such sensitive issues? And even if the respondent tries to tell the truth about his own drinking experiences and problems, to what extent can he be relied upon not to rationalize or suppress from memory some things in his past which he might rather forget?

The direct evidence on validity in such studies of problem drinking is indeed slender, consisting of a few isolated instances when some verifiable type of behavior was checked against official records. Fortunately, the limited evidence available indicates that respondents tend to be reasonably accurate in reporting such experiences as arrests for drunkenness, although they exhibit some tendency to place such experiences farther back in time than they actually occurred (Robins, 1966; Knupfer and Monsky, 1966). It is conceded that it is more likely that the percentages reported here for various types of problems associated with drinking represent understatements rather than overstatements of drinking problems. Thus these findings are reported not with any claim of absolute validity, but are coupled with many illustrations of two other finds of validation: concurrent validity (findings of relative prevalences of problems among subgroups congruent with comparative data from other sources); and construct validity (findings congruent with an established body of theory about the true interrelationships between various types of problems or the expected correlates of various problems).

The case for the relative validity of respondents' reports of their own behavior in this series of studies was advanced by Cisin as follows: "In pursuit of the validity question, it seems appropriate to point out that what is of interest here is not the detailed accuracy of any subject's report; the uniqueness of any individual and the reproducibility of his behavior should be the problem of clinical studies, not of gross, large-scale surveys. Rather, what is of interest here is the classification of individuals into rather broad categories. Thus the question of validity ought not to be asked about the *truthfulness* of any individual statements, but about the resultant *summary* classification of each individual" (1963, pp. 608–609).

Accordingly, the prevalence rates for the various types of drinking problems presented in the following chapters should not be considered absolute, immutable rates. Future studies will produce somewhat different rates, depending upon the types of problems covered, the number and kinds of questions asked to measure the problems, the base period covered (whether one year, three years, or longer), the ways in which the problem indices are scored, and other considerations. The chief value of prevalence rates from surveys of this type is to be found in relative comparisons within each survey—comparisons between the specific types of problems themselves, and comparisons of prevalence rates for various subgroups within the population. The next chapter presents such findings.

III Identifying Problem Drinkers

Past studies have indicated that we should expect to find substantial differences in rates of the occurrence of problems associated with drinking among certain subgroups in the national population, notably by sex, age, socioeconomic status, urbanization, and ethnocultural characteristics. This chapter presents findings on these subgroups, after first presenting some comparisons of differences in aggregate prevalence rates among the eleven specific types of problems.

Table 1 presents a simplified summary of the prevalence of each of the specific types of actual or potential drinking problems as having occurred during the last three years, this period having been chosen as a convenient span for measuring "current" drinking experience, since it coincided approximately with the period between the two stages of interviews in this study, and because a three-year span would make it more likely that more potential problems would be detected than if a one-year span had been used. At the bottom of Table 1 appear the findings on the "current problems score," which combine results for the eleven individual types of drinking-related problems.[1]

[1] Full details on all the items and the procedures for scoring the eleven

Each one of the individual problems entering into the overall Current Problems Score was scored as to its presumed severity or on the basis of the number of items answered affirmatively. Each type of problem was given equal weight in the overall current problems score (except for health problems, financial problems, and belligerence, which were given a lower maximum weight not because of their presumed lesser importance but because each included very few items). Generally, a fairly high overall current problems score of seven points or more (the dividing line used for many of the analyses in the following chapters) could be attained only by having problems in two or more areas, with at least one being rated as being in severe form; or problems in three or more areas, with at least two being at least moderate in severity; or problems in five or more areas, with at least one being moderate or severe; or slight problems in seven or more areas.

The chief specific problems for men shown in Table 1 were frequent intoxication, symptomatic drinking, psychological dependence, and problems with spouse or relatives. None of the specific problems showed a "high" rate for women in excess of the 4 per cent for health problems. Fifteen per cent of the men and 4 per cent of the women (and thus 9 per cent of the total) had what was judged to be a fairly "high" score on the combined index for the eleven problems taken together. The scoring procedures were perhaps rather arbitrary, though logical enough in giving the problems differential weights in accordance with their presumed severity; and scores were also affected by the number of items within a problem area which a respondent reported as being applicable.

Depending upon where one puts the cutting point on scores, one can represent the adult population as having a high rate of problem drinking (since 43 per cent of men, 21 per cent of women, and 31 per cent of the total reported having had some degree of one or more of the eleven types of problems during the three preceding years), or as having a relatively low rate (almost six out of ten men and eight out of ten women reported having none of these eleven actual or potential problems at any time during the last three years).

One out of six American male adults have at least a moderate potential problem of getting intoxicated fairly often; two out of five

individual types of problems and the combined current problems score are in the Supplementary Tables and Scoring Procedures, available from the author upon reimbursement for cost of reproduction.

Table 1. PREVALENCE OF DRINKING-RELATED PROBLEMS OVER THREE YEARS, BY SEX
(in percentages)

Type of Problem	MEN (N = 751)			WOMEN (N = 608)		
	None	Moderate	High	None	Moderate	High
1. Index of Frequent Intoxication[a]	83	3	14	97	1	2
2. Binge drinking	97	—	3	100	—	*
3. Symptomatic drinking[b]	84	8	8	93	4	3
4. Psychological dependence	61	31	8	85	12	3
5. Problems with current spouse or relatives	84	8	8	96	3	1
6. Problems with friends or neighbors	93	5	2	97	3	*
7. Job problems	94	3	3	98	2	1
8. Problems with police or accidents	99	—	1	99	—	1
9. Health[c]	88	6	6	93	4	4
10. Financial problems	91	6	3	98	2	1
11. Belligerence associated with drinking	88	8	4	93	5	3
Current Problems Score, combining results for the 11 specific problems. (High score: 7+ of a maximum of 58)	57	28	15	79	17	4

[a] Components: frequency and amount-per-occasion, and frequency of getting high or tight.
[b] Positive responses to such items as difficulty stopping drinking, blackouts, sneaking drinks.
[c] Physician told respondent to cut down drinking.

NOTE: All percentages in the tables in this book represent weighted findings (see Appendix A) projectable against the household population. Numbers (*e.g.*, N = 751) are the actual number of interviews in the group specified. Tables add horizontally for each sex. Totals may vary from 100 per cent because of rounding each figure to nearest whole per cent.

* Less than one-half of one per cent.

men and 15 per cent of the women appear to have at least some psychological dependence upon alcohol; and 12 per cent of men and 8 per cent of women said they had had something of a health problem associated with their drinking within the past three years. However, it is with some hesitation that the rates of real or potential problem drinking shown here are described as "prevalence" rates at all, since "prevalence" may be taken as connoting an absolute rather than an arbitrarily defined rate, as in the prevalence of a relatively clearly defined disease such as pneumonia.

For those wishing to bite the bullet and take a stand for a single prevalence rate, the writer recommends, for interim use only, the combined current problems score of seven or higher as denoting a fair likelihood that this level of overall score isolates most of those with a recognizable problem (or set of problems) related to drinking. However, the ultimate test of the utility of any particular set of arbitrary criteria as to what constitutes a potentially "severe" problem is whether in the long run the problem either becomes, or continues to be, of serious adverse consequences in relation either to the person's own long-term well-being from his own standpoint, or to his relations to other people. Thus the standards for what constitute a "severe" problem need to be tested by time: how does a problem of a certain type at time A relate to the same individual's well-being at a later time B? Exactly this type of test will be applied on these findings a few years hence, when the same respondents are to be scheduled for a reinterview and adverse experiences (including mortality rates) are evaluated in relation to the earlier scores on drinking problems.

In the interim, another criterion for the usefulness for these problems scores is whether they serve to differentiate between subgroups of people who might be expected to vary in their current problem rates, in the light of past studies which have shown a higher rate of problem drinking among men, those under sixty, those of lower socioeconomic status, those living in the largest cities, and those with certain social-psychological characteristics which will be described below. These scoring procedures yield results which are consistent with theory and with the findings of other studies in the past.

HOW PROBLEMS ARE RELATED

The degree to which the various problems are linked together is important in inferring the nature and significance of each type of problem, and also in showing whether the various types of problems are sufficiently interrelated to permit us to use one single index of problem drinking (such as the Current Problems Score discussed earlier) for some descriptions of various groups within the national household population. The set of eleven types of problems fares rather well in that regard, with intercorrelations ranging from .10 to .51. (The highest correlations are between symptomatic drinking and six of the ten other variables: index of frequent intoxication, psychological dependence, problems with spouse or relatives, problems with friends or neighbors, job problems, and belligerence). Another test of how well the various problems combine was the application of a principal components factor analysis, which found all but two of the variables loading on one single factor, the two exceptions being the two which accounted for a relative handful of cases (problems with police or accidents, and binge drinking).[2] Thus the available evidence indicates that the eleven types can be considered to be sufficiently interrelated to be combined into a single current problems score for certain analytic purposes, although the individual problems (plus a typology which takes into account the interactions among some of the major types of problems) will be analyzed against a number of demographic and other variables later in this chapter.

The interrelationships between the various types of problems are shown in another form in Table 2. Here the relationships are shown in percentage form, to put problems of various frequencies on a standardized basis to facilitate comparison. Some of the principal relationships to be gleaned from Table 2 are as follows: The types of problems with the highest mean number of other problems were those which were the least common. This is in part an artifact of the fact that if variables have a fair degree of intercorrelation, the ones with the lowest frequencies have the highest chance of occurring along with the other variables. It also may be a reflection of the "seriousness" of some of the problems: note that the highest means belong to binge drinking, problems with friends or neighbors, job problems, or problems involved with police or accidents. In the former instance, binge drinking probably rates low on a social acceptability scale; and the latter three problems imply a failure to manage one's drinking so as to escape the censure of people outside one's own household. Only one variable, "health," was the sole problem with a "high" qualifying

[2] See the Supplementary Tables, obtainable from the author.

Table 2. INTERRELATIONSHIPS OF SPECIFIC TYPES OF PROBLEMS
(Dichotomized at higher scores shown in Table 1)

Type of Problem	No. Persons Qual.	Mean No. Probs.	Had Only the One P.	1.	2.	3.	4.	5.	6.	7.	8.	9.	10.	11.	Overall Current Problems Score 7+
				Type of Problem, in Percentages											
1. Freq. Intox.	(134)	2.6	36	X	11	34	31	23	7	10	2	13	7	19	73
2. Binge drinking	(25)	4.5	7	54	X	65	35	56	16	32	14	32	12	39	93
3. Symptomatic dr.	(87)	3.4	15	47	18	X	32	38	12	13	12	28	5	30	82
4. Psychol. dep.	(91)	2.8	32	43	9	32	X	26	5	13	4	16	12	20	68
5. Spouse, relat.	(72)	3.4	23	39	19	47	32	X	17	18	4	27	13	28	77
6. Friends, neigh.	(16)	5.5	—	54	26	74	31	83	X	37	9	57	26	49	100
7. Job	(30)	4.3	6	42	27	42	42	45	20	X	17	36	26	30	94
8. Police, accid.	(13)	3.9	6	20	23	71	26	20	9	31	X	43	6	43	94
9. Health	(67)	2.6	53	20	10	32	19	25	11	13	8	X	8	15	47
10. Financial	(27)	3.3	30	31	11	16	41	34	14	27	3	22	X	30	66
11. Belligerence	(54)	3.4	32	40	16	46	31	35	12	15	11	20	14	X	56
Overall Current Problems Score 7+	(158)	—	—	59	15	48	40	37	10	17	9	24	12	25	X

NOTE: This table should be read horizontally; for example, the 134 persons qualifying as having a "high" score in Frequent Intoxication had a mean number of problems (including that one problem) of 2.6 out of 11.0. Of these 134 persons, 11 per cent qualified as having a "high" score on Binge drinking and (finally) 73 per cent qualified as having a Current Problems Score (overall) of 7+. Warning: means or percentages based on less than 30 persons should be interpreted with caution.

score for as many as half of those who reported it. As we have discussed earlier, "health" has an ambiguous status as a "problem" in any case, because it singles out those who have consulted a physician and who have been advised to reduce their drinking; many of those mentioning having received this advice were aging persons who may have been on the brink of reducing their drinking in any case. "Health" was mentioned as a problem by only 13 per cent of those who had a high score on frequent intoxication—which (unlike health) is most common among men in their twenties.

Frequent intoxication was most often found to be accompanied by symptomatic drinking and psychological dependence, and binge drinking most often was accompanied by symptomatic drinking and problems with spouse or relatives. Problems with friends and neighbors were accompanied in a majority of instances by frequent intoxication, symptomatic drinking, problems with spouse or friends, and health problems—another way of stating that it is plausible that by the time one's drinking draws remonstrances from friends and neighbors, it is likely that the person's behavior has become a problem to his own immediate family—or at least that his family and his drinking are incompatible.

Looking to the vertical column to the left of the table, almost all of those with "high" scores on binge drinking, problems with friends and neighbors, job problems, and police or accident problems also qualified for "high" scores on the overall current problems score. Inspecting the bottom horizontal row of the table, frequent intoxication, symptomatic drinking, and psychological dependence are seen as being the most frequent among those with high current problems scores; this is largely a function of the relatively high number of persons qualifying on these three types of problems. On a separate regression analysis, it was found that these three variables alone correlated .92 with the current problems score, thus accounting for 85 per cent of the variance on the current problems score, leaving the other 15 per cent to be accounted for by the eight other types of problems with lower rates of prevalence.[3]

SPECIFIC PROBLEMS AMONG SEX AND AGE GROUPS

Tables 3 and 4 summarize the current problems data and data on the eleven specific types of problems separately for men and women

[3] See the Supplementary Tables, available from the author.

of six age groups. All studies of drinking problems have found that more men than women have such problems, and a larger proportion of persons under fifty have drinking problems than do older persons. As would be expected, this national study confirms these general findings. However, when findings are inspected separately for men and women within each of six age groups, it is seen that somewhat different patterns of problems emerge:

> Among men (Table 3) drinking problems generally taper off sharply only after age fifty, but continue at a fairly high level until the age of seventy, while among women (Table 4) the prevalence of these problems becomes very slight indeed after the age of fifty. The general patterns of Current Problems are somewhat different for men of various ages than for women: among men, the prevalence of problems (in the aggregate) is highest among those in their twenties, conspicuously lower in the thirties and forties, and then tapering off somewhat in the fifties. On the other hand, relatively few women in their twenties report problems, with the bulk of problems for women appearing to be concentrated among those in their thirties and forties, with (again) a very sharp dropoff in the fifties. These differences between men and women are consistent with the inference that while men may generally get introduced to heavier drinking by other men when they are young, women more often get involved in heavier drinking relatively later, perhaps as a result of their husbands' or men friends' influence. Younger men show relatively higher prevalence of the specific problems of frequent intoxication and symptomatic (or addictive) drinking, problems with spouse or relatives, use of alcohol because of psychological dependence, and development of belligerence while drinking, while older men (especially those in their forties and fifties) show a higher prevalence than younger men of health problems; and women in their forties have a higher prevalence of drinking because of psychological dependence than is the case with younger or older women. Exceptions to the general downward trend in problems among the older men are the apparent increase in the rate of Symptomatic drinking among men in their fifties compared to those in their forties and the increase in the rate of health problems related to drinking among men in their forties and fifties compared to rates for younger men.

The findings shown in Tables 3 and 4 above are consistent with past studies of alcoholics insofar as the finding that a relatively small proportion of women over fifty and men over seventy appear to have serious drinking problems (Malzberg, 1960; Bailey, Haberman,

Table 3. SPECIFIC PROBLEMS ASSOCIATED WITH DRINKING AMONG MEN IN SIX AGE GROUPS (in percentages)

Higher Scores on Drinking-Related Problems[a]		Age Groups					
		21–29	30–39	40–49	50–59	60–69	70–Up
	N =	(104)	(156)	(180)	(143)	(100)	(68)
Current Problems Score 7+		25	16	17	13	12	1
Index of Frequent Intoxication		21	16	17	9	9	2
Binge drinking		6	3	3	2	3	—
Symptomatic behavior		19	8	6	10	2	—
Psychological dependence		15	5	12	9	4	—
Problems with spouse, relatives		16	7	8	9	5	—
Problems with friends, neighbors		2	2	1	3	2	—
Problems with job related to drinking		4	3	5	4	1	—
Problems with police or accidents		3	—	1	2	3	—
Health (physician said cut down)		6	5	7	9	4	1
Financial problems related to drinking		3	5	1	3	2	—
Belligerence associated with drinking		12	7	3	4	—	—

[a] For definitions of higher scores, see Table 1.

Table 4. SPECIFIC PROBLEMS ASSOCIATED WITH DRINKING AMONG WOMEN IN SIX AGE GROUPS (in percentages)

Higher Score on Drinking Related Problems[a]		Age Groups					
		21–29	30–39	40–49	50–59	60–69	70–Up
	N =	(92)	(129)	(157)	(106)	(64)	(60)
Current Problems Score 7+		2	8	7	2	1	*
Index of Frequent Intoxication		2	3	4	3	2	—
Binge drinking		—	1	1	—	—	—
Symptomatic behavior		5	5	4	1	1	—
Psychological dependence		1	4	7	2	*	*
Problems with spouse, relatives		1	3	1	1	—	—
Problems with friends, neighbors		1	—	1	—	—	—
Problems with job related to drinking		1	*	1	—	—	—
Problems with police or accidents		—	1	1	1	—	—
Health (physician said cut down)		3	5	4	4	2	1
Financial problems concerned with drinking		3	1	1	—	*	*
Belligerence associated with drinking		7	3	3	1	1	*

[a] For definitions of higher scores, see Table 1.
* Less than one-half of one per cent.

and Alksne, 1965; Drew, 1968; Gibbins, 1968). Findings regarding activities other than drinking, such as use of drugs (Winick, 1964) and sexual activities (Kinsey, Pomeroy, and Martin, 1948), consistently show the same general pattern of "maturing out" or "senescence" or "withdrawal." Where these national survey findings do differ from some of the statistics on labeled alcoholics is that a much higher relative proportion of persons in their twenties (as compared to those in their thirties and forties) show up in the survey as having drinking problems than is the case among labeled alcoholics (Malzberg, 1960, p. 6). Part of the reason for this is that it ordinarily takes many years of hard drinking before the problem drinker becomes publicly known as an "alcoholic"; and part of the reason may be that when persons persist in heavy drinking beyond their twenties, they tend to encounter a much higher level of intolerance of such conduct on the part of significant others. One implication from the standpoint of preventive medicine and public health is that it should be worthwhile to concentrate more intensively upon the young, so that problem drinking of people in their twenties less often hardens into what is finally perceived as "alcoholism" in their forties and fifties.

In the forthcoming final stage of this series of longitudinal studies, it will be possible to determine whether these age group differences are relatively constant reflections of the effects of physiological, sociological, and psychological forces upon individuals within our culture, or whether they may reflect only temporary influences—such as the lingering effects of Prohibition and repeal. If these age patterns are found to be at all enduring, the findings certainly point to the twenties through the fifties for men, and the thirties and forties for women, as the periods which are worthy of special attention from public health and social welfare workers.

SOCIOECONOMIC STATUS

Exploration of differences by socioeconomic level in the prevalence of the various types of drinking problems will shed further light both on the probable implications of the specific problems and on the fact that those of upper and lower status are rather dissimilar in their problem patterns even when age is held constant. Table 5 presents findings on the same specific problems (and overall Current Problems Score) as for the six age groups shown in Table 3, except that these are subdivided by socioeconomic status, using a variant of Hollings-

Table 5. Specific Problems, Men in Six Age Groups, Divided by Socioeconomic Status[a]
(in percentages)

		Higher Socioeconomic Status						
Type of Problem	N =	20's (53)	30's (85)	40's (106)	50's (73)	60's (45)	70's (20)	Total (382)
Frequent Intoxication		17	13	16	6	4	—	11
Binge drinking		2	1	1	—	—	—	1
Symptomatic drinking		21	6	4	5	—	—	6
Psychological dependence		11	5	13	7	4	—	8
Problems with spouse, relatives		11	5	7	5	4	—	6
Problems with friends, neighbors		—	1	—	—	—	—	*
Job problems		2	3	2	—	—	—	1
Problems with police, accidents		2	—	—	—	3	—	1
Health (doctor said cut down)		4	3	5	7	3	2	4
Financial problems		—	3	—	—	—	—	1
Belligerence		5	8	2	—	—	—	3
Overall Current Problems Score of 7+		18	13	12	6	8	—	11

		Lower Socioeconomic Status					
Type of Problem N =	20's (51)	30's (71)	40's (74)	50's (70)	60's (55)	70's (48)	Total (369)
Frequent Intoxication	25	20	19	12	13	3	16
Binge drinking	9	6	6	4	6	—	5
Symptomatic drinking	18	11	8	16	4	—	10
Psychological dependence	19	4	12	11	5	—	9
Problems with spouse, relatives	22	9	10	14	6	—	10
Problems with friends, neighbors	4	4	2	6	3	—	3
Job problems	6	4	9	8	2	—	5
Problems with police, accidents	3	—	2	3	3	—	2
Health (doctor said cut down)	8	7	10	10	6	—	7
Financial problems	7	8	3	6	3	—	5
Belligerence	18	5	4	8	—	—	6
Overall Current Problems Score of 7+	32	20	25	20	15	2	20

[a] Hollingshead's index of social position (1957).

* Less than one-half of one per cent.

head's index of social position (1957).[4] Here results are presented only for men, since the prevalence rates for women are generally too small to be particularly illuminating.

Rather consistently, Table 5 shows an apparent pattern of greater "maturing out" (or diminution) of drinking problems among those of higher socioeconomic status as they get older, than is the case among those of lower status. Particularly is this the case for frequent intoxication, symptomatic drinking, and all of the interpersonal problems (with spouse or relatives, friends or neighbors, jobs, and police or accidents). For example, on frequent intoxication, note that the rate has dwindled to 6 per cent and 4 per cent, respectively, among upper-status men in their fifties and sixties, in contrast to 12 and 13 per cent, respectively, among lower-status men; among upper-status men in their fifties, the rate for symptomatic drinking is 5 per cent; among lower-status men of the same age, the rate is three times as high, or 16 per cent.

Some of the reasons for these differences between upper and lower socioeconomic levels of men are analyzed in detail in a later chapter, in terms of some of the differences in social-psychological characteristics of the different socioeconomic levels; these include differences in tendencies toward greater alienation and lesser impulse-control on the part of those of lower status. One may hazard the guess also that the lower-status man finds his environment less supportive or tolerant if he drinks heavily at times; but one is tempted to infer that the differences in rates of drinking problems for lower-status and upper-status men are not merely a function of the older upper-status man's being in a better position to conceal his heavy drinking from the general public. The upper-status men also show a markedly lower prevalence of concealable type-of-drinking indices (frequent intoxication, binge drinking, and symptomatic drinking) as well as in the less concealable interpersonal types of problems. Thus one would modify the conclusions regarding trends by age groups discussed above (Table 3) by saying that while men of lower status have relatively little apparent shrinkage in the rates of drinking problems from their thirties through their fifties, men of upper socioeconomic status show a marked apparent lessening of their rates after the age of fifty.

Again, the term "apparent shrinkage" is used in relation to the

[4] As applied here, the index of social position takes into account the educational and occupational levels of the main earner within the household.

differences between age levels because it is possible that the differences between age levels is a function of historical considerations (for example, generations coming of drinking age before and after the repeal of Prohibition). This appears unlikely because there do not seem to have been corresponding dramatic increases in rates of arrests for drunkenness over the years since repeal; but the constancy of this apparent "maturing out" phenomenon is subject to further check through follow-up studies of the same individuals over a period of time. This phenomenon will be one of the main points for investigation in the final studies in this series, to be conducted several years hence. An additional analysis of the data on specific types of problems for these same age groups will be presented in the next section of this chapter, which deals with a typology in which the interpersonal types of problems are combined into one index.

TYPOLOGY

The usefulness of typologies, or combinations of types of drinking problems, should be explored whenever possible, in order to guard against concealing important interactions between types of problems which may affect the correlates of drinking problems among subgroups classified according to demographic or other characteristics. A number of typologies have been utilized in analysis of the San Francisco 1964 data by Clark and Knupfer, and by the present writer in analyzing the results from the two-stage Hartford survey. Clark (1966, p. 663) used several combinations of problems, including "excessive intake," "self-perceived drinking problems," "interpersonal problems" (including problems with police, at work, with spouse, friends, or troubles with aggressiveness), and "possible addiction or coping." Knupfer (1967, p. 978) used "social consequences" (much like Clark's "interpersonal problems"), "dependence" (self-perceived problems, use of alcohol for coping, and addictive symptoms), and "excessive intake" (prolonged drunks and frequent high intake). Cahalan used the following typology in the Hartford study: "interpersonal problems," "non-interpersonal problems only," "drank but no problems in last three years," and "never drank as often as once a year" (1968).

The sample in the 1967 national survey was materially larger than in the San Francisco and Hartford surveys, permitting the use of a somewhat more detailed six-category typology along similar lines, as follows:

Group 1. Those who said they had not drunk at all during the preceding two and one-half years constituted a "didn't drink" group in the typology. The distinction between the "didn't drink" and "no problem" groups was preserved because past regional and national studies in this series have shown that the abstainer tends to be quite different in characteristics from the light or moderate drinker (Knupfer and Room, 1970; Cisin and Cahalan, 1968; Cahalan, Cisin, and Crossley, 1969; Cahalan *et al.,* 1965; Cahalan, 1968).

Group 2. Those who had drunk at least a little during the most recent two and one-half years but who did not qualify in one of the following groups, were termed the "no problems" group.

Group 3. Persons who did not qualify for either the "interpersonal problems" or "implicative drinking" groups, described below, but who had drunk at least four drinks on some occasion during the prior two and one-half years and who also answered at least two of five questions in a way which indicated that a leading motivation for drinking was for personal reasons, were categorized as the "psychological dependence" group.

Group 4. Those who did not qualify for the "interpersonal problems" group were combined into an "implicative drinking" group[5] if they had a score of two or higher on the "implicative drinking patterns" index, that is, scored high on frequent intoxication, binge drinking, or symptomatic drinking. These persons' problems associated with drinking were assumed to be of lesser gravity than for the "interpersonal problems" group, since they denied that their drinking during the preceding three years had seriously affected their interpersonal relationships. They had to be rather heavy drinkers to get into this group; and the hypothesis will be tested, in a subsequent follow-up study, that these individuals would be more likely than more moderate drinkers to encounter social consequences in their drinking if they continue with their present style of drinking.

Group 5. The four "interpersonal" types of problems (with spouse or relatives, friends or neighbors, on the job, or with police or accidents) were singled out as indicating problems of relatively unambiguous seriousness in terms of the social consequences of these types of conflict or misunderstandings related to drinking. Persons having a

[5] Keller's term (1962) for drinking which arouses suspicions of alcoholism.

score of two or higher on the combination of these types of "interpersonal problems" were classified in Group 5 if they did not also belong in the "implicative drinking" group.

Group 6. Persons in this group were those who were classified as having a high score in both "implicative drinking" and "interpersonal problems." These were isolated as most likely to have the more serious types of problems related to drinking.

Table 6 presents the distribution of this problem-drinking typology for men and women of three age levels within each of two socioeconomic levels. Eighty-four per cent of the total appeared to have had no drinking problems of consequence; 6 per cent were registered in the implicative drinking group, 2 per cent in the interpersonal-only group, and 4 per cent in the group with both implicative and interpersonal problems. Men under sixty exhibited a higher rate of interpersonal problems relative to implicative drinking, compared to older men. Interpersonal problems also occurred relatively more frequently among lower-status men than among others. It will be seen that relatively more of the women, those of lower status, and older people were non-drinkers than was true for the others. The last two rows in Table 6 also show that lower-status women had much higher percentages of non-drinkers than upper-status women, though the lower-status women had the same rates for the three types of problems or potential problems. This is another way of saying that there is a smaller proportion of moderate drinkers among the lower-status women than among other women: if the tabulation had set aside the non-drinkers, the rates of problem drinkers among drinkers would have been higher for lower-status women.

Further analysis of the problem rates for men is presented below in Table 7, where twelve age and economic-status groups are shown. Six out of ten lower-status men in their twenties had some kind of problem or potential problem, and half were in the more consequential implicative drinking and interpersonal problems groups. Implicative drinking was high (relative to interpersonal problems) among lower-status men in their sixties.

The findings underscore the importance of preventive and remedial public health measures directed at men in their twenties and earlier, since the facts belie the stereotype that the prevalence of problem drinking is highest in the late thirties and early forties. Perhaps

Table 6. CURRENT PROBLEM-DRINKING TYPOLOGY, BY SEX, AGE, AND SOCIAL POSITION (in percentages)[a]

Sex, Age, and Index of Social Position (ISP)	N	(1)[b] Didn't Drink	(2) No Problems	(3) Psychol. Dependence	(4) Implicative Drinking	(5) Social Consequences	(6) Both (4) and (5)
Grand Total	(1359)	24	60	3	6	2	4
Total Men	(750)	15	58	5	11	4	7
Total Women	(608)	32	61	2	3	1	2
Men 21–39							
Upper ISP	(138)	5	67	5	14	4	6
Lower	(122)	11	47	4	18	7	13
Total	(260)	8	58	5	16	5	9
Men 40–59							
Upper ISP	(179)	11	65	8	9	3	5
Lower	(144)	22	46	2	11	6	12
Total	(323)	16	57	5	10	4	8
Men 60+							
Upper ISP	(65)	23	68	3	3	3	—
Lower	(103)	26	58	3	10	1	3
Total	(168)	25	62	3	7	2	2

Women 21–39							
Upper ISP	(123)	6	85	3	4	—	3
Lower	(98)	37	51	3	5	1	3
Total	(221)	22	67	3	4	1	3
Women 40–59							
Upper ISP	(133)	22	70	3	3	1	2
Lower	(130)	37	54	4	2	1	2
Total	(263)	30	62	3	3	1	2
Women 60+							
Upper ISP	(59)	36	62	—	1	1	1
Lower	(65)	62	37	—	*	—	1
Total	(124)	51	48	—	*	*	1
Men, Upper ISP	(382)	11	66	6	9	3	5
Men, Lower ISP	(369)	20	50	3	13	5	10
Women, Upper ISP	(315)	19	74	2	3	1	2
Women, Lower ISP	(293)	43	49	2	3	1	2

[a] Percentages may not always add to 100 horizontally, because of rounding.

[b] (1) Didn't drink during last two and one-half years. (2) Drank, no problems of apparent severity. (3) Psychological dependence only. (4) No severe social consequences, but implicative drinking (frequently intoxicated binge drinking, symptomatic drinking behavior). (5) Social consequences (problems with spouse, relatives, friends, neighbors, job, police or accidents), but no severe symptomatic drinking. (6) Both implicative drinking and social consequences.

* Less than one-half of one per cent.

Table 7. CURRENT PROBLEM-DRINKING TYPOLOGY, MEN IN SIX AGE GROUPS, BY SOCIAL POSITION (in percentages)[a]

Groups of Men	N	(1)[b] Didn't Drink	(2) No Problems	(3) Psychol. Dependence	(4) Implicative Drinking	(5) Social Consequences	(6) Both (4) and (5)
Higher Socioeconomic Status							
20's	(53)	5	57	6	16	6	10
30's	(85)	5	72	4	12	2	4
40's	(106)	8	63	7	11	4	7
50's	(73)	15	67	8	5	1	3
60's	(45)	27	62	4	4	4	—
70's+	(20)	16	84	—	—	—	—
Total Higher	(382)	11	66	6	9	3	5
Lower Socioeconomic Status							
20's	(51)	8	32	10	20	11	19

30's	(71)	13	59	—	17	4	8
40's	(74)	18	52	1	13	3	12
50's	(70)	26	40	4	9	9	12
60's	(55)	20	55	4	15	2	4
70's+	(48)	35	62	—	3	—	—
Total Lower	(369)	20	50	3	13	5	10
Total Men							
20's	(104)	7	44	8	18	9	15
30's	(156)	9	66	2	14	3	6
40's	(180)	12	58	5	12	4	9
50's	(143)	20	54	6	7	5	8
60's	(100)	23	58	4	10	2	2
70's+	(68)	29	69	—	2	—	—
Total	(751)	15	58	5	11	4	7

[a] Percentages may not always add to 100 horizontally, because of rounding.
[b] Key: see Table 6.

problem drinking is more memorable and conspicuous among those in their late thirties and early forties, both because many avoid becoming publicly labeled as "alcoholics" until they reach that age, and because drinking problems are more readily noticed if they occur in the lives of persons in age groups in which youthful "sowing of wild oats" is no longer as readily condoned. But these findings, as well as an independent replication of the same findings in a new 1969 national sample of men between twenty-one and fifty-nine (as yet unpublished), clearly demonstrate that the peak prevalence for almost all types of drinking problems is in the twenties rather than in older age groups.

These findings also reinforce the earlier findings from the same series of studies that the misuse of alcohol represents more of a threat to those of lower social status than to others (Cahalan, Cisin, and Crossley, 1969, p. 196). A majority among upper-status men in each of the six age groups were classified as not having discernible problems, while this was not true for lower-status men in their twenties.

Consistent with past studies (Mulford, 1964), size of city (or degree of urbanization) was found important in the prevalence of problem drinking, particularly as regards the prevalence of interpersonal problems.[6] Differences were particularly marked among men between forty and fifty-nine: apparently in this age group there is a greater tendency for men in small towns and rural areas to avoid interpersonal complications in association with their drinking than is true for men in their forties and fifties living in cities, particularly in cities of fifty thousand or more. It will be noted that psychological dependence is slightly, but consistently, higher in rate among those in larger cities than in smaller cities or rural areas. The same trend is true also, among men, for both of the two other types of problems.

The report of the national survey of drinking practices conducted by the Social Research Group in 1964–1965 showed that younger and older men of upper and lower socioeconomic status had different drinking patterns, depending upon whether they lived in larger or smaller cities (Cahalan, Cisin, and Crossley, 1969, p. 43). The highest proportion of abstainers and infrequent drinkers was found in the forty-five and over–lower-status–lower urbanization group, while the higher proportions of heavy drinkers was found in

[6] See Supplementary Tables and Scoring Procedures, available from the author upon request.

the twenty-one to forty-four–lower-status–higher urbanization group. The degree of urbanization appears to be related in different ways to drinking behavior depending upon age and social status; the earlier report speculated that it may be that these variations reflect different social pressures regarding drinking on the part of those of lower status, with greater social control in the smaller cities and rural areas (Cahalan, Cisin, and Crossley, 1969, p. 42).

An analysis of the interaction between socioeconomic status and urbanization in the rate of problem drinking also showed the same pattern.[7] The highest rate of having both interpersonal problems and implicative drinking behavior was in the group of younger men of lower social status in the largest cities, and the lowest rate was in the group of older men of higher status in the small and medium-size towns. Thus lower status and city size are cumulative in their apparent effects upon problem drinking: the term "apparent" is used because some of the cumulative effects may have been caused by in-migration of heavy drinkers to the larger cities or by some skidding downward in socioeconomic status as a result of drinking.

Somewhat different styles of drinking, and of motivations for and reactions to drinking, appear to be involved in the findings for the various types of drinking problems among the different ethnoreligious groups.[8] For example, the Irish Catholics, Latin-Americans or Caribbeans, and Negroes showed the highest rates of social-consequence drinking problems; the small group of British Catholics showed only implicative drinking as a problem; among Jews, drinking problems with social consequences would appear to be minimal.

Thus we have seen that there are differences in the types of drinking problems in various subgroups according to sex, age, socioeconomic status, urbanization, and ethnoreligious background. These differences appear to be congruent with the differences in the life-styles and stresses which might be expected among men as distinct from women, and among people of different age levels, social status, type of urbanization, and ethnocultural origins. Other differences in rates of drinking problems among these subgroups are presented in later chapters.

[7] See Supplementary Tables and Scoring Procedures, available from the author upon request.

[8] See Supplementary Tables and Scoring Procedures, available from the author upon request.

COMBINING BACKGROUND VARIABLES

We have just seen an analysis of how findings on a problem-drinking typology vary according to sex, age, socioeconomic status, size of city, and ethnocultural origin. These variables are worthy of special attention because they are about the most readily identifiable attributes that people have, and because public health and social action activities in the United States lend themselves to being directed toward subgroupings according to these variables, because special media and other channels of communication are available to permit considerable selectivity in dealing with these groups. Another reason for dealing with these variables as a group is that they are relatively stable characteristics, thus making more legitimate their use as independent variables for the purpose of predicting drinking problems or other social phenomena.[9]

Two separate multivariate analysis processes were carried out using these four variables in combination to predict problem drinking: sex, age, index of social position, and size of city.[10] (Ethnocultural origin was set aside because even in a sample of 1,359 the numbers in some subgroups were too small for these analytic purposes.) One of these analysis procedures was the stepwise multiple regression technique, in which first the single variable most highly correlated with the criterion variable (in this case, problem drinking) is singled out, and then the next variable which explains more of the remaining variance in problem drinking than any of the other variables; and so on until all variables have been accounted for. The advantage of this technique lies in its statistical power (higher statistical reliability of findings than some other methods, using the same size of sample) and its

[9] It can be argued that socioeconomic status and urbanization may change as a function of a person's drinking behavior (for example, losing jobs or drifting into lower-class work, or moving from a small town to a larger city "where the action is"). However, the socioeconomic indicator was a variant of Hollingshead's index of social position (1957), which does not change readily over such a short period of time as the three years between the two surveys, since its components are educational attainment and type of occupation rather than income; and relatively few persons moved from one size of city to another during the three-year period.

[10] The term "predict" is used, although some of the predicting data were drawn from the first survey and some from the second. Since the problem drinking data were gathered during the second survey, the process of estimation of problem drinking thus represented a combination of prediction from the first-stage and correlation from the second-stage data.

simplicity, in that it yields a single figure (R, the coefficient of multiple regression) as the index of the total variance on the criterion variable. The other technique is the AID (Automatic Interaction Detector) procedure, a non-parametric cross-tabulation procedure developed at the University of Michigan by Sonquist and Morgan (1964).[11] This analytic technique consists essentially of a series of cross-tabulations, applied so as to answer this question (Sonquist and Morgan, p. 4):

> Given the units of analysis under consideration what single predictor variable will give us a maximum improvement in our ability to predict values of the dependent variable? This question, embedded in an iterative scheme is the basis for the algorithm used in this program. . . . The program divides the sample, through a series of binary splits, into a mutually exclusive series of subgroups. Every observation is a member of exactly one of these subgroups. They are chosen so that at each step in the procedure, their means account for more of the total sum of squares (reduce the predictive error) than the means of any other equal member of subgroups.

As noted by Sonquist and Morgan (p. 2), the technique is appropriate for a situation (as in this instance of the correlates of problem drinking) in which the independent variables are "a mixture of nominal and-or ordinal scales (or coded intervals of an equal-interval scale) and the dependent variable is a continuous, or equal-interval scale."

The results on the first, or stepwise regression, method are shown in Table 8. Here it will be noted that sex was the single most effective predictor of current problems score, followed by age, then by city size, and finally by index of social position. The cumulative multiple regression or "R" was .27, which, when squared, is found to explain 7 per cent of the aggregate variance on the current problems score. While this is hardly a tremendous achievement in prediction, it at least demonstrates that we can make a prediction of someone's problem drinking which is significantly better than chance, even if all we know about the person is his sex, age, socioeconomic status, and size of city.

The advantages of the AID or Automatic Interaction Detector

[11] A procedure based upon the same principles, and differing only as to detail, was developed independently by Belson (1958, 1959) for analysis of survey data.

Table 8. MULTIVARIATE ANALYSIS OF BACKGROUND VARIABLES AGAINST CURRENT PROBLEMS SCORE (CPS) (Divided at Score of 7+ or higher)

Background Variables	Correlation with CPS (Pearson r)	Partial Correlation	Multiple Correlation (Stepwise Regression) (R)
Sex	.19	.20	.19
Age (6 groups)	.11	.13	.22
City size (6 groups)	.11	.12	.25
Index of Social Position (4 groups)	.08	.11	.27

procedure over that of the multiple regression procedure are that it permits one to detect the existence of nonlinear interactions between two or more variables in the determination of the problem drinking score, and that the technique singles out discrete subgroups with exceptionally high or low proportions of problem drinkers. As an illustration, Table 12 reveals the existence of several of these subgroups with high mean current problems scores: the branching "tree" or chart of sub-groups shows that men in the aggregate had 15 per cent with a "high" current problems score; that 34 per cent of the men in the cities of one million or more had a high score; and that among the remainder this percentage grew to 20 per cent for men of lower index of social position (ISP), to 23 per cent of men of lower ISP who were aged twenty-one to fifty-nine, and finally to 34 per cent for men of lower ISP aged twenty-one to fifty-nine who were residents of cities of fifty thousand or more. Among women, on the other hand, age was a better discriminator of problem drinking than socioeconomic status, although women as a group did not show much variance in problem drinking on these four variables. It will be noted that the AID procedure explained more of the variance in problem drinking (Figure 1, 19 per cent) than did the multiple correlation procedure (Table 8, 27^2 or 7 per cent). The reason is that the AID procedure permits taking into account the interactions between the variables.

For this specific comparison, it would appear that the AID technique is more useful than the multiple correlation approach in delineating specific groups with high problem-drinking scores. However,

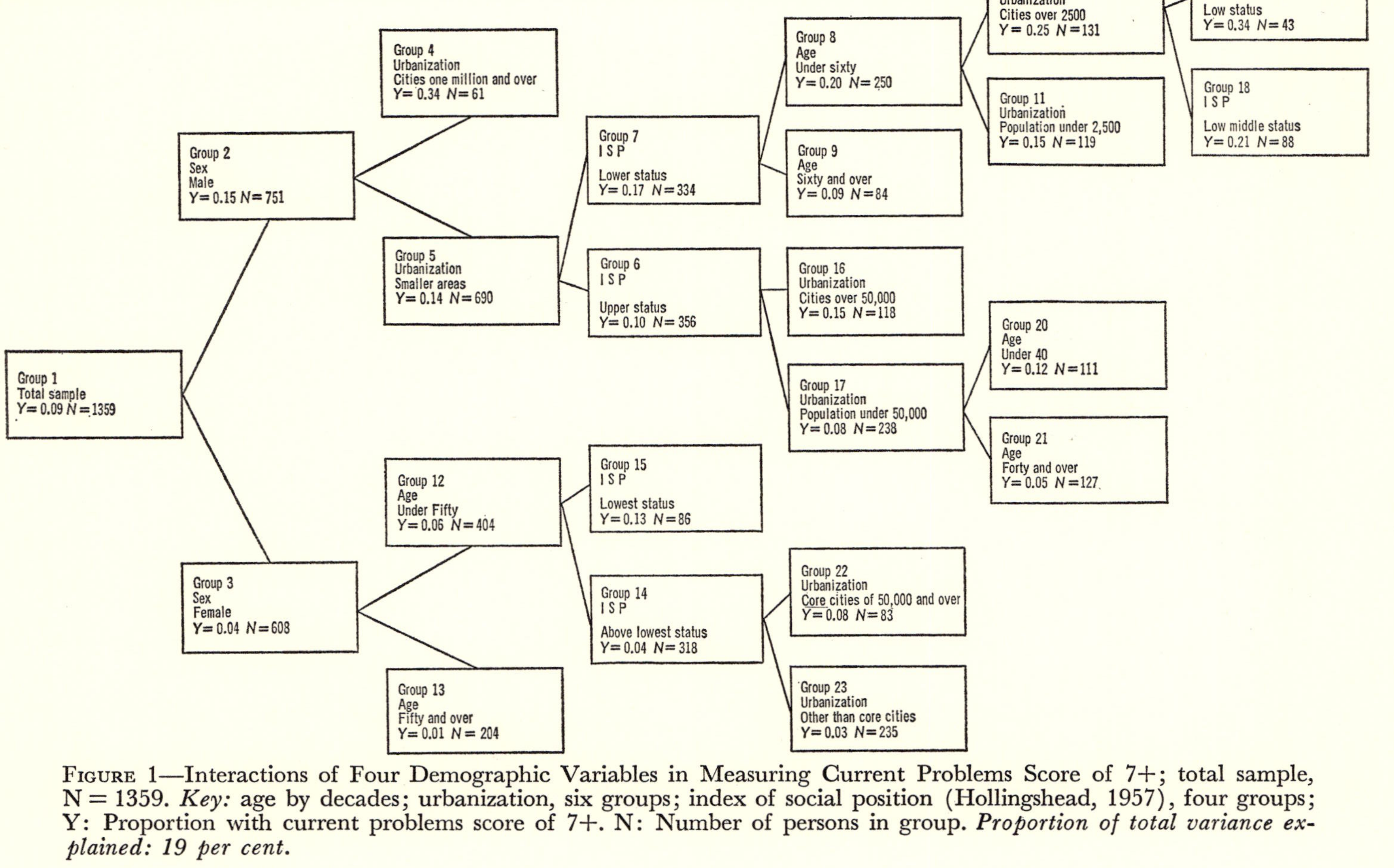

FIGURE 1—Interactions of Four Demographic Variables in Measuring Current Problems Score of 7+; total sample, N = 1359. *Key:* age by decades; urbanization, six groups; index of social position (Hollingshead, 1957), four groups; Y: Proportion with current problems score of 7+. N: Number of persons in group. *Proportion of total variance explained: 19 per cent.*

it is evident that even though either technique permits one to make a better-than-chance prediction of problem drinking on the basis of these four demographic variables, other factors are responsible for the bulk of the variance: for example, not all of the lower-status young men in large cities become problem drinkers. We will see that a substantial amount of additional variance in problem drinking can be explained by intervening variables of a social-psychological nature. The next chapter will discuss the process of identifying and measuring the social-psychological variables most highly correlated with problem drinking.

IV Social and Personality Characteristics

The previous chapter has shown that one can explain a modest but definite amount of difference in problem drinking by taking only four independent demographic variables into account: sex, age, social status, and urbanization. It is also known that certain social-psychological factors operate as intervening variables between the independent demographic variables and the drinking behavior to affect the rate of problem drinking. Most writers on alcohol have dealt with some of these intervening social-psychological variables, summarized by Plaut as follows:

> A tentative model may be developed for understanding the causes of problem drinking, even though the precise roles of the various factors have not yet been determined. An individual who (1) responds to beverage alcohol in a certain way, perhaps physiologically determined, by experiencing intense relief and relaxation, and who (2) has certain personality characteristics, such as difficulty in dealing with and overcoming depression, frustration, and anxiety, and who (3) is a member of a culture in which there is both pressure to drink and culturally induced guilt and

> confusion regarding what kinds of drinking behavior are appropriate, is more likely to develop trouble than will most other persons. An intermingling of certain factors may be necessary for the development of problem drinking, and the relative importance of the differential causal factors no doubt varies from one individual to another (1967, p. 49).

The great range of sociological, cultural, and psychological variables which can be invoked to account for variance in problem drinking provides a powerful incentive to try to reduce confusion, complexity, and redundancy by combining a limited number of variables in an interdisciplinary model which is simple enough for practical use, which explains an optimal proportion of variance in problem drinking, and which takes into account the interactions between a number of key variables. Before discussing such a model, however, it is necessary to review some of its specific components, divided into psychological and sociological-cultural aspects.

PSYCHOLOGICAL FACTORS

It is important to preserve a distinction between psychological factors related to alcohol use which have to do with the unique facets of an individual personality, and the general psycho-physiological characteristics which are common to most persons. The first set of attributes would be those (often rather long-lasting) specific personal characteristics of a type measured by various personality tests, which might make a difference in whether a person would be susceptible to alcohol or some other class or classes of drugs. It is presumed that most of these characteristics are a product of social learning, though some few may be genetically inherited. The second set of characteristics are those apparently universal and genetically determined ones which make all (or almost all) persons respond rather uniformly to at least some of a broad range of positive or negative reinforcers; these response characteristics come under the general field of habit-formation, and the seeking out of positive stimuli and avoidance of negative stimuli. In other words, while individual men differ in what they will learn because of their personalities, whether they will learn general response patterns of approach and avoidance is dependent upon man's innate psychological characteristics. Thus man is so constituted that certain drugs will tend to have a stimulating or depressing or mind-altering effect upon him; but whether he will continue to take certain drugs over a period of time will be dependent upon his personality—as well as many environmental factors.

First, we will consider some of the psycho-physiological implications of alcohol as it affects the vast majority of its users; and once we have been reminded of some of man's basic response patterns, we will consider personality traits that may be related to heavy use of alcohol. We should always remember that alcohol is a "drug" in that it is used to affect the central nervous system. Ausubel summarizes the role of drugs as follows (1958, p. 10):

> When we ask to what drugs can one become addicted, we must include a large number of drugs: stimulants such as cocaine, Benzedrine, and mescaline; depressants such as marijuana, opiates, and their derivatives; hynotics and sedatives such as bromides and barbiturates; and alcohol, tobacco, caffeine, and certain kinds of laxatives. Physical dependence, however, is a relatively rare phenomenon in the total picture of drug addiction. True physical dependence probably only develops in relation to opiate and opiate-like drugs, although characteristic withdrawal symptoms are sometimes found in chronic alcoholism and invariably in advanced cases of barbiturate addiction. Nevertheless . . . physical dependence is by no means the most important or most dangerous aspect of drug addiction. When it does take place it merely guarantees the occurrence of a relatively severe and invariable group of withdrawal symptoms. The actual prognosis of a case of drug addiction, however, is primarily a function of psychological and personality factors.

Whether a person will learn to depend upon any drug is contingent upon whether he receives any positive reinforcement from it. Part of this learning process is physical: his central nervous system learns to respond to the drug in a positively reinforcing way (such as to stimulate him or to quiet his anxieties), or else the purpose of taking the drug will have been defeated. But much of the learning process in the taking of alcohol or other drugs is cognitive or psychological in nature: the person must learn to anticipate certain favorable outcomes from taking the drug, and to recognize the effects as favorable. Thus Lindesmith's central thesis in his *Addiction and Opiates* is that a person's taking even such an addictive drug as morphine for a long enough period to build up physiological tolerance for large quantities of it will not result in true addiction unless the person learns to recognize the withdrawal symptoms as such and also recognizes that the withdrawal symptoms are related to the cessation of taking the specific drug of morphine (1968, p. 7). Thus in the development of a stubborn addiction to any drug, physiological and cognitive learning takes place, in obtaining a marked positive reinforcement from taking the drug plus a marked negative reinforcement if the drug is withdrawn.

In order to understand the differences between habituation and addiction in relation to alcohol as compared to other drugs, one must keep in mind the difference in the process of acquiring physical tolerance to alcohol as compared to other drugs. Jellinek summarizes one of these kinds of differences, in this case between alcohol and morphine, as stemming from the fact that while continued use of drugs in the morphine group produces a tolerance to amounts 20 to 100 times above the therapeutic dose and well above the usual lethal dosage, the acquired increased tolerance to ethyl alcohol surpasses the inherent or initial tolerance not more than 3 or 4 times. Jellinek goes on to point to the consequence of the difference in tolerance between morphine and alcohol as follows:

> The incidence of addiction in users of heroin is practically 100 per cent, and among users of morphine around 70 per cent, but among users of alcoholic beverages it is only 10 per cent at the maximum. Furthermore, addiction to drugs in the morphine group sets in after approximately 4 weeks of continued use, but addiction to alcohol requires a very high intake over a period of from 3 to 30 years [1960a, p. 118]. . . . One may ask why addiction to alcohol occurs in a relatively small minority of users only. The process of addiction to alcohol requires the continual consumption of large amounts of alcoholic beverages over many years. Such drinking behavior, however, is not favored by our culture. Consequently, mainly those are liable to expose themselves to the risk of alcohol addiction who have a special individual inducement, such as the inability to cope with tensions, or who are placed in one of the small cultural subgroups which accept a high alcohol intake as the norm [1960a, p. 120].

Jellinek expresses doubt whether the physical dependence upon alcohol among alcoholics is much of a factor in our culture, and appears to attribute much of the "habit" aspects of alcohol addiction to the cognitive or psychological aspects of the reinforcing properties of alcohol:

> The absence of manifestations of a physical demand for alcohol between drinking bouts or during a prolonged enforced period

> of abstinence casts grave doubts on the theory postulated by some proponents of nutritional and endocrine etiologies of alcoholism that craving exists at the onset of the heavy use of alcohol by the prospective alcoholic [1960a, p. 141]. . . . The demand for alcohol seems to be of a twofold nature. One part reflects the necessity to allay the distressing withdrawal symptoms, i.e., a physical demand; the other part reflects the obsessive belief that ultimately a sufficient amount of alcohol will bring about the tension reduction which, before the loss of control, was achieved quite easily [1960a, p. 146].

One can think of reasons why it takes a considerable period of time to build up physiological addiction: for many people, the drinking of alcoholic beverages is a gradually acquired taste. To learn how to get pleasantly and consistently euphoric from drinking alcohol is a fine art, particularly since alcohol is a depressant whose effects are highly dependent upon one's expectations, mood, and physical condition. Then when tolerance of higher blood alcohol levels begins to develop, the amount of alcohol required for an intoxicating effect tends to put a considerable strain upon the kidneys, liver, and other parts of the body. Also, high blood alcohol concentrations (unlike opiates) are usually accompanied by bad breath, unsteady gait, and other symptoms which can be unpleasant to one's "significant others"—so it is no wonder that instead of continuing to drink heavily until late in life, the figures shown for age groups in the preceding chapter indicate that the average heavy drinker tends to taper off sharply in his drinking when he gets into the forties and fifties.

Ausubel provides additional reasons why alcohol is a less effective drug (and, ostensibly, why it is a relatively inefficient addictive drug) when he says (1958, p. 55):

> The inadequate personality is not satisfied with alcohol because alcohol does not provide complete gratification of his hedonistic needs. Unlike the opiates, it is not in itself a complete mode of adjustment to life: primary needs are not wholly obliterated, an all-embracing sense of well-being and freedom from threat is not obtained, the kick is less rhapsodic, and fantasies are less grandiose and omnipotent. Alcohol is not a genuine euphoriant. Its chief psychological effect is not depression of the self-critical faculty but release of cortical inhibition of emotional expression, thereby intensifying pre-existing mood. Hence, depression may be precipitated as well as exhilaration. There is also a spurious appearance of euphoria because the loss of inhibitory control

makes speech and behavior seem buoyant and exuberant. Underneath the overt jocularity, however, may be much sadness and self-deprecation. Frequently the use of alcohol leads to motor incoordination, impairment of the sensorium, and disruption of higher mental processes. The essentially unaggressive opiate addict may also be particularly disturbed by the belligerency which alcohol generates.

But while alcohol differs from the opiates in major respects (such as in its side-effects, and in the period generally required for building up physiological tolerance for large quantities), for those who do once achieve addiction, it may well be similar to the opiates in what Seevers refers to as "secondary psychological dependence." Seevers said of opiates that "in confirmed addicts who depend upon 'street' sources for their supply, fear of the aversive symptoms from drug deprivation may even surmount the importance of reward, especially after tolerance development has diminished the initial intensity of the reward" (1968, p. 1266). Similarly, it is the author's impression, from limited observation, that chronic heavy drinkers tend to lose the "honeymoon" euphoric effect of alcohol at the same time they are developing a greater sense of suffering when they are without alcohol.

To summarize the weight of expert opinion about the psychophysiological aspects of the process of habituation and addiction to alcohol and other drugs: the process of addiction has to involve learning of both neural and other bodily tissues as well as a cognitive process involving anticipatory and perceptual processes. Another factor is that among those who have tried both drugs, true addiction to alcohol appears to be harder to achieve than addiction to opiates, even in our Western culture where alcohol is commonly accepted as a component of the good life, while the taking of heroin is generally viewed as highly deviant and dangerous. Since alcohol is a relatively ineffective addictive agent which usually takes many years of hard drinking to bring about a process of true addiction, the reinforcing properties of alcohol need to have a strong helping hand from personality and cultural factors in order to culminate in deep-seated alcoholism of Jellinek's Gamma variety, with increased tissue tolerance to alcohol, withdrawal symptoms and subjective "craving," and loss of control over drinking.

The process of addiction, whatever the drug, is a truly "vicious circle" in that increased dependence upon the drug tends to bring about changes in the person's behavior and values which render him more maladjusted to the outside world, which in turn brings about greater motivation to retreat into increased use of drugs. As Ausubel says (1958, p. 37):

> The fact that single doses of opiates produce euphoria in addicts is relatively unimportant. In and of itself it constitutes no evidence of any lasting psychological change attributable to drug addiction. The real danger in addiction lies in the more permanent change it induces in characteristic drive-motivated, drive-satisfying, and adjustive behavior. Drug addiction first becomes harmful when it gives rise to a changed way of life, that is, when the desire for euphoria permanently replaces all other socially useful drives, when activity satisfying the need for drugs replaces all other drive-satisfying activity, and when drug use becomes the primary adjustive mechanism in an individual's behavior repertory.

Turning now to our quest for social-psychological factors associated with problem drinking: thus far, many authorities have searched high and low for "the alcoholic personality," but in vain. In an extensive review of the literature, Syme (1957) failed to find any very promising evidence that the personality of problem drinkers or alcoholics had unique characteristics which could not be accounted for by other variables. Armstrong (1958), in his article "The Search for the Alcoholic Personality," reinforced the conclusion that past research is not very helpful in defining the alcoholic personality. Rosen (1960), in another review article, concluded that "alcoholics do not represent a unique personality type or a unique psychiatric nosological group" (p. 265). In a later article in the same vein, Armstrong (1961) emphasized the importance of studying the interactions, between psychological and sociocultural phenomena, pointing out that persons who are members of groups with extremely high acceptance of heavy drinking may show very little in the way of psychological complications, while persons who persist in drinking heavily even though they are members of groups with low tolerance for heavy drinking may show a high frequency of personality problems (p. 145).

In the same article Armstrong summarizes various psychoanalytic and psychological theories regarding alcoholism, including alcoholism as a flight from homosexual impulses, incestuous thoughts, and masturbatory guilt; alcoholism as a symptom of epilepsy and psychosis; addiction related to sadistic drives and oedipal conflicts; alcoholism as the result of a compromise between hysterical and obsessive compulsive neuroses; and escape from depression through the pharmacologically-produced magical sense of elation the patient craves. Armstrong also mentioned the self-destructive drives of the alcoholic; the alcoholic's unconscious need to dominate, together with feelings of loneliness and isolation; alcoholism as a character disorder distinguished by excessive demands, an inability to carry out sustained effort, and feelings of hostility and rage; the dynamic functions of alcohol as discharging anxiety, guilt, and shame, the narcotization of painful reality, facilitating symbolism through which one achieves the identity of status one desires, the achieving of infantile oral gratifications, masochistic functions, hostility functions, discharging homosexual impulses, enabling one to identify with preferred models such as parents. But in summarizing these various theories, Armstrong (1961) concludes that "we cannot . . . divorce our psychological concerns from the setting of the culture in which the patient is operating" (p. 144).

Any intensive study of behavior problems demonstrates the folly of simplistic psychological or sociological reductionism, in which only one or two variables are considered to be "the central cause" of behavior. There has been altogether too much of this reductionism in the recent past, during the days of the growing pains of psychology and sociology. As Albert Bandura, himself an authority in the field of clinical psychology, says about such reductionism:

> A social-learning model does not, of course, assume that behavior is determined exclusively by psychological variables. Genetic endowment and constitutional factors may set certain limits on both the types of behavioral repertoires that can be developed in a given person, and the rate of response acquisition. In certain cases, neurophysiological conditions may contribute to the observed behavioral malfunctioning. Moreover, biological and psychological factors typically interact in subtle and complex ways in producing certain patterns of behavior [1969, p. 61]. . . . In recent years there has been a fundamental departure from conventional views regarding the nature, causes, and treatment of behavioral disfunctions. According to this orientation, behavior that is harmful to the individual or departs widely from accepted social and ethical norms is viewed not as symptomatic of some kind of disease but as a way that the individual has learned to cope with environmental and self-imposed demands. Treatment then becomes mainly a problem in social learning rather than one in the medical domain. In this conceptual scheme the remaining

> vestiges of the disease-demonic mode have been discarded. Response patterns are not viewed as symptoms and their occurrence is not attributed to internal, pernicious forces [p. 10]. . . . Psychopathology is not solely a property inherent in behavior but reflects the evaluative responses of social agents to actions that violate prescribed codes of conduct. The social labeling of a given response pattern as a pathological expression is, in fact, influenced by numerous subjective criteria including the aversiveness of the behavior, the social attributes of the deviator, the normative standards of persons making the judgments, the social context in which the behavior is performed, and a host of other factors. Consequently, the same response pattern may be diagnosed as "sick" or may be normatively sanctioned and considered emulative by different groups, at different times, or in different environmental settings [p. 62].

Bandura is an outstanding exponent of a growing general perspective in American psychology which is particularly compatible with an interactionist point of view in explaining problem drinking, that of "operant conditioning," built upon the principles of B. F. Skinner (1953).[1] As yet few operant-conditioning theorists have commented on the obvious implications of their point of view for problem drinking and alcoholism, although the operant approach is being used increasingly. According to the operant conditioning theory, behavior which is reinforced immediately tends to be repeated, while behavior which is rarely reinforced tends to be extinguished. Operant conditioning theory has important implications both for better understanding of problem drinking and for more effective treatment, particularly since addictive drinking generally appears to be built up only gradually over a period of many years. The sociocultural and personality attributes of the individual in his unique environment interact to make alcohol the "solution" to certain individuals in certain circumstances over a long period of time. As Levy (1958) has pointed out, alcohol becomes habituating (here equivalent to reinforcing) when it economically "solves" a large variety of the individual's problems in a specific way, and when—as a consequence of excessive drinking—there is a breakdown of social functioning which can be assuaged (in an ego with a scarcity of resources) only by further drinking (p. 658). Ferster, Nurnberger, and

[1] Skinner explains the use of the word "operant" by saying, "the term emphasizes the fact that the behavior *operates* upon the environment to generate consequences" (1953, p. 65).

Levitt (1962) express the operant conditioning concept in drawing an analogy which helps to explain the twin paradoxes of why it could be that addictive drinkers will persist in drinking in the face of the social opprobrium which inevitably follows heavy drinking, and why obese people continue to overeat even though the consequences should be obvious to them, by saying that "the long-term or ultimate aversive consequences of obesity are so postponed as to be ineffective compared with the immediate reinforcement of food in the mouth" (p. 87), and that hangover symptoms and the full impact of heavy drinking are not suffered until considerable time has elapsed, whereas the pleasant effects of drinking provide an immediate reinforcement to more drinking. Much of the same point of view is expressed by Conger (1956), who infers that persistence in excessive drinking is the result of such a gradient of reinforcement, including the anxiety-reducing effects of continued drinking to postpone redoubled anxiety from thinking about (or experiencing) the social punishment to come. Two additional reinforcement aspects of heavy drinking can be inferred in the writings of MacAndrew and Garfinkel (1962), who found the sober-self and drunk-self self-portrayals of problem drinkers were markedly dissimilar, with the excessive drinkers evidently getting special reinforcement in the assertiveness which alcohol brings about or permits; and in the interpretations of another study by Storm and Smart (1965), who cited results of studies of animals (which showed that there was little transfer of training from drugged to undrugged conditions, and vice versa) to support the speculation that it might be easier for long-term alcoholics to learn more effective methods of coping with their problems if the lessons were applied when they were drunk than when they were sober.

The operant conditioning and social-psychological interactive perspectives are fully compatible with the early writings of Knight (1937a, 1937b), who discusses the "essential" versus the "reactive" alcoholic. The "essential" alcoholic (whose personality demands immediate gratification) has a much poorer prognosis than does the "reactive" alcoholic (who may have fallen into the habit of heavy drinking temporarily, because of temporary environmental influences). In describing the "essential" alcoholic, Knight sums up as follows:

> It is quite apparent that the patient has now gotten into a typical neurotic vicious circle, and one which is immensely complicated by the intertwining with it of the alcoholism. Let us describe this

> sequence. His childhood experiences have given him a personality characterized by excessive demands for indulgence. These demands are doomed to frustration in the world of adults. He reacts to the frustration with intolerable disappointment and rage. This reaction impels him to hostile acts and wishes against the thwarting individuals for which he then feels guilty and punishes himself masochistically. As reassurance against guilt feelings and fears of dangerously destructive masochism and reality consequences of his behavior, he feels excessive need for affection and indulgence as proof of affection. Again the excessive claims, doomed to frustration, arise, and the circle is complete. The use of alcohol as a pacifier for disappointment and rage, as a potent means of carrying out hostile impulses to spite his parents and friends, as a method of securing masochistic debasement, and as a symbolic gratification of the need for affection is now interweaving itself in the neurotic circle" [1937b, p. 546].

Rudie and McGaughran (1961) have replicated Knight's earlier study comparing "essential" and "reactive" alcoholics, coming to the conclusion that "Knight's distinction between these classes of alcoholism appears to be an essentially useful and valid one that can serve to reduce variance in future research with alcoholics" (p. 665). Substantially the same two types of excessive drinkers were unearthed by Ferguson (1968) in her subsequent study of Navajo drinking, although she uses the term "recreation drinkers" and "anxiety drinkers" rather than "reactive" and "essential" alcoholics: "The anxiety drinkers need something more [than brief rehabilitation and redirection]. Their trouble appears to lie at a much deeper level . . . Such people need help on the unconscious level where conflicts are producing the anxiety which underlies excessive drinking" (p. 167).

Quantitative studies of problem drinking also lend support to the reinforcement or operant-conditioning point of view, particularly as regards the role of anxiety and a feeling of alienation from society as being involved in repetitive problem drinking. Knupfer (1968) found, in her San Francisco survey, an association between psychosomatic complaints and problem drinking, and between "face-stuffing" (smoking, eating) and problem drinking (p. 7), as did Haberman (1969); and Bailey, Haberman, and Alksne (1965) and Haberman (1965) found a similar association between psycho-physiological symptoms and alcoholism. In experimental studies with college men who answered anxiety-depression questions before, during, and at the end of cocktail parties, Allan F. Williams (1965a) found that the problem drinkers were self-critical and tended to endorse adjectives suggestive of neurosis (p. 594); and that while anxiety and depression decreased significantly at low levels of alcohol consumption, anxiety and depression tended to increase at high levels of consumption (Williams, 1965b, p. 692)—perhaps suggesting one reason why heavy drinking calls for more drinking to relieve "hangovers." As regards the tendency toward alienation, or the perception of being powerless, unloved, and unable to control one's own destiny (which we will see later as being highly correlated with anxiety and depression), Boalt, Jonsson, and Snyder (1968), in summarizing one hundred studies on alcohol, concluded that "alcoholism and to a certain extent alienation hang together with other expressions of unsocial behavior and with a disreputable background" (p. 7).

Finally, Reinert (1968b) rather neatly summarizes the operant conditioning and social-psychological interactive points of view regarding problem drinking when he says, in his recent article, "The Concept of Alcoholism as a Bad Habit":

> The evidence seems to be that the phenomenon of addiction or the potentiality for addiction is too widespread to justify looking for esoteric explanations in aberrant physiology or psychology. It seems closer to being a universal condition of human beings which must be explained by some universal mechanism. In view of this and in view of the great benefits of alcohol to mankind . . . it is certainly as valid to ask why someone does not become alcoholic as to ask why he does, and it introduces a new perspective that may contribute to our understanding of the role of good habits and of other compelling interests in the prevention of alcoholism. . . . Giving a central position to the concept of alcoholism as a bad habit makes possible the integration of the findings and points of view about the condition better than any other conception. Psychological and physical factors when they exist can fall into place as contributing but not essential factors and the findings of the sociologists nicely explain the backgrounds necessary to begin the process of learning to be an alcoholic. This process involves the discovery that alcohol can serve several important functions such as give pleasure, reduce pain and fear, raise self-esteem, offer a socially recognized identity, etc. Eventually using alcohol becomes inextricably bound to a myriad of common social situations or emotional states in much the same way that the use of tobacco has for those who cannot stop smoking [pp. 44–45].

SOCIOCULTURAL FACTORS

The importance of considering both psychological and sociocultural factors has been borne out by a number of descriptive studies on drinking behavior, including the first national probability sampling on American drinking practices (conducted by the author and colleagues), in which it was tentatively concluded that "whether a person drinks at all is primarily a sociological and anthropological variable rather than a psychological one" (Cahalan, Cisin, and Crossley, 1969, p. 200), but that certain measures of personality are useful in explaining some of the variations in heavy drinking (and thus, presumably, problem drinking). The contingent relationship between psychological and sociocultural characteristics in relation to problem drinking also has been pointed out by Cisin and Cahalan (1968) in comparing abstainers and heavy drinkers in the 1964–1965 national survey, in that the *choice* of means of artificial escape from one's daily problems is dependent upon the culture's permissiveness concerning specific substances for specific groups, but that a person's *abuse* of a substance (alcohol, drugs, food) is also dependent upon his personality and his immediate environment (p. 20).

The "interactionist" (or social-psychological) point of view in problem drinking and mental illness is given additional support in the views of Rose (1962), who points out that the differential between men and women in such a "psychological" problem as the onset of involutional melancholia may be accounted for by a social-psychological theory about the changes in life roles (pp. 544–545); by Maddox and Borinski's (1964) findings on the interaction of social status and personality structure in the use of alcohol among Negroes (p. 666); and by Glatt and Hills' (1968) finding that the interaction of early deprivations and unsatisfactory home and neighborhood environments with personality maladjustments contribute materially to alcohol abuse among the young (p. 189). Trice (1956), after citing Bowman and Jellinek (1941) that "no personality constellation leads of necessity to addiction," sums up the interactionist position by saying that "the time is long overdue when researchers in the alcohol field will look upon alcoholism as a *process,* not a single-factor, one-way, cause and effect result" (1956, p. 40). Even Jellinek, who looked long and hard to try to find an "alcoholic personality," concluded (1952) that there probably was no such personality isolable from environmental influences:

> By and large, these reactions to excessive drinking—which have quite a neurotic appearance—give the impression of an "alcoholic personality," although they are secondary behaviors superimposed over a large variety of personality types which have a few traits in common, in particular a low capacity for coping with tensions. There does not emerge, however, any specific personality trait or physical characteristic which inevitably would lead to excessive symptomatic drinking. Apart from psychological and possibly physical liabilities, there must be a constellation of social and economic factors which facilitate the development of addictive and nonaddictive alcoholism in a susceptible terrain.

Jellinek also emphasized the necessity for an interactionist point of view by noting that a society's norms for conduct can play a large part in determining whether "deviant" behavior will be contingent upon the deviant's personality: "In societies which have a low degree of acceptance of large daily amounts of alcohol, mainly those will be exposed to the risk of addiction who on account of high psychological vulnerability have an inducement to go against the social standards. But in societies which have an extremely high degree of acceptance of large daily alcohol consumption, the presence of any small vulnerability, whether psychological or physical, will suffice for exposure to the risk of addiction (1960a, pp. 28–29).

Whether the specialist has a primary orientation toward psychological, physiological, or sociocultural explanations for problem drinking, mosts authorities sooner or later come to social-psychological interactionist conclusions. Thus Jellinek (1960b) in recapitulating the process of development of "the problems of alcohol," describes how the use of alcohol is first attached to symbolic and ritual behavior in society and then spreads because of tension-relief to the point that "the once sacred object becomes a substance of everyday use," which in turn facilitates excessive use for relief from tension, with ultimately alcohol becoming not "an original source of a problem but . . . a means for solving it and . . . a means out of which more and more problems arise"—problems involving vested interests in the supply and control of alcohol, which clash with "emotionally oriented reform forces" (p. 202). Bacon (1957) also, while emphasizing the sociological factors in alcoholism, stresses the interaction of personality characteristics with sociocultural phenomena; and Blum (1967) points out that the distinction between normal and problem drinking is a social one: "The drinking troubles the normal person has are ones that he and his society are fully prepared to accept as the price of being able to continue to drink" (p. 44).

The application of an interactionist social-psychological perspective to drinking problems is in keeping with the current emphasis in epidemiology and public health upon studying the ways in which various physiological, psychological, and cultural influences operate to affect health and behavioral adaptation to stress.[2]

Specific studies of the association of sociocultural factors in alcoholism as measured in longitudinal studies include Robins' (1966) St. Louis study, William and Joan McCord's (1962) study in suburban Boston, and Swiecici's (1968) study in Warsaw which covered an eleven-year period. In all these longitudinal studies, and in de Lint's (1966) retrospective study of alcoholics, a strong association was noted between broken homes, economic deprivations, and exposure to heavy drinking as factors in the development of excessive drinking and related kinds of delinquency. Some of the strongest associations between sociocultural factors and alcoholism or sobriety are noted in comparative studies of special ethnic groups, such as the Irish (who have a high rate of alcoholism), and the Jews and old country Italians and Chinese (who are noted for their sobriety even though most members of these groups do drink); these studies are summarized by Snyder (1962, 1964a, 1964b), who notes, in regard to a comparative study of primitive societies by Field (1962), that higher inebriety appears to be more in evidence in societies with kinship systems which are more amorphous, fragmented, or unstructured: that group solidarity appears to be an important factor in low rates of alcoholism (Snyder, 1964a, p. 208); and since it is likely that the prevalence of neuroses and psychoses as a reflection of stress among the Irish and the Jews must be rather comparable, the difference in alcoholism between these groups must be a function of their differences in normative orientations regarding the act of drinking, plus the use of different functional equivalents or alternatives to excessive drinking (Snyder, 1964b, p. 17).

A number of sociologists have emphasized the impact of roles and norms on drinking behavior. Illustrations include Clark's (1964) discussion of sex and marital status roles in alcoholic beverage usage, especially differentials in going to bars, and Mizruchi's concepts of norms as setting different limits on the enforcement of values regard-

[2] For an excellent recent review of epidemiological concepts, see Plaut (1966).

ing appropriate drinking behavior (1967; Mizruchi and Perucci, 1962). Jackson (1965), while not discussing problem drinking specifically, has contributed a useful concept concerning the range of tolerable behavior and its potential effect on behavior, whereby a narrow range of tolerable behavior would be associated with more disapproval and negative reinforcement. Abu-Laban and Larsen (1968) and Larsen and Abu-Laban (1968) have applied drinking-norms concepts to their analysis of data on a study in Edmonton, where they found that "prescriptive" (or positive hortatory) norms were associated with social-effects (or non-addictive) types of drinking, "nonscriptive" norms (or failures of norms to prescribe) were associated with personal-effects (or tension-relief or escape) drinking, and "proscriptive" ("don't drink") norms were associated with a higher-than-average rate of abstinence from drinking.

The principal impression which one derives from reviewing the literature on the sociocultural correlates of problem drinking is that there is much need for an integration and consolidation of the various perspectives into a more limited set of models for explaining problem drinking and associated kinds of behavioral problems. While the multivariate model which is presented below does not pretend to incorporate all relevant points of view into a single comprehensive model, it is intended as a step in this direction.

MULTIVARIATE MODEL

As illustrated earlier in this chapter, there is such a variety of variables which have been employed in past studies to help to explain problem drinking that some efforts at consolidating the variables into a smaller number is essential, both for scientific parsimony and for ease in communication of research findings. Communication becomes very much of a problem in dealing with a longitudinal study such as the one being reported, in which we are concerned with not only the relationships between independent and intervening (demographic and sociocultural) variables and dependent (problem drinking) variables at one point of time, but also the relationships between independent and intervening variables at the earlier stage to predict scores on dependent variables at a later stage; and also correlating change in independent and intervening variables with change in the dependent variable. Since 150 questionnaire items in Stages I and II of the national survey were used in measuring demographic and social-psychological variables to be correlated with drinking and problem drinking, the added analytic complexities of the longitudinal design made it imperative to reduce the data to a minimum number of variables in order to avoid inflicting several hundred thousand statistical comparisons upon the reader. Further, the concepts gleaned from past descriptive studies of drinking behavior now make it possible to arrive at a selective few variables which, when taken together, can be efficient predictors of changes in problem drinking in the future. One key requirement of a social-psychological model to predict problem drinking is that it be specific enough to be applicable to the special field of alcohol abuse in the American culture. An appropriate model was found in the work of Jessor and his associates (Jessor *et al.,* 1968; Graves, 1967) at the University of Colorado in the Tri-Ethnic Project, in which Spanish-speaking, Indian, and Anglo-American members of a relatively isolated Colorado community were contrasted in a study of the correlates of deviance, including problem drinking.[3] The theoretical framework for the Tri-Ethnic study may be summarized thus:

Sociological concepts were drawn from Merton's (1957) theory of social structure and anomie, and from the theories of Cloward and Ohlin (1960) regarding delinquent gangs: these theories predict that deviant behavior is more likely to occur when the expectation of maximizing one's attainment of goals or preferred outcomes through deviant behavior is higher than the expectation of attaining one's goals through conforming behavior. Consolidating these theories, Jessor and associates (Jessor *et al.,* 1968) focused upon three sociocultural substructures which should correlate with deviance: the opportunity structure (or the channels of access to the achievement of goals valued in the American culture), the normative structure (identification of the values and goals toward which striving is to be directed), and the social control structure (or the socially patterned opportunities for learning and performing deviant or other behaviors). Jessor's combined central sociological hypothesis is this: "The magnitude of deviance rates at a given location in society will vary directly with the degree of value-access disjunction, anomie, and access to illegitimate means characterizing that location" (p. 78).

[3] Again, the terms "deviance" and "deviant" are not intended to have a pejorative connotation, but rather are defined as departures from norms of behavior. It should also be recognized that what is "deviant" to the majority of people may be socially approved behavior within subgroups in which the behavior is frequently practiced.

In their psychological concepts, Jessor and his colleagues drew heavily upon the "social learning" theories of Rotter (1954). The resultant personality system is summarized by Jessor and colleagues as follows: *"The likelihood of occurrence of deviant behavior will vary directly with the degree of personal disjunction, alienation, belief in external control, tolerance of deviance, and tendencies toward short time perspective and immediate gratification characterizing an individual at a given moment in time"* (Jessor *et al.*, 1968, p. 111).

The "social learning" approach to behavior deviancy is consistent with the "differential association" approach of Sutherland (1955), in which it is recognized that in order for deviant behavior to attain sufficient social reinforcement to be persisted in, the individual must find some encouragement from subgroups which are formed on the basis of "like seeks like." Bandura, like Jessor a clinical psychologist in background, independently reinforces the "social learning" perspective as against those who consider much deviant behavior as being psychopathological or sociopathological:

> The idiosyncratic behavioral content [of behavior] is obviously learned rather than physiologically produced. Nor do capacity variables account for gross deficits in motor, conceptual, or affective responses that are clearly within a person's capabilities. Unfortunately, deviant behavior is often prematurely attributed to physiological determinants, an attribution which results not only in therapeutic pessimism, but also effectively retards further psychological investigation of behavioral phenomena [1969, p. 61]. . . . Although drinking behavior is initially most often acquired under nonstress conditions, a habitual social drinker will experience stress reduction on many occasions. Once alcohol consumption is thus intermittently reinforced, it will be readily elicited under frustrative or aversive conditions. Therefore, alcoholism typically results from habituation after prolonged heavy social drinking acquired within the context of familial alcoholism [p. 535].

Jessor and his associates, in analyzing the data on drinking problems and other deviant behavior in their tri-ethnic study, combined these sociocultural and social-psychological concepts in their scoring of aggregates of relevant questionnaire and interview items into a number of indices which, when taken together, served to explain substantially more of the variance in drunkenness and other deviant behavior than would have been accounted for by using any one index alone.

The general model applied in the Tri-Ethnic study was applied subsequently in modified form by the present author in a two-stage community study in Hartford (Cahalan, 1968), which yielded findings which were congruent with those of the Tri-Ethnic study despite rather considerable differences in emphasis in content, populations, and the specific procedures used in analysis of data. The same general concepts, again with further adaptations, have now been applied to the data in the present national survey. The Colorado and national studies differ materially in content, populations covered, and analysis procedures. However, despite these differences, it will be seen in the next chapter that the findings of the national survey bore out the principal findings of the Colorado study of Jessor and associates in every major particular.

The following six social-psychological molar intervening variables[4] were developed out of combinations of 150 items which were applied to the same respondents in both the 1964–1965 and 1967 interviews: (1) attitude toward drinking; (2) environmental support for heavy drinking; (3) impulsivity and non-conformity; (4) alienation and maladjustment; (5) unfavorable expectations; (6) looseness of social controls. The selection and scoring of items within each of the six variables was determined through use of a combination of factor-analytic and multiple correlation procedures. Details on the individual items are available from the author.

The rationale for the six intervening molar variables, and a summary of their content, is given below:

(1) Attitude toward drinking. The findings of this national survey are that highly favorable attitudes toward drinking are strongly correlated with problem drinking. While there are many definitions of "attitudes," ranging all the way from that of psycho-physiological aspects of "set" or *aufgabe* or perception to cognitive and self-conscious values or norms, this writer sees these various definitions as various manifestations, on different levels, of the same basic process of acquiring habits through reinforcement of one's behavior—in this case, of acquiring favorable attitudes toward drinking because drinking is re-

[4] The term "molar" is used here to differentiate a broad composite variable made up of many items or scales, as distinct from "molecular" variables made up of single items or scales. These are considered as "intervening" variables, which intervene between the independent variables (here, demographic variables such as sex, age, socioeconomic status, and urbanization) to be associated with an increase or decrease in the rate of problem drinking.

warding to the individual. Some might claim that favorable attitudes toward drinking may be more the reflection of an attempt to justify one's past drinking than the result that the rewards one gets from drinking are responsible for the favorable attitudes. Certainly this evolution of attitudes through self-justification of one's drinking does happen in some instances, but the writer strongly subscribes to Allport's general conclusion that "attitudes are dynamic forces; they *cause* behavior" (1950, p. 172). While the findings are not absolutely conclusive, the weight of the evidence presented later in this study indicates that attitudes are more important in the development of habits of drinking than drinking is important in the development of attitudes toward drinking.

The specific items making up the combined molar score of attitude toward drinking included the following: a four-item "social drinking" Guttman scale (for example, I drink because the people I know drink), plus single items on how much the respondent would miss drinking if he had to give it up, the opinion that "drinking does more good than harm," the opinion that "good things can be said about drinking," and the respondent's selection of an above-average number of drinks as appropriate for his own drinking, and his agreeing that "I enjoy getting drunk once in a while."

(2) Environmental support for heavy drinking. When drinking is social behavior, excessive drinking is learned behavior—behavior learned from others. One's drinking tends to be influenced by one's associates not only because one's significant others teach how and when and how much to drink, but also because they reinforce drinking behavior (either positively or negatively) by both their example and by their expressed or implied attitudes toward drinking. Heavy drinking seldom develops full-blown overnight; it is an acquired taste, taught by others.

The expectation is that those who are exposed to heavy drinking, and to permissiveness on the part of others toward heavy drinking, will be more likely than others to become problem drinkers. The questions making up this molar variable total twenty-one items, including items on how many persons from the neighborhood or from work, or among one's friends, drink a lot; whether the respondent had relatives or friends with drinking problems; one's parents' attitudes toward drinking; whether one's father, mother, spouse, or some other significant person drank above-average amounts upon occasion; and the respondent's guesses that his significant others would think it would be all right for him to drink above-average amounts (eight drinks or more) upon occasion.

(3) Impulsivity and non-conformity. Since heavy drinking is frowned upon by most members of the society, for one persistently to indulge in heavy drinking one must be either impulsive and short-term-oriented, or deliberately non-conformist—unless one is successful in managing one's environment so that it consists almost exclusively of persons who are tolerant of heavy drinking. The variable of "impulsivity and non-conformity" contains items similar to those in Jessor's "belief in external control," "tolerance of deviance," and "short time-perspective" measures (Jessor *et al.,* p. 111). The variable is also much the same as the MMPI factor II, termed "ego control" by Block (1964, p. 115). The hypothesis here would be that those who are impulsive or rebellious, or who have flexible moral codes in general, would be expected to drink more heavily than others, either as a short-cut toward goals (of pleasure, or relief from unpleasant reality) or as an expression of defiance of others. The association of the "impulsivity and non-conformity" variable and problem drinking has been borne out independently through a qualitative analysis of data from the longitudinal Berkeley Growth Study by Jones (1968), who found that "a core of traits described the problem drinkers as undercontrolled, impulsive, and rebellious. . . . The results indicate that alcohol-related behavior is to some extent an expression of personality tendencies which are exhibited before drinking patterns have been established" (p. 2).

In the present study, several sets and items were combined to make up this molar variable: a four-item religious fundamentalism Guttman scale; a four-item impulsivity Guttman scale; a seven-item impulsivity scale from an earlier California study; a two-item "anger score"; an eleven-item internal-external control scale (measuring perceptions of one's ability to control one's environment); and a twelve-item attitudes toward deviance scale (both of the latter adapted from the Tri-Ethnic study, Jessor *et al.,* 1968).

(4) Alienation and maladjustment. This molar variable is related to Jessor's "personal disjunction" and "alienation" scales (1968) and is obverse to the MMPI factor I, termed "ego-resiliency" by Block (1965, p. 111). Those scoring as highly alienated or maladjusted would tend more often than others to adopt the use of alcohol to re-

lieve tensions and anxieties and fears of failure. It would be expected that the correlation between the "alienation and maladjustment" variable and problem drinking would be somewhat lower than the correlation between "impulsivity and non-conformity" and problem drinking, both because there is a wide range of possibilities that are more socially approved than alcohol to alleviate tension and anxieties, and because women and the elderly (who tend to be above average in their alienation and maladjustment scores) find that relief of problems through drinking is less acceptable than is true for other groups with lower alienation and maladjustment scores.

Several sub-areas were combined to make up the alienation and maladjustment score: neuropsychiatric complaints, as measured by a five-item neuropsychiatric complaints Guttman scale and a nine-item adaptation of the Langner (1962) scale; alienation, as measured by a four-item alienation Guttman scale (Cahalan, Cisin, and Crossley, 1969) and a thirteen-item alienation scale from the Tri-Ethnic study (Jessor *et al.,* 1968); a six-item non-helpfulness score (for example, how much one could count on people in time of trouble); a four-item irritability index (how often irritated by conditions in one's environment); and single items on one's desire for a different occupation, worrying about getting ahead, and rating of one's present level of happiness and one's happiness when a child.

(5) Unfavorable expectations. The hypothesis here is that those who feel they have (or can obtain) access to their expectations are less likely than others to resort to excessive use of alcohol. This independent molar score was made up from thirteen items, ten of which constituted an expectation score related to outlook regarding future relationships with family and friends (adapted from the Tri-Ethnic study of Jessor *et al.,* 1968), with the remaining items dealing with their general expectations regarding meeting their own goals in life.

(6) Looseness of social controls. Since the norm for drinking in America is generally that of moderation, the hypothesis is that the greater the number of close primary-group ties a person has, the more likely it is that he will live up to the norm of moderation. In this study, only five items of this nature were included: the respondent's marital status, whether he had close friends from the neighborhood, and his primary-group ties. As will be seen, this variable was found to be correlated with problem drinking, but not markedly; it is expected that the current national study in the same series, in which a larger number

of primary-group ties are being explored and in greater detail, will result in a finding of a higher correlation of looseness of social controls with problem drinking than was found in this first national study of problem drinking.

GROUP DIFFERENCES

As a preface to the analysis of the association of the six social-psychological molar scores with problem drinking which is to be presented in the next chapter, some subgroup differences in scores on these six variables and on their combined total are summarized as follows.[5]

Sex, age, and social position: The largest differences were found in relation to alienation and maladjustment, where the women had somewhat higher scores than the men. This is consistent with the findings of studies in which women were found to be more prone than men to check positive responses to inventories measuring psychosomatic complaints (Knupfer, 1968). Those of lower social status had materially higher scores than did the others. While there was little difference by social status on impulsivity and non-conformity, young men and women (aged twenty-one to thirty-nine) had significantly higher scores (were more impulsive and less conformist) on this variable than was true for older persons. The differences among the six specific variables tend to cancel each other out when the variables are brought together in the aggregate total score, on which differences by sex, age, and socioeconomic status were inconsequential.

Concerning sex, age, and urbanization: In their attitude toward drinking there was little difference within men between twenty-one and thirty-nine according to whether they lived in larger or smaller towns, but there was a substantial difference among men between forty and fifty-nine, the pattern being similar to that for looseness of social controls. Evidently social controls and prevalent attitudes concerning the acceptability of heavy drinking may be operating to make for a lesser rate of problem drinking among middle-aged men in the smaller towns than in the larger cities—a finding which is shown in the next chapter.

For environmental support for heavy drinking, those in towns or rural areas under 2,500 were consistently lower than others in mean score. This is particularly the case with men from forty to fifty-nine

[5] Details are in the Supplementary Tables and Scoring Procedures, obtainable from the author.

and women from twenty-one to thirty-nine; the smaller communities are less permissive concerning heavy drinking for people in these groups than is true for the larger cities.

For looseness of social controls (or thinness of bonds to primary-group members), there were very substantial differences among all groups except for men between twenty-one and thirty-nine. As noted elsewhere, this finding is paralleled by differences in the rate of problem drinking, which is relatively lower among both men and women ages forty and older who live in the smaller towns than is the case for the younger men. This difference in social controls is understandable because young men in small as well as large towns have the mobility, energy, and perhaps the motivation to cast off personal ties to a greater extent than is true for older persons. The finding of a higher rate of problem drinking among the younger men in all sizes of cities also may be affected by a greater degree of public permissiveness, almost everywhere, toward the young men's "sowing their wild oats."

The net effect of the six variables upon the aggregate total mean was to bring about a generally higher "risk score" (in terms of potential for problem drinking) among those in the larger cities than for those in the smaller towns. This expectation is borne out in the findings to be reported in the next chapter.

We may now examine the mean scores on independent variables for ethnoreligious groups. On attitude toward drinking, Irish Catholics as a group were found to have the most favorable attitudes, and this group is reported later as having an above-average rate of problem drinking. In environmental support for heavy drinking, Catholics were above average and conservative Protestants below average. This is consistent with the findings on the rate of problem drinking (see the next chapter). For alienation and maladjustment, again the Latin-Americans and Caribbeans and Negroes have the highest average.

For unfavorable expectations, the Latin-Americans and Caribbeans and Negroes have the highest (least optimistic) score, which is consistent with their generally low socioeconomic status. Looseness of social controls had a higher mean (fewer primary-group controls) for Catholics, those of Latin-American or Caribbean background, Jews, and Italians. The former two had an above-average rate of problem drinking, the latter two a below-average rate. Perhaps the inconsistencies are a function of the small sizes of some of these subsamples. While these findings for these various ethnoreligious groups do not reflect any enormous and consistent differences, enough differences were found in these indicators of life-style and outlook to warrant continued concentration on differences in drinking behavior in these groups, which are presented in some detail in the next chapter.

Since the variable of environmental support for heavy drinking will be demonstrated to be one of the two most important intervening variables in predicting the rate of problem drinking, some further discussion of subgroup differences in "the climate of drinking" is in order. Two sets of questions constitute the principal components of this environmental support variable: one consisted of four items which asked the respondent whether he knew (or could guess) whether four of his "significant others" (father, mother, spouse, and another person important in his life from outside his household) ever had drunk as many as four drinks at any one time; and the other series of items asked the respondent to guess what would be the largest number of drinks that the same "significant others" would think appropriate for him (the respondent) to drink at any one time. The findings of these exposure-to-drinking and permissiveness items are summarized in supplementary tables (not presented here) for the three variables of sex by age by socioeconomic status, sex by age by size of city, and ethnoreligious group.

In environmental support for heavy drinking within sex, age, and socioeconomic groups, a somewhat higher proportion of men than of women were aware (or would guess) that their fathers ever drank as many as four drinks upon an occasion, and more women reported their husbands as drinking that many drinks than believed this was true for their fathers.[6] Almost twice as many men (56 per cent) as women (27 per cent) reported that they themselves had drunk four or more drinks on one or more occasions during the preceding two and one-half years.

Within each sex, in almost all socioeconomic comparisons respondents of higher socioeconomic status reported a higher percentage of heavy drinkers among their significant others than was true for those

[6] Obviously, a larger proportion of women than of men reported their spouses as drinking four or more drinks upon occasion; and that artifact alone is responsible for the finding that a slightly higher proportion of women than of men reported that one or more "significant others" drank four or more drinks at least occasionally.

of lower status. Thus it will be seen that while a larger proportion of persons of lower socioeconomic status themselves have drinking problems, those of upper status tend more often to be exposed to heavy drinking than are those of lower status. The responses of younger persons may be more accurate than those of older persons, as judged by comparisons of findings on respondents' reports of their fathers' drinking: since their reports were supposed to be based on observations of the father's maximum drinking as observed by the respondent over the respondent's lifetime, it would be logical to expect that accurate reporting would yield reports of heavier drinking for fathers on the part of older persons, since they would be reporting on a maximum over a longer period. However, both among men and women, older respondents tend to report significantly lower levels of heavier drinking (of four or more drinks per occasion) by their fathers.

Findings on permissiveness of the "climate of drinking" in terms of respondents' estimates of how many drinks their significant others would deem appropriate for the respondents themselves to drink on any occasion show about the same patterns as for the exposure findings. In general, a larger percentage of significant others were reported to be permissive of four or more drinks per occasion for men than for women respondents; and fewer lower-status and older respondents reported such permissiveness than was true for upper-status and younger respondents. The largest difference in permissiveness by socioeconomic status was for younger higher-status men, where a much larger proportion reported their significant others (and themselves) as being permissive of four or more drinks-per-occasion than was the case for the younger lower-status men. However, the abrupt shrinkage in the percentages of permissiveness for those over thirty-nine illustrates how social norms regarding appropriate drinking may be having a profound influence upon decreasing the level of drinking among older persons—even after all due allowance is made for any tendencies on the part of heavy drinkers to project their own permissiveness over onto their significant others.

To summarize environmental support for heavy drinking, by sex, age, and urbanization groups: in general, the level of environmental support was found to be materially higher for both men and women in the larger cities, being particularly low for respondents in towns or rural areas under 2,500 population. The differences in exposure and permissiveness by size of city indicate that the "drinking climate" in small towns is a much more austere one than in large cities. The findings thus are congruent with the finding (reported in the next chapter) of a systematically higher rate of drinking, and of problem drinking, in the larger cities than in the smaller towns.

To summarize environmental support for heavy drinking among ethnoreligious groups: a significantly higher proportion of Catholics (particularly Irish Catholics) reported being exposed to significant others who drank at least four drinks on some occasions. A fairly high rate of exposure to heavier drinking was also reported by those of British liberal Protestant backgrounds, Germans, Italians, and those of Latin-American or Caribbean extraction. Jews had a relatively low percentage reporting being exposed to significant others who ever drank as many as four drinks per occasion.

As regards the respondent's perception of permissiveness among his significant others for his own drinking, the same patterns in general prevailed as for exposure to heavier drinking, except that in general the levels of permissiveness were lower than the rates for the estimated drinking of one's significant others (for example, the significant others appear to drink more than the respondent reports they want him to drink).

PREDICTION

Only data gathered in the first stage permit a true prediction of problem drinking during the approximately three years between Stages I (the 1964–1965 survey) and II (the 1967 survey) of the survey, because the measurement of the independent and intervening variables preceded the measurement of the dependent variable of problem drinking. However, items from the Stage I intervening variables by themselves do not constitute a very balanced list: the Stage I survey had only one item on unfavorable expectations, and only three on looseness of social controls. There had been no detailed plan to conduct a later survey concentrating on problem drinking, because the primary objective of the Stage I survey was to cover a broad range of descriptive items regarding drinking behavior and attitudes of many kinds—thus only a limited number of questions were asked at Stage I concerning certain of the intervening variables.

Combining the intervening variables from the two stages has the effect of striking a compromise between making a true prediction (from Stage I variables to Stage II reports of problem drinking) and having a correlation between independent and intervening and dependent variables measured at the same point in time (as regards these variables and problem drinking as reported at Stage II). Thus the combined Stage I and II intervening variables somewhat overstate the prediction which would have been attained if all the 150 items had been asked at Stage I, and somewhat understates the correlation which would have resulted if all the 150 items had been asked at Stage II. The combined Stage I and II variables, however, are used extensively in preference to the Stage-I-only variables because the combined data provide a much better representation of content for all of the six intervening variables than the Stage I data alone.

In the new national survey now being completed, most of the items covered in either Stage I or II (plus additional items) are being applied, both to get a correlation with problem drinking reported in the same interview, and to predict future problem drinking to be measured in the projected final Stage IV survey about 1975. Data from these improved replications of the Stage I and II surveys will be used to provide a further check on the reliability of the findings from the combined Stage I and II intervening variables presented in this report. It is believed that in the interim, the findings from the combined data can be used with a reasonable degree of confidence as indicating the direction (if not entirely the extent) of predictions of problem drinking to be measured in future surveys.

An indication of the similarity of the findings which would be derived if solely the Stage I data had been relied on in predicting problem drinking, rather than the combination of Stage I and II data, is available through measurement of the correlations of scores at I compared to the combined I and II scores. It should be noted that the overall correlation for the combined molar scores was .85, and that the correlations for the six individual molar scores ranged from .70 to .92.[7] Thus it would appear that findings from the Stage I and I and

[7] A few scales which were applied at both Stages I and II enter into the molar scores for each study and thus increase the correlation between findings for Stage I and for Stage I and II over the correlations which would have ensued if there was no overlap in content between Stages I and II. The items were an impulsivity Guttman scale, an alienation Guttman scale, a neuropsychiatric complaints Guttman scale, a social drinking scale, and an item on how much one's close friends drink. Since each scale in the molar variables entered into the variable with a weight of only a single item, and since the five duplicate scales were widely distributed over the six molar variables, the duplication of

II data are sufficiently similar to permit the use of either set of data for some purposes. Since the Stage I and II data are more reliable because based on a greater number and balance of items, more emphasis is put upon the combined data in the analyses of the correlates of problem drinking presented in the next chapter.

The intercorrelations of both the Stage I and I and II molar scores were similar for the two sets of figures, and the intercorrelations were relatively low, with the exception of the association between attitude toward drinking and environmental support for heavy drinking (.42 for Stage I data alone and .55 for Stages I and II combined). The intercorrelations were low enough to permit a fair-sized additive multiple correlation between the combination of the six variables and the dependent variable of problem drinking. It will be seen in the next chapter, however, that some of the individual molar variables had relatively low correlations with problem drinking, thus limiting the multiple correlation of the combined variables with problem drinking to a rather moderate level.

As discussed earlier, the only data in this national study which permit a true prediction in a prospective (forward) direction of problem drinking reported in the 1967 Stage II survey are the data gathered on the same individuals in the earlier 1964–1965 Stage I survey. A multiple correlation of the six social-psychological variables measured at Stage I against current problems score (for problems reported at Stage II as having occurred during the past three years, the period approximating the time between Stages I and II) obtained a resultant multiple correlation of .28 between all six variables and problem drinking (or .31 for men and .22 for women).

From one standpoint, a multiple correlation of .28 may not appear to be a very effective prediction: it accounts for only about 8 per cent of the variance in problem drinking. However, from other standpoints this might be considered quite creditable: it was made about three years in advance of the followup study which measured problem drinking; it was based on very limited numbers of items for certain social-psychological variables; and these six variables do not take into account such important primary independent variables as age, socioeconomic status, urbanism, and ethnocultural background—

---

these scales could not have had a material effect on the correlation between the Stage I and I and II molar variables.

of which more will be said in the next chapter. In any event, the forecast is about on a par with many other forecasts derived from using various types of personnel tests to predict later success in various types of jobs. The main implication is that the outcome is sufficiently encouraging to lead to hopes that much better forecasts of problem drinking will be made, using the same general multivariate model, when better data than that from the Stage I survey become available.

Table 9 presents a multivariate analysis of the six social-psychological variables against current problems score (divided at the high score of seven points) when the six variables consisted of items which were applied at either Stage I or Stage II. The combined Stages I and II items yielded a multiple correlation of .38 for the total sample —materially higher than the correlation for Stage I items alone.

Table 9. Multivariate Analysis of Social-Psychological Scores against Criterion of Current Problems Score (1964–1967), Combined Prediction and Correlate Analysis (N = 1,359)

Combined items from 1964–1965 (prediction) and 1967 (concurrent) studies	Number of Items (Total, 150)	Correlation with Criterion (Pearson r)	Partial Correlation	Stepwise Multiple Correlation
Attitude toward drinking	13	.35	.27	.35
Alienation and maladjustment	55	.10	.10	.37
Impulsivity and non-conformity	43	.18	.06	.38
Environmental support for heavy drinking	21	.24	.04	.38
Unfavorable expectations	13	.09	.01	.38
Looseness of social controls	5	.13	.00	.38

The first four variables—attitude toward drinking, environmental support for heavy drinking, impulsivity and non-conformity, and alienation and maladjustment—accounted for virtually all of the variance in the multiple correlation. The remaining two variables (unfavorable expectations, and looseness of social controls) have negligible partial correlations with the current problems score after taking into account the partial correlations of the leading four variables. However, each of these two variables had a significant correlation with problem drinking when considered alone; and hence they are being retained within the battery of intervening variables because they may help to account for some variance in problem drinking under some circumstances.

It will be noted that the lion's share of the multiple correlation between the six variables and problem drinking in Table 9 was accounted for by one variable, attitude toward drinking—composed of items on whether the respondent would miss drinking if he had to give it up, whether he agreed that "drinking does more good than harm" rather than the converse, felt that good things could be said about drinking, and that the reasons of sociability were important in his drinking.[8] It could be argued that attitude toward drinking is a dubious variable for the prediction of problem drinking unless it is fully established that the attitudes existed prior to the development of the problem drinking, on the grounds that favorable attitudes toward drinking might be a dissonance-reducing consequence of problem drinking rather than a cause, or that some third factor could account for both the attitudes and the problem drinking. However, attitudes really must be considered in predicting human behavior, for attitudes are usually themselves prime motivating forces rather than epiphenomena whose contaminating effects are to be excluded where possible. Some writers go as far as Allport, who said in discussing causal factors in *The American Soldier:* "To my mind we have clear evidence here that attitudes are dynamic forces; they *cause* behavior. . . . Nothing ever causes behavior excepting mental sets (including habits, attitudes, motives). To hold education or any other background factor constant is to imply that it alone may directly determine behavior. It is illegitimate to bypass in this way the personal nexus wherein all background influences must be integrated. Background factors never directly cause behavior; they cause attitudes; and attitudes in turn determine behavior" (1950, p. 172).

This still leaves unanswered the objection that even though attitudes are important determinants of behavior, and even though the attitudes toward drinking were measured at Stage I (before the report of problem drinking at Stage II for the period between the two stages),

[8] Full details on the component items making up each of the social-psychological variables may be obtained from the author.

part of the correlation between attitudes and drinking problems may have been a function of heavy and problem drinking preceding or concurrent with the formation of favorable attitudes toward drinking. While this no doubt is true to some extent, findings to be discussed in Chapter Five demonstrate that there is sufficient evidence concerning the role of prior attitudes in changing the components of problem drinking (heavier intake, and drinking for relief of problems) to indicate that prior attitudes are as much (if not more) of a causal factor in problem drinking than problem drinking is a causal factor in determining attitudes. Accordingly, attitude toward drinking will be retained as one of the six social-psychological variables in the analysis of findings throughout this section.

The procedures involved in the multiple correlation presented in Table 9 provide an extremely conservative statement of the association between the social-psychological variables and problem drinking, because the distribution on the dichotomy of problem drinking is highly lopsided, with only 9 per cent in the group with high current problems scores; and such an extreme 91–9 split reduces the top limit of the potential correlation. Table 10 demonstrates that the association between social-psychological and current problem drinking score is much higher, in terms of practical ability of predicting problem drinkers from the social-psychological "risk score" than might be assumed from the multiple correlation of .38.[9] In Table 10, note that for men, if the sample is divided into six groups according to their social-psychological "risk score," only two per cent of the lowest-risk group (lowest social-psychological scores) had a rather high current problems score, whereas 51 per cent of men in the highest-risk group had a current problems score of 7 or more points.

Chapter Five will discuss the combined effects of basic background independent variables (such as sex, age, socioeconomic status, and urbanization) plus the social-psychological "risk score" intervening variables (of attitude toward drinking, environmental support for heavy drinking, alienation and maladjustment, impulsivity and non-conformity, looseness of social controls, and unfavorable expectations) in predicting current problem drinking.

[9] From this point on, the combined score for the six social-psychological molar variables will be referred to as the "risk score," when they are used to predict problem drinking. The term is used to mean that the higher the "risk score," the greater the likelihood of a high problem drinking score.

Table 10. ASSOCIATION OF CURRENT PROBLEMS SCORE WITH SOCIAL-PSYCHOLOGICAL RISK SCORE: COMBINED 1964–1965 AND 1967 DATA, MEN, WOMEN, AND GRAND TOTAL[a]
(in percentages)

Current Problem Score (within last three years)		Social-Psychological Score: Lowest Score 22–26	2nd Score 27–28	3rd Score 29–30	4th Score 31–32	5th Score 33–34	Highest Score 35–40	Total
	N	(133)	(139)	(160)	(141)	(98)	(80)	(751)
Men: Score 7+		2	3	10	17	30	51	15
	N	(90)	(109)	(150)	(110)	(84)	(65)	(608)
Women: Score 7+		—	1	3	4	12	19	4
	N	(223)	(248)	(310)	(251)	(182)	(145)	(1359)
Grand Total: Score 7+		1	2	6	10	20	36	9

[a] The "risk score" consisted of the six social-psychological components shown in Table 9. Each of the six components was given equal weight by standardizing each score (to a mean of .50 and standard deviation of 10) and summing the six sub-scores to get the total risk score.

V Predicting Problem Drinking

Independent and intervening variables may be combined in many ways to predict the dependent variable of problem drinking. In this analysis, basic demographic variables such as sex, age, socioeconomic status, and degree of urbanization are used as the independent variables because commonly they precede both the criterion to be predicted (in this case, problem drinking) and such intervening variables as are influenced by generally somewhat more ephemeral personality and environmental factors. The six social-psychological molar variables were chosen as intervening variables after a lengthy winnowing process involving the scanning of many tabulations of items and groups of items from this national survey and its predecessors in the series, factor analyses of large pools of items, and an examination of the findings of other studies.

The four independent variables in combination were found to have a multiple correlation (Table 8) of .27 with current problems score. An interaction analysis, also presented in Chapter Three, showed that sex was the most important single factor (among demographic favorables) in predicting problem drinking, and that the highest proportion of persons with a "high" problem drinking score (35 per cent) discovered in interrelating these four variables was for men, of lower socioeconomic status, under sixty years of age, and living in cities of more than fifty thousand population. The six intervening variables (social-psychological "risk scores") were found to have a multiple correlation (Table 9 above) of .38 with current problems score, and "attitude toward drinking" was found to be the single most important moderator variable in predicting problem drinking. Before analyzing the combined correlates of independent and intervening variables, let us examine the relationships of the social-psychological "risk scores" to drinking-related problems when we consider individually several of the major independent demographic variables (such as sex, age, socioeconomic status, urbanism, and ethnocultural background).

Table 11 shows the association of "risk scores" (three groups rather than the six groups in Table 10) with problem drinking score, separately for men and women within each of the three age groups. There is quite an orderly progression in the prevalence of the more severe drinking problems: the range is from virtually zero problems among both men and women sixty or older of lowest-risk score, to 38 per cent for the youngest men (twenty-one to thirty-nine) of highest-risk scores. Men in all age groups have a higher percentage with

Table 11. Association of Current Problems Score with Social-Psychological Risk Score, Men and Women, by Age Groups

	N	Per Cent with Current Problems Score of 7+
MEN		
Age 21–39		
Risk Score		
Lowest	(61)	2
Medium	(97)	11
Highest	(102)	38
Age 40–59		
Risk Score		
Lowest	(120)	5
Medium	(97)	11
Highest	(106)	33

Table 11. (Continued)

Age 60–Up		
Risk Score		
Lowest	(91)	—
Medium	(49)	10
Highest	(28)	32
WOMEN		
Age 21–39		
Risk Score		
Lowest	(54)	—
Medium	(74)	6
Highest	(93)	10
Age 40–59		
Risk Score		
Lowest	(89)	1
Medium	(98)	3
Highest	(76)	15
Age 60–Up		
Risk Score		
Lowest	(56)	1
Medium	(45)	—
Highest	(23)	3
TOTAL BY AGE GROUPS		
MEN		
Age 21–39	(260)	20
Age 40–59	(323)	15
Age 60–Up	(168)	8
WOMEN		
Age 21–39	(221)	5
Age 40–59	(263)	5
Age 60–Up	(124)	1

a higher prevalence of problems than is true for women in comparable age groups, even when social-psychological risk scores are held constant. The prevalence of problem drinking among women is negligible except among those under sixty in the highest-risk group, while the proportions of men with current (fairly recent) drinking problems are fairly high for those of medium or high-risk scores at all three age levels. It is thus obvious that the sex difference itself makes a difference in the prevalence of problem drinking which is not fully explained by the social-psychological variables in the risk scores. Further analysis, later in this book, will help to explain some more of the difference in prevalence of drinking problems between men and women. The obvious factors to consider would be the roles that are taken on by being a man or a woman—including the greater constraints in this culture against heavy drinking as well as in sanctions against heavy drinking, and differences in the culturally prescribed alternative outlets for relief from stress available to women and to men.[1]

Still looking at Table 11, regarding results by age group: at least for men, there is a remarkably similar prevalence of drinking-related problems from age group to age group when risk score is held constant. This implies that there is not a great deal that is unique about age level per se (in relation to problem drinking) that is not measured by the risk score: men sixty and over of highest risk score show almost the same prevalence as the same group among those between thirty and forty-nine, and those in the high-risk thirty to forty-nine group in turn show a prevalence that is not much lower than among the high-risk twenty-one to thirty-nine group. Thus we would appear to have little ground for saying that the tapering off of drinking-related problems among older men is primarily a function of energy level—for older men with a higher risk score still maintain a high prevalence of problems related to drinking.

Earlier, in Chapter Three (Table 5), it was shown that the prevalence of problem drinking was found to be higher among those of lower socioeconomic status than among those of higher status. The interaction of the independent variable of socioeconomic status with two social-psychological "risk score" groups is shown in Table 12, in which sex and age are held constant. In Table 12 we see again that *within* each sex and socioeconomic group (except for women of sixty or older) those of higher-risk score have a higher prevalence of problem drinking than those of lower-risk scores. In addition, we can see that among men, those of lower status have a consistently higher prevalence of problem drinking; but this is not true for women—such a relatively small proportion of lower-status women drink at all (see Table 6)

[1] The first national study in this series found that while more men than women relied upon drinking and smoking for relief when depressed or nervous, more women than men relied upon the oral activities of eating, taking tranquilizers, or taking other pills or medicines, which was also the case for such activities as working harder, church or prayer, and talking with friends or relatives (Cahalan, Cisin, and Crossley, 1969, p. 151).

Table 12. Association of Current Problems Score of 7+ with Social-Psychological Risk Score, Men and Women by Social Position (Hollingshead, 1957)

	MEN		WOMEN	
	N	Per Cent	N	Per Cent
Age 21–39, Higher ISP[a]				
Risk Score				
Lower	(60)	—	(58)	2
Higher	(78)	26	(65)	9
Total	(138)	15	(123)	6
Age 21–39, Lower ISP				
Risk Score				
Lower	(58)	12	(46)	2
Higher	(64)	34	(52)	11
Total	(122)	25	(98)	5
Age 40–59, Higher ISP				
Risk Score				
Lower	(101)	3	(76)	1
Higher	(78)	20	(57)	9
Total	(179)	10	(133)	4
Age 40–59, Lower ISP				
Risk Score				
Lower	(84)	10	(74)	2
Higher	(60)	42	(56)	12
Total	(144)	22	(130)	5
Age 60+, Higher ISP				
Risk Score				
Lower	(53)	1	(41)	1
Higher	(12)	29[b]	(18)	5[b]
Total	(65)	6	(59)	2
Age 60+, Lower ISP				
Risk Score				
Lower	(76)	5	(54)	—
Higher	(27)	24[b]	(11)	—[b]
Total	(103)	10	(65)	—
Total, Higher ISP				
Risk Score				
Lower	(214)	2	(175)	2
Higher	(168)	23	(140)	9
Total	(382)	11	(315)	4

Table 12. (Continued)

Total, Lower ISP				
Risk Score				
Lower	(218)	9	(174)	1
Higher	(151)	36	(119)	10
Total	(369)	20	(293)	4

[a] Index of social position (Hollingshead, 1957).
[b] Caution is advised in accepting these specified results at face value, since they are based on very small samples.

that it sets a low ceiling on the chances of their getting into trouble because of drinking.

Table 13 shows differences in prevalence of problem drinking by size of city, separately for men and women in each of three social-psychological "risk score" groups. Again we find a regular progression, with almost 40 per cent of men of higher-risk scores in the larger cities having higher problem scores, as against almost zero for women of lowest-risk scores who live in places of less than 2,500. It is also evident that those in any of the three sizes of city have about the same prevalence of problems associated with drinking as the men in either of the other city-sizes when risk-group is held constant.

Table 13. Association of Current Problems Score of 7+ with Social-Psychological Risk Score, Men and Women, by Urbanization

MEN	N	Per Cent
Large Cities[a]		
Risk Score		
Lowest	(60)	4
Medium	(87)	12
Highest	(117)	39
Medium Cities		
Risk Score		
Lowest	(68)	1
Medium	(70)	15
Highest	(74)	28
Small Cities		
Risk Score		
Lowest	(144)	3
Medium	(86)	7
Highest	(45)	38

Table 13. (Continued)

WOMEN		
Large Cities		
Risk Score		
Lowest	(42)	1
Medium	(79)	—
Highest	(103)	12
Medium Cities		
Risk Score		
Lowest	(61)	1
Medium	(75)	7
Highest	(59)	8
Small Cities		
Risk Score		
Lowest	(96)	*
Medium	(63)	4
Highest	(30)	13
TOTAL BY SIZE OF CITY		
Men		
Large Cities	(264)	21
Medium Cities	(212)	14
Small Cities	(275)	10
Women		
Large Cities	(224)	5
Medium Cities	(195)	5
Small Cities	(189)	3

[a] Large is 50,000 or more; medium is between 50,000 and 2,500; small is less than 2,500.

* Less than one-half of one per cent.

It would appear that the principal reason why men in the larger cities show such a high prevalence of drinking problems is that this group includes a higher proportion of higher-risk people—and not that larger cities per se somehow "cause" much problem drinking. The real question then becomes, why are the mean "risk scores" on certain variables—such as environmental support for heavy drinking, looseness of social controls, and attitudes toward drinking—higher for those in larger cities than for those in small towns and rural areas? The inferences drawn are that the lower level of social controls and a more permissive "drinking climate" definitely play a part in this difference in problem drinking among those in larger and smaller cities or towns, but that the higher level of alienation and maladjustment in the larger cities may not be as important a factor in problem drinking as the other variables which are more specifically related to drinking norms and social controls over conduct. In any event, these findings certainly do point up the high prevalence of drinking-related problems in our larger cities.

The final table in this series testing the association of intervening variables with problem drinking is Table 14, which presents findings for three major religious groupings: "liberal Protestants" (members of denominations which do not have an official stand against drinking), "conservative Protestants" (denominations which have taken official stands against alcohol), and Catholics. Again we see that when risk score is held constant, the results for the three groups are rather similar at each level of risk. However, the Catholics have a higher aggregate proportion of persons with higher problem scores, as a function of the fact that they have a higher proportion of persons with higher-risk scores. As in other studies (Bales, 1944; Glad, 1947; Snyder, 1958; Knupfer and Room, 1967), Jews were found to have a very low prevalence of problems related to drinking.

We have now presented, in some detail, the associations of several independent variables (including sex, age, socioeconomic status, degree of urbanization, and religion) with current problems score, as further affected by interactions with the combined six social-psychological intervening variables. We have seen a great degree of difference in the prevalence of problem drinking among the groups covered, ranging from a low of zero among women sixty or older of lower social status and of lower risk score, to a high of 42 per cent among men forty to fifty-nine of lower status and of higher risk score (Table 12). Certainly the findings of these multivariate cross-tabulations and multiple regressions have demonstrated that a few key variables account for a considerable amount of the explained variance in the correlates of problem drinking. However, there exist multivariate analytic techniques which can enable us to test the effects of additional variables.

Use of multiple regression methods represents a statistically

Table 14. Association of Current Problems Score with Social-Psychological Risk Score, by Religious Groups

	N	Per Cent with Current Problems Score of 7+
Liberal Protestants[a]		
Risk Score		
Lowest	(93)	1
Medium	(83)	6
Highest	(87)	23
Conservative Protestants[b]		
Risk Score		
Lowest	(295)	1
Medium	(232)	7
Highest	(113)	27
Catholics		
Risk Score		
Lowest	(75)	4
Medium	(120)	7
Highest	(188)	21

Note: Sample sizes were sufficient for this detailed analysis for these three general groups only. Aggregate proportions with Current Problems Scores of 7 or higher were as follows: Jews (27), 4 per cent; liberal Protestants (263), 8 per cent; conservative Protestants (640), 7 per cent; Catholics (383), 13 per cent.

[a] Liberal Protestants: classified on basis of church's stand on use of alcohol, denominations which do not advocate total abstinence; includes Episcopalian, Presbyterian, Lutheran, Unitarian, and so on.

[b] Conservative Protestants: denominations recently favoring complete abstinence; Baptists, Methodists, United Church of Christ, Congregationalists, Disciples of Christ, and Evangelical United Brethren.

efficient multivariate method of predicting problem drinking from a combined set of independent variables, *if* the consequent assumption of linearity of relationships is sufficiently valid to provide assurance that no serious bias might result from the concealment, in the multiple regression process, of important interactions among certain variables. However, much variance remains to be explained by variables which are non-monotonic in nature: such nominal (non-ordinal) variables as occupation, race, region, national origin, and religion; and the multiple regression process cannot deal with these except through the statistically inefficient and interaction-concealing process of dichotomizing each variable through using a series of dummy variables (for example, Irish and non-Irish, Jewish and non-Jewish, and so on). Another limitation of the regression procedure is that it yields results that are more difficult to interpret and to apply in epidemiological studies intended for use in public health programs, in which tables of prevalence rates (expressed in percentages of viable subgroups in the population) ordinarily are required.

Thus in dealing with a phenomenon such as problem drinking which can be expected to involve interactions between physiological, psychological, and sociocultural variables, linear multivariate analysis methods and partial correlations cannot do the job alone. However, it is also obvious that the traditional cross-tabulation approach is also inadequate on several counts. One is that two-variable or three-variable cross-tabulations probably are too simplistic to account for an adequate amount of variance in problem drinking. Another is that if one attempts to account for more than about three variables in a series of cross-tabulations, if the sample is large it takes an enormous number of "fishing expeditions" to determine which variable to cross-tabulate and which subgroups to combine within each variable in order to explain the maximum amount of variance that is congruent with existing hypotheses. And if the sample is small, the series of successive cross-tabulations has to be very limited because of the small numbers in the individual cells.

Fortunately, there is available a multivariate technique which does a reasonably efficient job of explaining variance by a logical series of binary "splits" to isolate cells of subgroups which differ significantly upon a criterion (or dependent) variable. It is the AID (Automatic Interaction Detector) computer-programmed procedure of Sonquist and Morgan (1964), described in Chapter Three. There, results were contrasted for the AID approach and a stepwise multiple regression, in analyzing the association between four independent variables (sex, age, socioeconomic status, and urbanization) and problem drinking. Below, the same type of parallel comparison is demonstrated, for the same four independent variables plus the six intervening social-psychological variables.

The multiple regression for the four independent variables plus the six intervening variables is shown in Table 15 as being .42. Attitude toward drinking, alienation and maladjustment, sex, and index of social position are shown to be the four leading variables of the ten. As is usual when so many variables are utilized, very little additional variance is explained by the last five variables.

Table 15. MULTIVARIATE ANALYSIS OF BACKGROUND VARIABLES AND SOCIAL-PSYCHOLOGICAL RISK SCORES AGAINST CURRENT PROBLEMS SCORE (Divided at Score of 7+)

Variables	Correlation with Current Problems Score (Pearson r)	Partial Correlation	Multiple Correlation (Stepwise Regression) (R)
Attitude toward drinking	.35	.25	.35
Index of social position (2 groups)	.08	.13	.38
Sex	.19	.14	.40
Alienation and maladjustment	.10	.08	.41
Impulsivity, noncompliance	.18	.06	.42
Age (6 groups)	.11	.05	.42
Environmental support of heavy drinking	.24	.03	.42
City size (6 groups)	.11	.02	.42
Unfavorable expectations	.09	.01	.42
Looseness of social controls	.13	.00	.42

The total explained variance with the ten variables thus is about 18 per cent ($.42^2$), leaving about four-fifths of the variance in problem drinking score to be explained by other factors, including unreliability in measurement. However, the predictive utility of the combined independent (demographic) variables and intervening (social-psychological) variables actually is considerably better than indicated by this multiple regression, in part because the multiple regression procedure penalizes any prediction utilizing a skewed distribution such as that for problem drinking, in which the great mass of the sample was piled up at one end, like the shoulders and hump of a dinosaur, with a rapidly dwindling tail of problem drinkers; and in part because the multiple regression procedure assumes a straight-line or at least monotonic relationship between the predictor and criterion variables, without taking into account any interactive relationships between the predictor variables.

A more realistic picture of the predictive power of the ten combined independent and moderator variables is shown in the AID (Automatic Interaction Detector) procedure in Figure 2. This figure, prepared according to the same principles as Figure 1 in Chapter Three (except that it includes the six intervening variables in addition to the four independent variables shown in Figure 1, shows that use of the interaction analysis makes it possible to isolate one group of sixty persons with 63 per cent having a "high" (7+) current problems score. This group consisted of men with highly favorable attitude toward drinking who were also high on the impulsivity and non-conformity variable and also high on environmental support for heavy drinking. It will also be noted that the AID procedure resulted in explaining 23 per cent of the variance in problem drinking, or more than the 18 per cent explained via the multiple regression.

When it is considered that having a "high" current problems score (of 7+) is a minority phenomenon shown by only 9 per cent of the total, the fact that the multivariate procedure has made it possible to identify subgroups of as high as 63 per cent with high current problems scores indicates that research methods based on similar principles should, when refined, result in the development of pencil-and-paper measures which can predict problem drinking with high accuracy.

The analyses of independent variables shown in Table 8 and Figure 1 were limited to four in which there was a consistent or monotonic relationship between problem drinking score and the various values for the variable (for example, the three age groups and the three size-of-city groups each exhibited a trend in problem drinking score, with the youngest persons having the highest rate and the oldest the lowest, and with those in large cities having the highest rate and those in the smaller areas having the lowest). The comparisons of the multiple correlation and the AID procedures were limited to variables with

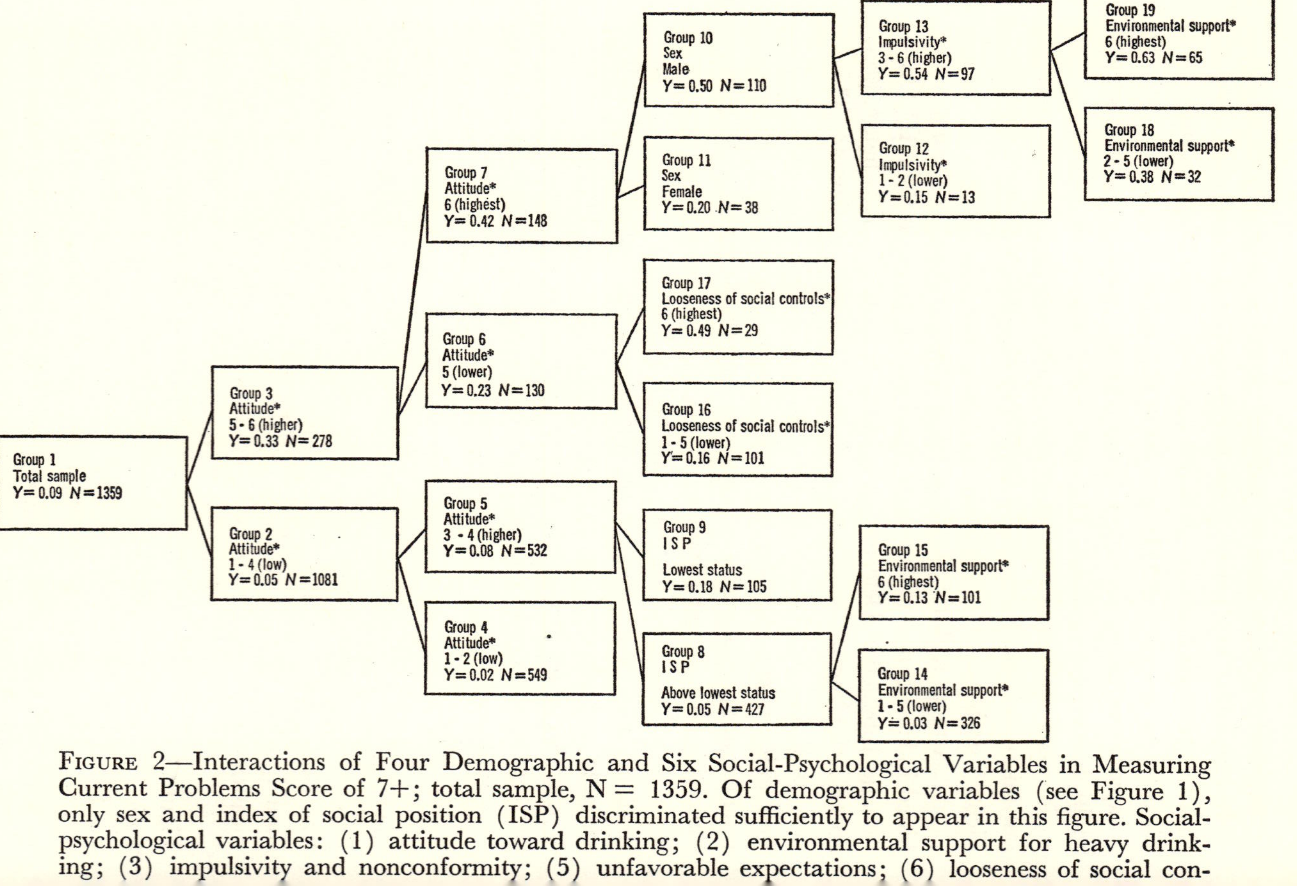

FIGURE 2—Interactions of Four Demographic and Six Social-Psychological Variables in Measuring Current Problems Score of 7+; total sample, N = 1359. Of demographic variables (see Figure 1), only sex and index of social position (ISP) discriminated sufficiently to appear in this figure. Social-psychological variables: (1) attitude toward drinking; (2) environmental support for heavy drinking; (3) impulsivity and nonconformity; (5) unfavorable expectations; (6) looseness of social con-

monotonic relationships to problem drinking because non-monotonic or non-linear relationships are inappropriate for multiple correlation unless one artificially restricts the range of values within a variable. In addition, a separate AID analysis was conducted in which ten independent variables were used, along with the same six social-psychological intervening variables. The eight independent variables were singled out for study because separate cross-tabulations revealed that they were correlated with problem drinking. The variables for this AID analysis were as follows: Independent variables: sex; age in decades, twenty-one through seventy plus; race and national ancestry, utilizing separate dichotomies (dummy variables) for each ethnic group; urbanization, in six size groups, from farm to central cities of one million or more; education, three groups; main earner's occupation, four groups —managerial and professional, clerical and sales, foremen and craftsmen and farmers, semiskilled and unskilled and service workers; marital status; religion, utilizing separate dichotomies (dummy variables) for each group. Intervening variables (the six social-psychological variables): attitude toward drinking; environmental support for heavy drinking; impulsivity and nonconformity; alienation and maladjustment; unfavorable expectations; looseness of social controls.

AID multivariate analyses were conducted, using the above six molar social-psychological variables and eight demographic variables, with the dependent (or Y) variable being the mean (or proportion) who had a current problems score on Stage II of seven or more points. The interactions, computed separately for men and women, are shown in Figures 3 and 4.

Interactions for Men (Figure 3): The variable of attitude toward drinking provided the first key split for the single variable accounting for the largest share of the variance in problem drinking. The utility of the AID approach from a public health or epidemiological viewpoint is that it enables us to single out a subgroup of men of most-favorable attitude toward drinking who also had a high score on environmental support for heavy drinking, and among whom 58 per cent had a high current problems score; and this group is further divisible upon education, yielding one small group of eighteen high school dropouts with 81 per cent having a high problems score. Men with extremely low rates of problem drinking were those with an unfavorable attitude toward drinking who were also low in impulsivity and non-

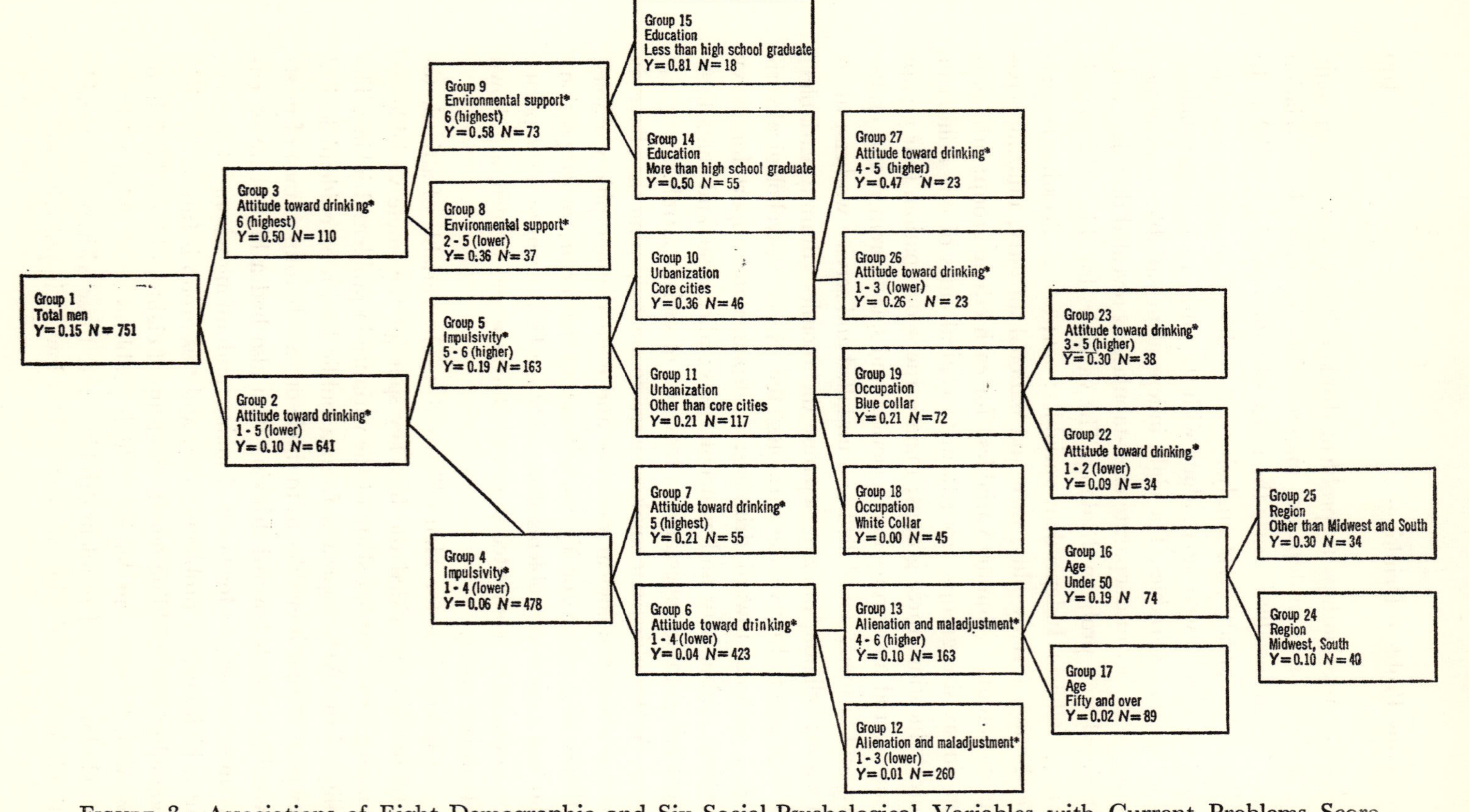

FIGURE 3—Associations of Eight Demographic and Six Social-Psychological Variables with Current Problems Score of 7+, Results for Men, N = 751. Note: four of the social-psychological and five of the demographic variables discriminated on current problems score sufficiently to appear in this figure. Social-psychological variables are as in Figure 2, and indicated by asterisks. *Proportion of total variance explained:* 28 per cent.

conformity and who were also not highly maladjusted, or who were age fifty or older.

Interactions for Women (Figure 4): The interactions for women were necessarily less complex than for men, because relatively few (only 4 per cent) of the women had a higher current problems score. The difference between men and women on the interactions is that the AID procedure explained a fairly healthy 28 per cent of the variance for men (Figure 3), but only 17 per cent of the variance for women (Figure 4). The highest scores among women were found among those who had a very favorable attitude toward drinking and also had either higher alienation and maladjustment scores or lived in large cities. Another small group with an above-average proportion (for women) of those with high problem-drinking scores were those who were not very favorable in attitude toward drinking but who were black.

To summarize the general implications of the interactions of the variables which have been explored above: the AID approach does provide information which assists in delineating viable subgroups of high and low rates of problem drinking—in ways which are not provided through the traditional multiple regression methods presented earlier in this chapter. One general finding was that in most instances it took interactions between combinations of demographic and social-psychological characteristics to find groups with either a very high or very low rate of problem drinking.

Another indication from the AID analyses is that the one variable closest to the MMPI type of maladjusted-personality test, namely the alienation and maladjustment variable, was *not* found to be very powerful in discriminating blocks of persons with a high problem-drinking score, except within the small group of women (Table 16) with a very favorable attitude toward drinking. This is consistent with the past findings of Syme (1957), Armstrong (1958), and others that there does not appear to be such a thing as a clear-cut "alcoholic personality."

Thus the higher potency of psychological than of demographic factors in predicting problem drinking have not been established by the data to hand. Further and more detailed longitudinal studies will be needed to establish more exactly the contingencies in which various factors play a precipitating or supporting role in the development of problem drinking. In any case, however, these analyses have estab-

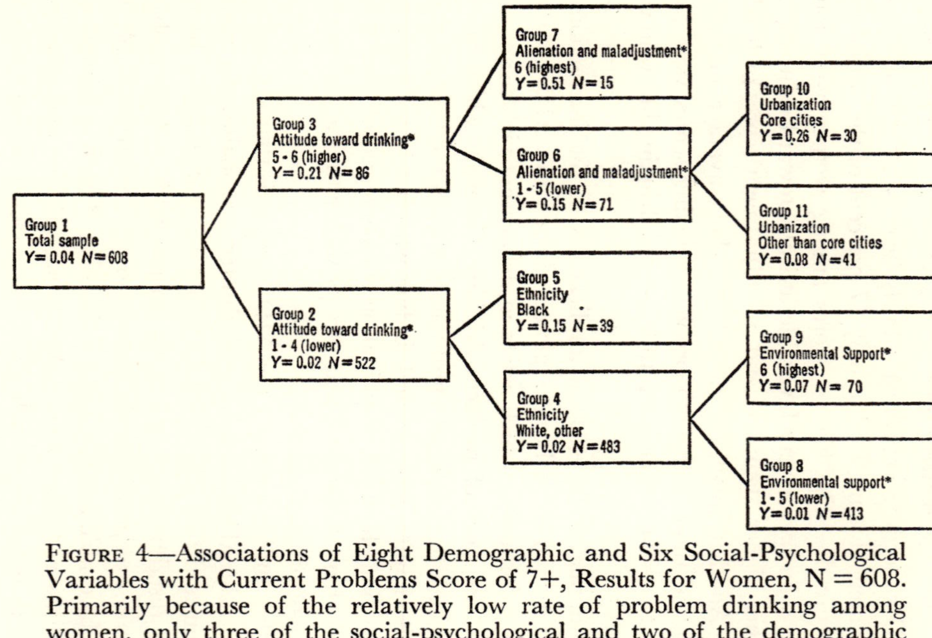

FIGURE 4—Associations of Eight Demographic and Six Social-Psychological Variables with Current Problems Score of 7+, Results for Women, N = 608. Primarily because of the relatively low rate of problem drinking among women, only three of the social-psychological and two of the demographic variables discriminated on current problems score sufficiently to appear in this table. Social-psychological variables are as in Figure 2, and indicated by asterisks. *Proportion of total variance explained: 17 per cent.*

lished the principle that interactions between psychological and demographic factors can be important in predicting problem drinking.

Again, it should be remembered, as shown earlier, that the chief single variable in predicting problem drinking score is the person's attitude toward the usefulness and importance of alcohol in his life. While other psychological attributes not specific to alcohol (for example, alienation and maladjustment) deserve further study, the findings presented earlier amply indicate that there should be a high payoff in concentrating upon the origin, exact characteristics, and causal sequence of the development of attitudes about drinking as such attitudes relate to the onset and changes in the severity of problem drinking in individuals over a period of time.

VI Patterns of Change

A primary goal of the present series of studies is the ultimate measurement at two or more points in time of the correlates of changes in behavior related to drinking problems, so that changes in an individual's life experiences can be related to later changes in his drinking behavior. Since the detailed range of drinking problems was not covered until Stage II (1967) of the current program, the more detailed analyses of correlates of change will not be possible until another measurement of the same range of drinking problems is conducted in about 1975. However, the first two stages of the series of surveys yielded some information on the correlates of change, some of it through comparisons of data obtained in the Stage I (1964–1965) and Stage II (1967) surveys, and some of it from questions asking respondents to recall past changes in their drinking behavior.

INDEX

The Stage I and II surveys repeated a number of the same items which measured two kinds of drinking problems, psychological dependence and frequent intoxication, thus making it possible to measure change which occurred in the three-year interval between the two stages. The psychological dependence measure consisted of five questions on the use of alcohol to deal with depression or nervousness, or to forget one's problems and worries, and the frequent intoxication index was derived from items on the frequency of drinking five or more drinks per occasion of drinking.

All persons were scored on this combined index of problem drinking and classified as either "high" or "low" on their separate responses in the Stage I and Stage II surveys. Six per cent of the sample showed a decrease in score during the three years between Stages I and II; 9 per cent showed an increase in score; 6 per cent were scored "high" at both stages; and the remaining 79 per cent were scored as "low" on these potential problems at both stages. Thus 15 per cent of the sample were found to have changed up or down in "high" or "low" scores in the short space of three years.

The correlation between the current problems score (measured at Stage II) and the index of problem drinking score (which is a part of the current problems score) at Stage II, was .71; or, in other words, 50 per cent of the variance in the more detailed current problems score was accounted for by the index of problem drinking measure. The practical utility of the shorter index of problem drinking measure is seen in the finding that of those who had a score of 7 or higher on the current problems measure, 83 per cent had a score of 1 or higher on the index of problem drinking score; and of those who had a score of less than 7 points on the current problems measure, only 9 per cent had a score of 1 or higher on the index of problem drinking measure. These findings indicate that the index of problem drinking measure may be used with a reasonable degree of confidence in a preliminary exploration of changes in problem drinking, until another measurement is carried out with the full set of problem-drinking questions.

Two types of data on changes in social-psychological variables were available to test their connection with changes in the index of problem drinking. One was a set of twelve items which were asked in identical form in Stages I and II. Table 16 represents the findings on the association between the changes in problem drinking index and changes between Stages I and II in the responses on these twelve items. Here only the findings for men are presented, for only these showed enough change in the index of problem drinking within the three-year span to be of interest.

The findings on these cross-tabulations can be summarized as follows: A consistent (though usually slight and statistically non-significant) change in the expected direction (more change toward drinking problems on the part of those suffering an "unfavorable" change in their status on the independent variables) occurred among men on all of the items except satisfaction in reaching life's goals. These findings are consistent with earlier findings on a few available measures of change in drinking behavior which indicated that some of the key variables involved are age (Williams, 1967; Cahalan, 1968) and changes in social and psychological influences (Cahalan, 1968). Inferences which can be drawn from retrospective studies done at single points in time (including the findings in this study, reported later) indicate the apparent importance of the same variables—of age and change in social and psychological influences—in affecting change in drinking behavior.

The principal implication to be drawn from these findings is not that these isolated items constitute in themselves an efficient battery of items with which to predict change in problem drinking over time. Rather, the findings do demonstrate that there is a sufficient association between changes in a person's outlook and life experience and a change in his drinking behavior, over even as short a period as less than three years, to lend encouragement to later measurements of changes in drinking problems through utilizing a larger and better-balanced set of items in both the independent and dependent variables to measure changes over a longer span of time.

Future studies of the association between change in people's life circumstances should take into account the possibility that even some kinds of apparently favorable change (such as upward economic or social mobility) may be associated with increases in problem drinking. This is the implication of recent studies which indicate that change per se tends to be stressful (Holmes and Rahe, 1967; Rahe and Arthur, 1968). Further, change in one's life circumstances may mean at least a temporary lessening in the social controls impinging on one, with the consequent possibility of an increase in problem drinking.

HISTORY

Returning now to the more detailed data on drinking problems in the full current problems score, based on eleven types of drinking problems or potential problems reported for the three years prior to

Table 16. ASSOCIATION OF CHANGE IN INTERVENING VARIABLES BETWEEN STAGES I AND II WITH INCREASE IN PROBLEM DRINKING INDEX (findings for men)

Change in Moderator Variables	Lessened Risk of Increase in Problem Drinking (N)	Increase in Problem Drinking (Per Cent)	Increased Risk of Increase in Problem Drinking (N)	Increase in Problem Drinking (Per Cent)
Impulsivity score	(292)	14	(135)	17
Alienation score	(254)	14	(221)	17
Neurophysiological complaints score	(265)	12	(181)	17
Non-drinking oral activity score	(169)	15	(192)	17
Satisfaction in reaching life's goals	(170)	20	(136)	12
Marital happiness	(90)	14	(86)	22
Change in marital status	(25)	28	(26)	44
Death of parent or child in past two-and-half years (approx. time between Stages I and II, death considered higher risk than no death)	(632)	14	(117)	17
Someone moved from R's household in two-and-one-half-year period (removal considered higher risk than no removal)	(584)	13	(167)	19
Evening outside activity score	(163)	13	(187)	21
How often drinks served with friends (less vs. more often)	(76)	12	(211)	18
"Social drinking" score (higher score rated higher risk)	(107)	15	(128)	19

NOTE: Table should be read as follows. Of the 292 persons with change to a lower impulsivity score in Stage II, 14 per cent showed increase in problem drinking score; of the 135 with change to a higher impulsivity score, 17 per cent showed increase in Problem Drinking.

the Stage II interview: questions were also asked, in most instances, on whether the person ever had the problem. While the data do not permit an analysis of the full range of change in drinking problems because not all types of drinking problems were covered for the past as well as for the last three years, and the data do not lend themselves to measurement of the incidence of problems for the first time during the last three years,[1] the data are useful in yielding a preliminary measurement of the characteristics of those who used to have certain problems but no longer have them—or at least report themselves as not having had them during the last three years.

By inspecting the ratio between current problem-drinking scores and the non-current former-problem scores, it is possible to infer a change in problem drinking—for example, a higher current-to-former ratio indicates an increase in problem drinking within the last three years, and a lower current-to-former ratio indicates a decrease.

Table 17 presents findings on the history of problem drinking for three demographic groupings: sex, age and index of social position. Each subgroup is reported in terms of four percentages: those who have had fairly severe problems during the last three years as evidenced by a current problems score of seven or higher, those who had a former score of seven or higher but not during the last three years, those who drank but reported never having problems which would qualify them for a score of seven, and those who said they never drank as often as once a year.

Table 17 shows the distributions of current and former drinking problems for the total, and for men and women in each of three age groups, each further subdivided into two socioeconomic groups. It will be noted that the proportions of those with fairly serious former (but not current) problems are 9 per cent for the total, 16 per cent for men and 3 per cent for women; and that the range of former (not current) problems range from a high of 22 per cent of the oldest men of lower socioeconomic status (index of social position) to a low of 2 per cent among several of the groups of women.

In general, the results by age fit one's expectations insofar as the finding that younger persons show a higher ratio of current to for-

[1] The current problems score includes both those who reported problems during the last three years when the questions were in those terms, and those who reported the problem currently (for example, in response to questions of "Do you have this experience . . . ?") when the questions referred to current or recent experiences without stipulating a time span.

Table 17. History of Problem Drinking: Current or Former Problems Scores by Sex, Age, and Social Position (in percentages)

Sex, Age, and Index of Social Position (ISP)	N	Never Drank	Drank, Never Problem Score of 7+	Former Problems Score of 7+, Not Current	Current Problems Score of 7+
Grand Total	(1359)	19	64	9	9
Total Men	(751)	8	61	16	15
Total Women	(608)	27	66	3	4
Men 21–39					
Upper ISP	(138)	4	68	13	15
Lower	(122)	7	50	18	25
Total	(260)	5	60	16	19
Men 40–59					
Upper ISP	(179)	6	68	17	10
Lower	(144)	9	53	17	22
Total	(323)	7	61	17	15
Men 60+					
Upper ISP	(65)	17	70	7	6
Lower	(103)	10	60	22	10
Total	(168)	13	64	16	8
Women 21–39					
Upper ISP	(123)	5	88	2	6
Lower	(98)	31	61	3	5
Total	(221)	19	74	2	5
Women 40–59					
Upper ISP	(133)	19	74	3	4
Lower	(130)	33	60	2	5
Total	(263)	27	66	3	5
Women 60+					
Upper ISP	(59)	36	61	2	2
Lower	(65)	49	43	9	—
Total	(124)	43	50	6	1
Men, Upper ISP	(382)	7	68	14	11
Men, Lower ISP	(369)	8	53	19	20
Women, Upper ISP	(315)	17	76	2	4
Women, Lower ISP	(293)	35	57	4	4

Note: Current problems occurred within the last three years (the approximate period between survey Stages I and II).

mer problems, among both men and women. However, the findings may reflect tendencies toward forgetting or minimization of former problems on the part of men sixty or older, since these older men had a combined current and former report of problems (warranting a "severity" score of seven or more points) totaling only 24 per cent, as against 35 per cent for men under forty: but logically, the older the person, the greater the likelihood of his *ever* having had a drinking problem. While the differences may reflect a recent increase in problem drinking among the young, there is little independent evidence that this is the case.

Findings by index of social position in Table 17 show a substantially higher proportion of lower-status men reporting having had drinking problems, particularly current drinking problems. This difference between lower-status and upper-status men is concentrated among those under sixty. Lower-status men sixty or older have a relatively high rate of former drinking problems.

Tabulations were made of findings on former and current drinking problems for men and women of three age groups, for each of three urbanization groups.[2] Among men, within each of the three age groups, there was a smaller percentage reporting current problems among those in places of under 2,500 (including rural respondents) than among those living in urban areas. In general, the ratio of current to former problems was higher in the larger cities, especially for men forty or older; in other words, there appears to be a tendency for men in small towns and rural areas to "mature out" of the problem-drinking group at an earlier age than those living in cities of fifty thousand or more.

Thus on the basis of two measurements of an index of problem drinking separated by a three-year span (Tables 16 and 17) and changes in problem drinking as reported by respondents) the findings demonstrate that the methods of measurement used in these surveys are sufficiently sensitive to detect changes in problem drinking, in as short a period as three years. Problem drinking changes, and is correlated with changes in the lives of the respondents. Again, later studies in this same series should produce even sharper findings on the correlates of changes in independent variables and problem drinking, because the later studies will cover a longer time span during which changes can occur.

[2] Available in the Supplementary Tables, upon request to the author.

QUESTIONS OF CAUSALITY

The findings reported above are strongly indicative of a correlation between certain short-term changes in social-psychological characteristics or life events and changes in problem drinking. However, it must be remembered that since the independent and dependent variables were measured at just two points of time, there is no absolute proof that the changes in social-psychological variables preceded the changes in drinking. Thus it is not possible to make conclusive inferences on the basis of the data now available that any of the changes in social-psychological characteristics "caused" the changes in drinking; such inferences would be possible only if a daily or monthly diary were kept of both changes in the person's social-psychological characteristics and changes in his drinking behavior, or if a Stage III followup survey is conducted which can relate changes in social-psychological characteristics between Stages I and II to changes in drinking behavior occurring between Stages II and III.

However, there does exist an analytic technique which will permit inferences as to which variable, the presumed "independent" or the presumed "dependent" variable, is more likely to be causal of the other. This technique, known as "cross-lagged correlations," recently has been applied in a fairly wide range of sociological, psychological, and economic research situations. The basic logic behind the use of the technique is that if the correlation between variable A at Stage I and variable B at Stage II is higher than the correlation between variable B at Stage I and variable A at Stage II, then one can infer that variable A has a higher probability of having had a causal effect on variable B than the converse (Pelz and Andrews, 1964; Campbell and Stanley, 1966, Rozelle and Campbell, 1969).

In the present study, the hypothesis concerning cross-lagged correlations between overall "risk score" and problem drinking is that if the "risk score" is to be considered a legitimate predictor rather than merely the consequence of changes in problem drinking, the prediction forward from "risk score" at Stage I to the index of problem drinking at Stage II should yield a higher correlation than the postdiction (or backward prediction) from "risk score" at Stage II to the index of problem drinking score at Stage I. Table 18 presents these comparisons in correlations, separately for men and women, and for both sexes for each of three age groups, as well as for the grand total.

Table 18. Cross-Lagged Correlations between Social-Psychological Risk Score and Score for Index of Problem Drinking

	N	Use of "Risk Score" for Forward Prediction[a]	Use of "Risk Score" for Postdiction[b]
Men 21–39	(260)	.41	.23
Men 40–59	(323)	.37	.24
Men 60+	(168)	.32	.30
Total men	(751)	.36	.24
Women 21–39	(221)	.23	.26
Women 40–59	(263)	.28	.24
Women 60+	(124)	.34	.15
Total women	(608)	.27	.24
Grand total, Men and Women	(1359)	.32	.24

Note: The means and standard deviations of the "risk score" for Stages I and II were standardized, for comparability.

[a] Stage I "risk score" correlated with Stage II index of problem drinking score (Pearson r).

[b] Stage II "risk score" correlated with Stage I of index of problem drinking score (Pearson r).

In all but one of the comparisons for the six sex-age groups, the use of "risk score" at Stage I to predict index of problem drinking score at Stage II yielded a higher correlation than the postdiction of index of problem drinking score at Stage I from the later Stage II "risk score." In three of the six sex-age groups the differences in correlations were substantial, particularly for the relatively heavy-drinking group of men aged twenty-one to thirty-nine.

While the differences are generally small, the findings furnish preliminary evidence that the combination of the six intervening molar variables making up the social-psychological "risk score" do a better job in predicting later problem drinking than problem drinking does in predicting later "risk scores." While the term "cause" should not be used in this instance because variables other than problem drinking or "risk scores" may have been responsible for the findings, it certainly can be said that these findings provide additional evidence that the social-psychological variables in combination have more effect on later problem drinking than problem drinking has upon the independent "risk score" variables taken as a whole. The findings thus lend encouragement for the use of these types of "risk scores" in future studies of changes in problem drinking.

It is believed that the application of another stage in this series of longitudinal studies will yield ever sharper differences in predictions and postdictions as measured through the cross-lagged correlation technique, because a later measurement will make it possible to compare findings when a large number of identical independent-variable items are asked at two successive stages, with a consequent increase in reliability. The addition of another stage will also make it possible to make legitimate comparisons of the net prediction-postdiction differences in apparent causal sequence on the part of each of the six specific "risk score" variables (for example, alienation and maladjustment, attitude toward drinking, and so on), on which too few items were asked in identical form in Stages I and II to permit firm comparisons of the six individual "risk score" variables.

The position has been taken in this book that attitudes and perceptions regarding the importance of alcohol in one's life play a key role in determining later tendencies toward encountering problems in relation to drinking. Earlier it was reported that if a person had a high score on the "attitude toward drinking" items at Stage I (including such items as missing drinking a lot if one had to give it up, believing that drinking does more good than harm, or finding it important to have something to drink on social occasions), he was more likely than others to have a higher current problems score when reinterviewed three years later. This finding is not conclusive proof that the prior attitudes "caused" (or contributed to) the problem drinking, because it is possible that the person with a high Stage I problem-drinking score already had a high score on problem drinking at the time of Stage I, when his attitudes toward drinking were measured—and thus the attitudes may not have preceded the problem drinking.

It is not possible to put this issue to conclusive test until there are three stages available in a longitudinal study, to demonstrate whether changes in attitudes between Stages I and II are accompanied by changes in problem drinking between II and III. However, it is possible to infer to some extent what the effects of attitudes upon later drinking behavior are likely to be, through cross-tabulations of attitudes at Stage I against problem drinking scores of the same individuals at Stage II, in which the level of drinking at Stage I is held constant. (The level of drinking at Stage I is used as a substitute for the level of problem drinking, which was not measured at Stage I.) This cross-tabulation would test whether even among those who at Stage I said they never drank as many as five drinks on any occasion, those who had the more favorable attitudes toward alcohol would show up with higher drinking-problem scores at Stage II than those who also never drank very many drinks per occasion but who had been above the average in rating alcohol favorably.

Table 19 presents the results of such a cross-tabulation. It is seen that there is a modest, but consistent, difference in the proportions of persons with high Stage II current problems scores depending upon their attitudes toward alcohol, even when level of drinking at Stage I is held constant. (These differences are more marked for men than for women, perhaps because men are under fewer constraints against changing their behavior in the direction of heavier drinking if they so desire.) Again, these findings are not as satisfactory a measure of the effects of attitudes toward drinking upon drinking behavior as will be provided by a later step in the series of longitudinal studies, in which changes in attitudes can be compared conclusively against subsequent changes in a range of types of problems related to drinking. However, they do indicate that attitudes can contribute to the development of drinking problems—although it is well-recognized that attitudes and behavior tend to be a reciprocal process, starting first with one or the other, and with each reinforcing the other as time goes on.

In both Stage I and II of the national survey, a number of questions were asked concerning past changes in drinking behavior and reasons for such changes. Since some of the questions call for the respondent to search his memory for events which happened many years ago, it is likely that the results of such retrospective questions are subject to some forgetting and distortion (Knupfer, 1963). However, since all questions are "retrospective" in the sense that they involve respondents' recollections of events which happened before the time of interview, these questions about past changes in drinking behavior differ from questions about more immediate events only in the degree of accuracy they can attain. While retrospective reports of events which may have happened many years ago should not be accepted with as

Table 19. Attitudes Toward Drinking (Stage I) as a Predictor of Problem Drinking (Stage II) with Amount of Drinking at Stage I Held Constant

Attitudes toward Drinking at I With Amount of Drinking Constant	Proportion with High Current Problems Score (7+) in Stage II Survey					
	Men		Women		Total	
	N	Per Cent	N	Per Cent	N	Per Cent
Low drinking level (never 5 drinks on any occasion)						
More favorable attitudes toward drinking	(114)	7	(156)	3	(270)	4
Less favorable attitudes	(330)	2	(322)	*	(652)	1
Sub total	(444)	4	(478)	1	(922)	2
High drinking level (5 drinks on some occasions)						
More favorable attitudes toward drinking	(196)	37	(73)	25	(269)	33
Less favorable attitudes	(111)	29	(57)	21	(168)	26
Sub total	(307)	34	(130)	23	(437)	30
Combined Low and High levels of drinking						
More favorable attitudes toward drinking	(310)	24	(229)	8	(539)	17
Less favorable attitudes	(441)	9	(379)	3	(820)	5
Grand Total	(751)	15	(608)	4	(1359)	9

* Less than one-half of one per cent.

much confidence as reports on very recent events, the information can be of considerable value when it is taken into consideration along with other findings.

The answers to some questions about past drinking behavior are presented in Table 20. Findings are presented separately for men and women, each divided into three groups: those who drink or have drunk but who did not achieve a problem score of seven or more points, those who have a problem score of seven or more for their drinking as recalled prior to three years ago (but not for current drinking), and those who have a current (last three years) problem score of seven or more. (These questions on drinking behavior obviously exclude those who say they never drank as often as once a year.) For convenience in presentation, as well as to highlight the differences between groups, the person's status on problem drinking is used as the independent variable or percentage base (for example, findings are analyzed in terms of the proportion of current or past problem drinkers who were younger than eighteen when they started drinking, rather than in terms of the proportion of persons who started drinking before age eighteen who are current or past problem drinkers.) Table 20 is a summary table in that only the most salient portion of the information on each item is presented: that is, it presents the proportions who started drinking before the age of eighteen but not the percentages for those who started drinking after eighteen; and it gives the principal reasons for drinking more or less now, but omits the many types of reasons which were mentioned by relatively few people.

Significantly more of those who were current or former problem drinkers (with a score of seven or higher) started drinking when they were younger than eighteen. A majority of the current problem drinkers had had a drink less than a day prior to the interview. While relatively few current problem drinkers had drunk their last previous drink alone, solitary drinking was more common among women current problem drinkers than among other women who drank. Relatively more of the current problem drinkers had drunk their most recent drink in a restaurant or bar, a place where presumably there were fewer social controls exerted by significant others than would be true for drinking at home.

A majority of the current problem drinkers reported that they had tried at some time or other to cut down on or quit drinking, and more than 80 per cent of these had tried to cut down within the last three years. While about half of the current problem drinkers who had tried to cut down said that a reduction in drinking was currently in effect, less than ten per cent of them said that a reduction had lasted as long as three years.

Thus one of the attributes which helps to distinguish the current problem drinkers from others is that while most of them have tried to cut down on their drinking and many of them had some success in making a temporary reduction, very few had made a long-lasting reduction—which almost follows by definition, for many of those who made a long-lasting reduction in their drinking thereby removed themselves from the current-problem-drinker class. But in any event, the findings indicate that even those with fairly severe current problem drinking problems do show a considerable fluctuation in their drinking—which implies that there are frequent occasions in the life of the average problem drinker when it would be easier to mobilize the drinking-control resources of the individual and his environment more effectively than at other times.

Principal reasons offered for drinking less than formerly showed relatively little difference between the current problem drinkers and others, except that male current problem drinkers emphasized "health reasons" less often than did other males, and women current problem drinkers mentioned "fewer opportunities" to drink than was true for the other women. For all classes of drinkers, the principal reasons given for drinking less were financial reasons, more responsibilities, and lessened need or desire to drink, and social reasons. Relatively few mentioned ethical or moral or religious or guilt-tinged reasons (for example, "sets bad example") as reasons for having cut down on drinking.

As for reasons given for drinking more than formerly, current problem drinkers did not differ materially from others. The chief reasons given by all classes of drinkers were that they could afford it better, and social reasons. Relatively few emphasize that they were drinking more because of tensions or special problems. Thus when asked free-answer questions as to the reasons for their drinking more or less than previously, all classes of drinkers tended to give rather impersonal and non-moralistic responses. This may reflect a tendency on the part of the average to heavy drinker to "keep his cool" and his defenses up in talking about his drinking; or it may indicate that most changes in drinking are *not* accompanied by high emotionalism or moralizing.

Table 20. Relationship of Drinking Behavior to History of Problem Drinking

Drinking Behavior		History of Problem Drinking (in percentages)					
		MEN			WOMEN		
		Drank, Never Problem Score of 7+	Former Problems Score of 7+, Not Current	Current Problems Score of 7+	Drank, Never Problem Score of 7+	Former Problems Score of 7+, Not Current	Current Problems Score of 7+
	N[a]	(369)	(207)	(54)	(397)	(54)	(36)
Started drinking before age of 18		18	28	28	11	27	17
Had a drink less than a day ago		37	39	55	18	23	62
Had most recent drink alone		19	14	15	6	9	17
Most recent drink in restaurant or bar		21	25	37	21	15	26
Had tried to cut down on or quit drinking		19	68	58	11	47	70
	N	(62)	(121)	(68)	(43)	(32)	(24)
Had tried to cut down within last 3 years		42	34	81	63	48	95
	N	(62)	(116)	(64)	(42)	(30)	(22)
Some reduction has lasted until the present		73	83	51	64	88	48

Some reduction had lasted 3 years or longer		53	57	8	26	51	2
Drinking less than formerly (Stage I responses)	N	(158)	(71)	(67)	(107)	(12)[b]	(24)
Principal reasons for drinking less now							
Financial (can't afford)		18	22	29	8		10
Change out of military service		14	16	7	—		2
Social reasons		11	17	7	17		14
Fewer opportunities		15	10	11	6		24
More responsibilities		21	28	26	14		4
Less need or desire		19	15	14	19		16
Health reasons		12	18	7	9		8
Drank more than formerly (Stage I responses)	N	(107)	(30)	(48)	(112)	(6)[b]	(17)[b]
Principal reasons for drinking more now							
Financial (can afford)		23	21	24	13		
Social reasons		23	14	14	43		
Job-related reasons		9	6	12	1		
More opportunities now		9	6	13	2		
Enjoy it more now		8	20	9	11		

Table 20 (*continued*). RELATIONSHIP OF DRINKING BEHAVIOR TO HISTORY OF PROBLEM DRINKING

Drinking Behavior		History of Problem Drinking (in percentages)					
		MEN			WOMEN		
		Drank, Never Problem Score of 7+	Former Problems Score of 7+, Not Current	Current Problems Score of 7+	Drank, Never Problem Score of 7+	Former Problems Score of 7+, Not Current	Current Problems Score of 7+
Six specific reasons for increasing drinking during last three years	N[a]	(369)	(207)	(54)	(397)	(54)	(36)
Friendships and social life		10	8	22	12	19	36
Health reasons		2	—	3	2	1	7
Marriage or home circumstances		1	1	11	1	9	33
Work or employment situation		6	3	16	2	3	9
Financial position		1	*	12	2	9	13
For religious reasons		—	1	1	1	—	—
Six specific reasons for decreasing drinking during last three years							
Friendships and social life		10	11	19	8	7	23

Health reasons	7	13	29	7	4	38
Marriage or home circumstances	2	5	13	2	—	9
Work or employment situation	3	1	12	1	—	10
Financial position	2	5	11	2	12	21
For religious reasons	1	4	5	1	3	20
N	(369)	(207)	(54)	(397)	(54)	(36)
Experiences after drinking during last three years						
Felt happy and cheerful	50	44	86	47	54	82
Became life of the party	11	13	49	7	12	47
Found all worries disappeared	7	11	33	5	17	49
Felt sleepy	34	41	72	41	47	57
Had difficulty walking straight	12	18	58	9	26	47
Passed out	*	2	14	1	9	26
Felt very sad	3	6	27	5	17	42
Had hangover or severe headache	17	26	72	15	36	75
Was loud or boisterous	4	14	42	4	16	29

[a] The last previous number (N) above percentages is the base for the percentages below it.
[b] Too few persons in these subgroups to permit analyses.
* Less than one-half of one per cent.

A somewhat different emphasis is provided by results from direct (categorical rather than free-answer) questions about reasons for increasing or decreasing drinking revolving around six specific life areas—friendships and social life, health reasons, marriage or home circumstances, work or employment situation, financial position, and religious considerations. The current problem drinkers rated all these considerations as important reasons for either increasing or decreasing their drinking during the preceding three years, more often than was true for other drinkers. Particularly frequent as a reason for increasing drinking among current problem drinkers was "friendships and social life"; and "marriage and home circumstances" (presumably a home atmosphere conducive to heavy drinking, or an unhappy marriage, or both) was mentioned particularly often by the women who were current problem drinkers. "Health" was most often rated as important as a reason for decreasing drinking, with "friendships and social life" again fairly prominent. Here "religious reasons" was rated as important by one-fifth of the women current problem drinkers.

The final set of questions had to do with experiences after drinking during the last three years. Rather considerable differences are seen in the responses of those with fairly high current problem-drinking scores as compared to other drinkers. The chief differences were on the items "had a hangover or severe headache," "had difficulty walking straight," and "became the life of the party," although substantially more of the current problem drinkers than others reported each of the nine types of experiences as applicable to themselves during the last three years. The fact that more than 80 per cent of the current problem drinkers rated themselves as having "felt happy and cheerful" after drinking points to one of the principal reinforcements which are obtained from drinking on the part of those who drink to excess. (Almost as many—or three-fourths—of the current problem drinkers also reported they "had a hangover or severe headache"; but, as pointed out elsewhere, the reinforcement of being "happy and cheerful" tends to be a more immediate—and therefore a more effective—reinforcement for heavy drinkers than is the eventual hangover.) In any event, the findings of these nine types of drinking experiences provide a further demonstration that those who are problem drinkers are more susceptible to both the positive and negative effects of drinking than is true for other drinkers.

To summarize: the weight of the findings on these questions

about past changes in drinking behavior reinforces the other findings in this two-stage national survey which indicate that changes in drinking behavior are usually highly susceptible to social influences. Drinking (and even heavy drinking) is highly social behavior; and social forces appear to play a paramount part in determining the onset and the end of problem drinking.

VII Summing Up the National Survey

This summary of research findings gives primary emphasis to the facts uncovered in the national survey. The final chapter will discuss the implications of the study for public health and preventive medicine, therapy for drinkers with problems, and future research on alcohol-connected problems. Most of the research discussed in this book is based upon the results of a national study of a sample of 1,359 persons, initially interviewed in a national probability (random) sampling of drinking practices of adult residents of households throughout the United States (exclusive of Hawaii and Alaska) in 1964–1965 (Stage I) and reinterviewed in 1967 (Stage II). The study is the second phase in a longitudinal program of research, which began in the early 1960's with a broad study of many details of drinking practices and will be completed in a longer-term assessment of changes in problem drinking to be conducted in the 1970's.

This study is quite unlike most past analyses of the correlates of alcoholism and problem drinking, which usually have been confined to those who have been institutionalized or otherwise have become formally labeled as "alcoholics." Here the population sampled was the *household* population, thus skipping most institutionalized or derelict "alcoholics" unless they were living in what the census defines as a "household" at some time during the period of the initial field work in 1964–1965. This sampling decision was based on the conviction that many of the phenomena measured in past studies of "alcoholics" really reflected the process of institutionalization and de-socialization more than they measured the correlates of problem drinking per se. The plan adopted was to follow up an essentially "normal" (or non-institutionalized) adult population over a period of years, so as to chart the course of the development or decline of drinking-related problems as they occur. While the institutionalized population was not covered in these surveys, it is expected that the findings will be helpful to understanding the process of becoming an institutionalized or derelict "alcoholic."

In preferring to study the correlates of "problem drinking" rather than those of "alcoholism," more than a narrow semantic distinction is at issue. We have tried to avoid using the concept of "alcoholism" in these descriptive studies of the general population. Part of the reason for not using the concept of "alcoholism" is to avoid any implication that such descriptive surveys are capable of substituting for medical or clinical diagnoses of advanced states of alcohol addiction. Further, over the years Jellinek's concept of the "addictive alcoholic" has been misapplied, resulting in much tunnel vision, ambiguity, and pejorative labeling of those with perhaps short-term adjustment problems as being irreversibly addicted, all with the unintended frightening of some problem drinkers away from seeking treatment, and the discouraging of developing new ways of helping persons with problems associated with alcohol.

RATES

The national survey of the correlates of problems related to alcohol utilized the definitions of Plaut that "problem drinking is a *repetitive* use of beverage alcohol causing physical, psychological, or social harm to the drinker or to others" (1967, pp. 37–38); and of Knupfer that "a problem—any problem—connected fairly closely with drinking constitutes a drinking problem" (1967, p. 974). Both definitions are in keeping with a research strategy which uses a fairly wide net which ultimately should enable us to determine which potential drinking problems turn out to be associated with later serious consequences in the lives of the people who have them. Thus the definitions of "drinking-related problems" used in this survey were based upon two principles: one is to include socially defined "problem" behaviors which are so regarded by the individual himself or by his significant others (such as his wife, his friends, his employers, or the police). The other principle is a public health or medical one, in which interim acceptance is given as "problems" to certain types of behaviors or symptoms which may not be regarded as problems by the person, but on which there is a reasonable degree of consensus among medical and psychiatric authorities that these (such as addictive drinking, frequent drinking to intoxication, and going on binges) are indicative or predictive of problems. Again, continued refinement over a period of years in the interim set of types of problems used in this study will help to determine which types of problems (or potential problems) are the most likely to have serious long-term consequences for the individual or for society.

A sharp distinction should be made between the utility of a list of problem behaviors in describing differences between subgroups in the population, and the use of the same drinking-problem scoring procedures in conducting detailed assessment of individual behavior in arriving at clinical diagnoses and prognoses of "alcoholism." Whether a symptom really is likely to indicate a real problem very much depends upon circumstances: the person's age, sex, social status, the nature and history of his relationships with his significant others, the reasons behind a given bit of drinking behavior, the chronicity of the behavior, and the like. It is also difficult in a survey conducted at a single point in time to determine which came first, the drinking or the problem. Thus it should be borne in mind that these potential "drinking problems" may vary in their implications and consequences in individual cases.

Prevalence of the eleven specific types of problems or potential problems was measured in terms of occurrence within the last three years (see Table 1). The most frequent specific current problem for men was frequent intoxication, followed by symptomatic drinking behavior ("symptomatic" of possible alcohol addiction), problems with spouse or relatives, and psychological dependency upon alcohol. Women's responses were quite different: no specific problems were numerous among the women, the leading one being that a physician had advised them to cut down on their drinking for reasons of health.

A current problems score was devised from combining the results on the eleven specific types of problems, with the individual problems being scored differentially according to their presumed severity and the number of experiences within a problem area: for example, a person could attain a current problems score of seven or more only if he had at least one type of problem in a form which most authorities would call rather severe *and* at least one other in mild form, or two problems in moderate form and one in mild form, or one in moderate form and four in mild form, or seven problems in mild form. Fifteen per cent of the men and 4 per cent of the women (9 per cent of the total sample) had a current problems score of seven points or more; and this level of problem-drinking score was used as the primary dependent variable in most of the analyses of the correlates of problem drinking in this book.[1] However, a majority (57 per cent of the men and 79 per cent of the women) denied having experienced any of the eleven types of potential problems during the previous three years.

Among men, drinking problems were found to taper off sharply only after age fifty and continued at a fairly high level until the age of seventy, while among women very few had drinking problems after the age of fifty. The patterns of current problems also differ for men and women in that among men the prevalence of problems is highest for those in their twenties, conspicuously lower for those in their thirties and forties, and then tapering off among men in their fifties. On the other hand, relatively few women in their twenties had drinking problems, with the bulk of problems being concentrated among those in their thirties and forties, with a very sharp dropoff among women in their fifties. These sex differences are consistent with the inference from other findings that men generally get introduced to heavier drinking by other men when they are young, and that women tend to get involved in any heavier drinking somewhat later in life, probably often through the influence of their husbands or men friends.

These findings are consistent with past studies that the proportion of alcoholics among the elderly is very small, and are consistent with the pattern of "maturing out" which has been observed also in the use of drugs and in sexual activities. However, a much higher pro-

[1] Again, as discussed in Chapter Three, there is nothing sacred about using a current problems score of seven as a cutting point rather than a score of four or a score of twelve, for example. Later reinterviews of the same sample will help determine which cutting points are most predictive of the later development or continuance of apparently severe problems.

portion of persons in their twenties showed up in this survey as having drinking problems than in studies of the age levels of labeled alcoholics, which generally show a higher prevalence in the thirties and forties. The difference is presumed to stem in part because it ordinarily takes many years of hard drinking before the problem drinker becomes publicly known as an "alcoholic," and in part because when people persist in heavy drinking beyond their twenties, they tend to encounter a much higher level of intolerance of such conduct as being "unsuitable for your age" on the part of their significant others.

A special analysis revealed a consistent pattern of apparently greater shrinkage or "maturing out" of drinking problems among men of upper status after they had reached the age of fifty, compared to lower-status men (Table 5). Some of the differences might be accounted for in terms of greater alienation and lesser impulse-control among those of lower status. Some of the difference also may stem from the fact that lower-status men are in a poorer position to conceal their heavy drinking from their employers, their spouses, the police, or the neighbors; but the upper-status men show not only an apparently higher rate of shrinkage in their fifties of interpersonal problems due to drinking, but the upper-status men also show an apparent shrinkage of the more readily concealable indices of heavy drinking, binge drinking, and admitting to symptoms of potential alcohol addiction. (The term "apparently greater shrinkage" is used because it is possible that the differences by age groups may be in part a result of special historical factors like Prohibition or repeal rather than long-term age differences; but this appears unlikely in view of the fact that rates for arrest for drunkenness among younger persons apparently have not grown materially in the last generation.) In any case, these differences by socioeconomic status indicate that at least at the present time, the lower-status man in his fifties or sixties probably is contributing more than his share of the more severe types of drinking problems.

In the forthcoming final stage of this series of longitudinal studies, it will be possible to determine whether these age group differences are relatively constant reflections of the effects of physiological, sociological, and psychological forces upon individuals within our culture, or whether they may reflect only temporary influences of such factors as Prohibition or repeal. If these age patterns are found to be at all enduring, the findings certainly point to the twenties through the sixties for lower-status men, and the thirties and forties for women, as the periods which are worthy of special attention by practitioners and researchers.

Analysis using a typology of problem drinking found that problems entailing obvious social consequences (problems with spouse or relatives, friends or neighbors, concerning one's job or with the law or police) were more common—relative to other problems—among men under sixty (particularly in cities of fifty thousand or more, and particularly among men of lower socioeconomic status), and among Irish Catholics, those of Latin-American or Caribbean origin, and Negroes, and extremely uncommon among Jews. These differences appear to be congruent with the differences in acting-out tendencies which would be expected among men in contrast to women, among younger, lower-status men (particularly in the more abrasive and alienated larger cities) and among various ethnoreligious groups which differ in their styles of expressing their tensions and aggressive tendencies.

SOCIAL-PSYCHOLOGICAL CORRELATES

To investigate the relationship between problem drinking and other variables, a multivariate analysis was conducted in which 150 survey items from both Stage I and Stage II were combined into six social-psychological variables (attitude toward drinking, environmental support for heavy drinking, impulsivity and nonconformity, alienation and maladjustment, unfavorable expectations, and looseness of social controls). These six social-psychological variables and demographic variables (sex, age, socioeconomic status, and urbanization) were then correlated with current problems scores.

It was found that all these variables bore some relationship to problem drinking; and the ten variables taken together yielded a multiple correlation with current problems score of .42 (Table 15). The lion's share of the variance in problem drinking was accounted for by one variable, attitude toward drinking; and this variable and the other one with a specific reference to alcohol (environmental support of heavy drinking) had higher correlations with problem drinking than did the other variables which did not directly refer to alcohol. This is certainly understandable, since attitudes of expectation of benefits from alcohol (and perceptions of permissiveness concerning use of alcohol) are specific to alcohol, while stresses related to the other four variables can be mitigated in many ways other than by drinking.

The psychological variables of alienation and maladjustment

and impulsivity and non-conformity were also correlated with problem drinking, although less strongly. While attitudes and environments favorable to drinking are more crucial among the correlates of problem drinking, the psychological variables were found to interact with attitudes and environments in being associated with a fairly high level of problem drinking among certain subgroups.

For most of the analyses of social-psychological correlates of problem drinking, the six social-psychological variables were combined to make a "risk score," the "risk" referring to the danger of being a problem drinker. Analysis showed that the social-psychological "risk score" does a fairly effective job of predicting problem drinking—particularly when combined with such independent variables as sex, age, social status, urbanism, and ethnic group. The following summary discusses some of the relationships of social-psychological "risk scores" to drinking problems when the independent variables of sex, age, social position (or socioeconomic status), and urbanism are taken into account. Details are shown in conjunction with the cited tables presented earlier in the text.

Table 11 shows results by sex for three age groups for three levels of social-psychological "risk score," based on the combination of the six independent variables discussed above. We can see an orderly progression in prevalence of more severe problems, from practically zero prevalence among women sixty or older of low risk score, to 38 per cent for men twenty-one to thirty-nine of high risk score. Men in all age groups have a higher percentage with higher problem scores than is true for women in comparable age groups, even when risk scores are held constant.

Regarding results by age group (see Table 11), at least for men, there is a remarkably similar prevalence of drinking-related problems from age group to age group when the risk score is held constant. This implies that there is not a great deal that is unique about age level per se that is not measured by the risk scores. Thus the tapering off of drinking-related problems among older men is not exclusively a function of energy level—for older men with a higher risk score still maintain a high prevalence of problems related to drinking.

Table 12 shows findings by index of social position. It is seen that among men within each of three age groups, those of lower status have a higher prevalence of problem drinking. The reasons for a higher prevalence of problem drinking among the lower-status men are interpreted as arising from a combination of factors, including relative lack of protection or tolerance from society and one's significant others, fewer options for recreation and tension release, a greater level of alienation and anxiety, and more of a tendency to act out one's aggressiveness on the part of lower-status persons as compared to those of higher status, as well as the possibility that some of the lower-status men in the sample who were problem drinkers had skidded to a lower status because of their drinking. Within each subgroup by social position (except for women sixty or older), the higher the social-psychological "risk score" the higher the rate of higher scores in current problems, particularly among men forty to fifty-nine of lower status, where the rate of current problems scores of seven or more reached 42 per cent.

In size of city (Table 13), especially for men, there is a consistent trend for the larger cities to be associated with a higher rate of problem drinking. When city size is subdivided by "risk score," again we find a regular progression, with 39 per cent of men of higher-risk scores in the larger cities having higher problem scores, as against almost zero for women of lowest-risk scores who live in places of less than 2,500. It is also evident that men in any of the three city sizes have about the same prevalence of problems as the men in either of the two other city sizes when risk-group is held constant. The inference drawn from findings of this study is that a lower level of social controls and a more permissive "drinking climate" in the larger cities may be primarily responsible for much of the difference in problem drinking in larger and smaller cities or towns, rather than the often-presumed higher level of alienation and maladjustment among those living in larger cities.

A special analysis of the interactions of sixteen variables in accounting for the correlates of problem drinking found that among men (Figure 3), the group with the highest rate of problem drinking (81 per cent with a current problems score of seven or more points) was the small group of eighteen persons who had an extremely favorable attitude toward drinking, plus a high score in environmental support for heavy drinking, plus having been high school dropouts.

In general, the findings bear out the conclusion that both sociological and psychological factors are important in the development of problem drinking. The sociological—that is to say, the external environmental—factors determine whether the individual is encouraged or permitted to drink heavily; and the psychological factors can operate to help to bring about or to maintain a level of drinking which may be above that normally encouraged or permitted for the person's environment. Thus if one sets aside the major factor of attitude toward drinking, it was found that for men the external environmental factors played a more conspicuous role among the correlates of problem drinking (Figure 3), while for women the variable of alienation and maladjustment appeared to be more influential than the sociological factors (Figure 4). It may well be that the differences here between men and women in the correlates of problem drinking stems from the greater general disapprobation of heavy drinking on the part of women, which may account for the finding that women with drinking problems are found to have higher scores on psychological maladjustment than did the men with drinking problems: it is speculated that it takes more psychological pressures for a woman than for a man to persist in problem drinking, in the face of general disapprobation of heavy drinking for women.

CHANGES

Man is not a static creature when it comes to his drinking behavior. His drinking usually changes from time to time, with consequent changes in the potentials for problems connected with drinking. An inquiry into changes in drinking (and into the reasons for changes) is essential for an understanding of the ways in which drinking problems develop.

Comparison of current and non-current drinking problem scores can provide a rough measurement of change in problem drinking. As previously noted, 9 per cent of the total sample (15 per cent of the men and 4 per cent of the women) had what we considered to be fairly severe current drinking problems. Asking about their past experiences, we found that an additional 9 per cent of the total sample (16 per cent of men and 3 per cent of women) said they had had such problems in the past. Comparing drinking problems for various age groups yields the expected pattern, with relatively more of those sixty or older showing a higher ratio of former to current problems than was reported by those under forty, thus providing further confirmation of the "maturing out" process which was inferred from comparison of the ranges of current problem drinking among the various age levels.

Findings by social position show that those of lower status not only had a higher rate of current problem drinking but also had a higher rate of former problem drinking than was true for others. There is considerable evidence here also (Table 19) that lower-status men are less likely to "mature out" of their problem-drinking status when they reach their forties and fifties: lower-status men age forty to fifty-nine show a higher ratio of a "high" level in current as against former problems (22 per cent to 17 per cent) than was found for higher-status men of the same age (10 per cent "high" level currently compared to 17 per cent for former problems). Similarly, findings by size of city show a generally higher ratio of current to former problems in the larger cities, especially for men forty and older: men in smaller towns and rural areas apparently tend to "mature out" of the problem-drinking group at an earlier age than those living in cities of fifty thousand or more. It may be that the lower level of social controls and the more permissive "drinking climate" in the larger cities plays a part in the apparent persistence of problem drinking to a more advanced age among men in the larger cities.

While only the Stage II interviews covered many types of drinking problems in detail, both Stages I and II included enough questions to make it possible to measure change between the two stages in two important elements in drinking problems, psychological dependence and frequent intoxication, which were combined into an index of problem drinking. Use of the index found that 22 per cent of the men and 9 per cent of the women had changed their problem drinking status materially within the short period of three years between the two stages of the study, thus indicating that many people may be going into, and out of, the problem drinking group more often than has been supposed. This finding could have important implications for encouraging intervening in the process of change so as to reduce the level of problem drinking.

A test of the sensitivity of measures of change in drinking problems in relation to changes in the situation or life experiences of the individual was provided by twelve items which had been measured at both Stages I and II. Analysis showed that drinking problems increased or decreased in relation to change in eleven of the twelve items, which included such varied questions as marital happiness, how often drinks are served when one is with one's friends, non-drinking "oral activity score" (reliance on eating, smoking, or use of tranquilizers or other drugs to alleviate stress), an impulsivity score, an alienation score, a neurophysiological complaints score, change in marital status, and the death of a parent or child.

These findings do not "prove" that changes in these independent-variable measures were "the cause" of changes in drinking behavior. However, the outcome of this analysis is encouraging in that it demonstrates that (a) significant changes in drinking behavior *do* occur which are measurable over as short a span as three years, and (b) changes in drinking behavior are found to be correlated with changes in the individual's status and experiences over the course of time, in ways which are clearly consistent with expectations.

These surveys uncovered a number of findings about respondents' recollections on their drinking behavior which should prove useful in planning future research and action programs. Among the more significant points are the following: An above-average proportion of those with a higher level of problem drinking started drinking earlier in life—almost three-fourths before the age of twenty. Those with higher problem-drinking scores who had *increased* their drinking in the past gave as principal reasons their financial ability, "social reasons" (influences of others), and having more opportunities or time for drinking. Relatively few emphasized drinking more because of increases in tensions or other problems of living. Similarly, on reasons for drinking less at some time, drinkers who reported having decreased their drinking emphasized financial reasons, their increased problems and responsibilities (again as a reason for drinking *less,* not more), having less need or desire for drink, becoming older and more mature, and health reasons. Mentions of ethical or moral or religious or guilt-tinged reasons for cutting down on drinking were relatively infrequent. Thus findings both as regards increases and decreases in drinking emphasize environmental and role factors rather than psychological factors (such as tensions associated with more drinking, or feelings of guilt associated with less drinking).

Considerable fluctuation in drinking behavior was found, even among those with relatively high problem-drinking scores. Fifty-eight per cent of the men and 70 per cent of the women with higher problem-drinking scores said there had been a time when they had tried to cut down on drinking; about half of those who had tried to cut down said they had tried to cut down during the preceding year; and about two-thirds of those who said they actually had cut down said the reduction had lasted less than a year; but about half of those who said they had cut down said the reduction was in force at the present time. This high rate of change in drinking behavior as measured on a retrospective basis is borne out by separate measurements in the 1964–1965 and 1967 surveys, in which during that short period 15 per cent of the total persons interviewed had moved into, or out of, the group reporting themselves as drinking five or more drinks per occasion at least some of the time.

The finding that even those with fairly severe current drinking problems do show a considerable fluctuation in their drinking, implies that the average problem drinker frequently has occasions when it would be easier to mobilize the resources of the individual and his milieu to bring his drinking under better control. In short, problem drinking need not be regarded as always being a stubborn "disease." Future research should be focused upon what types of "critical incidents" (Flanagan, 1954) are closely associated with movement into and out of problem-drinking status, so as better to determine how preventive measures and therapy may be better-tailored to intervene more effectively in reducing the incidence of problem-drinking behavior.

VIII New Directions

This has been an interim study of problem drinking in the United States; and until more evidence is in, it is hazardous to draw many firm conclusions. However, all of the evidence is never in; and many of the findings demand discussion now, in the hopes that some of the questions raised will bear some fruit in contributing toward constructive dissatisfaction with the ways in which problems related to alcohol are perceived and handled by the general public and by many practitioners and professional alcohologists. Accordingly, this chapter presents some of the implications which this national study of drinking problems may have for social research and remedial programs concerned with problems related to alcohol and perhaps with problems related to certain other types of mind-altering drugs.

IMPLICATIONS

Experience with these short-term longitudinal studies of drinking practices indicates the need for increased research emphasis upon several areas, as noted below. This series of studies, along with the prior San Francisco studies (Clark, 1966; Knupfer, 1967), has demonstrated that it is possible to measure prevalence and change in drinking problems through general population surveys, with a degree of precision sufficient to be useful to social scientists studying deviant behavior in general, as well as to public health workers in the field of alcohol and mental health.

The relationships between the combination of six broad social-psychological variables and drinking-related problems was found to be high enough to lend encouragement to the future utilization of relatively brief questionnaire instruments to predict the development of various problems related to alcohol.

The various social-psychological factors measured in this study (attitude toward drinking, environmental support for heavy drinking, impulsivity and nonconformity, alienation and maladjustment, unfavorable expectations, and looseness of social controls) were found to differ in their predictive value depending upon such demographic characteristics as sex, age, social position, urbanization, and ethnoreligious status—indicating the need to control for such factors in predicting the prevalence of problem drinking.

There should be more studies of the formative period of twelve to twenty years of age, to supplement these studies of the population twenty-one and older. The surveys of the adult population indicated that a higher-than-average share of those who were problem drinkers in later life tended to report their having started drinking at an early age; and it is important to measure the correlates of early heavy drinking at an early point in time if valid findings are to be achieved.

More intensive follow-up studies should be conducted among persons who recently have either changed their status from heavy or problem drinking to light or non-problem drinking, or changed from nonproblem or nondrinking behavior to heavy or problem drinking. While the available surveys have put some emphasis on questioning those who have changed their drinking habits, concentrating inquiry upon the events immediately preceding the change should be most helpful in providing additional clues as to why such changes occur.

Regarding longitudinal studies, the present series of surveys includes a 1969 national survey on the correlates of problem drinking among men in the age group (twenty-one to fifty-nine) most associated with heavy drinking. An additional follow-up study is contemplated for the mid-1970's, in which persons initially interviewed in the 1964–1965 survey (and reinterviewed in 1967) or in the 1969 survey will be reinterviewed, thus measuring trends in individual drinking over a ten-year span. There is need for additional qualitative studies of individuals on a short-term panel basis, to chart with greater precision the temporal sequence between changes in an individual's environment, behavior, attitudes, and values and his drinking behavior. Such panel studies could build upon the precedents established by Lolli's study in Italy (1958), in which food habits and drinking habits were charted over time, and the Finnish study of Ekholm (1968), in which drinking behavior of individuals was recorded at intervals over a period. These panel studies could be set up as an adjunct to national or local surveys in which persons with especially interesting patterns (for example, those who reported recent changes in drinking behavior or recent changes in environmental stress) would be studied intensively, with frequent measurements, over a period of time.

As a preliminary to measuring consequences of potential problems, the present study has followed the research strategy of using interim definitions of potential problems which are intended to include the widest possible range of direct or indirect indicators of alcohol dependence and potential injury to the drinker and to society. In later follow-up interviews with the same individuals covered in these 1964–1965 and 1967 surveys, intensive inquiry will be directed at the consequences of the symptoms of potential drinking problems measured earlier: whether the individual's health appears to have suffered, whether his economic and social position appear to have deteriorated, and whether his relationships with other people have been injured because of excessive drinking. Only through such a process of validation of the early signs of problem drinking against some later measure of longer-term conseequences will it be possible to arrive at a consolidated inventory of the correlates which are highly predictive of later serious disadvantages to the individual and society.

As a corollary, longer-term longitudinal studies should study human success as well as human failure; it will be important to assess the factors which help to explain how many of those who were excessive drinkers in early or middle life managed to reduce their drinking to a level tolerable to themselves and to their associates. Such an analysis of the correlates of kicking the habit of excessive drinking, including study of the resources mobilized by both the individual and his significant others—family, friends, work associates, social agencies—should be informative to those working in the broad field of mental health as well as to those who are concerned with preventive medicine and patient treatment or therapy in the specific field of excessive use of alcohol.

CULTURAL FACTORS

The powerful influence of cultural considerations in problem drinking has been established in many studies in the past. These studies are too numerous to review here; they are readily available in either Pittman and Snyder (1962) or MacAndrew and Edgerton (1969). To the extent that ethnic comparisons can be drawn from the data from this national study, the findings of past studies were borne out (for example, Jews were found to have a very high proportion of those drinking occasionally but very few problem drinkers, and those of Irish background, especially Irish Catholics, were found to have an above-average proportion of problem drinkers). In addition, if cultural is broadly interpreted to include all cohesive subgroups whose members have a consciousness of group belongingness and who interact with each other, the present study found that cultural factors were among the most useful ones in predicting problem drinking.

Cultural factors this study found to be highly relevant to problem drinking, in addition to ethnic and religious background, included sex, age, social class, and urbanization. The findings were that those of Irish and Latin-American or Caribbean origin, younger men (under sixty), those of lower social status, and residents of large cities had a higher prevalence of problem drinking than did members of other groups. Such cultural subgroups are the most visible and viable from the practical standpoint of future efforts to control problem drinking—for it is easier to direct remedial campaigns at distinct cultural subgroups than to direct campaigns at an undifferentiated mass of people. The most effective control programs are likely to be ones which entail face-to-face contact in group situations. Thus special attention in research and action programs must continue to be directed toward cultural subgroups which are the most susceptible to problem drinking. Again, since drinking is such a heavily social-cultural phenomenon, prevention and treatment of problem drinking needs to use cultural forces, and particularly the influences of primary groups such as the family and peer groups, in setting and maintaining appropriate norms for drinking behavior. That cultural forces in drinking behavior are very strong is borne out not only by the considerable subgroup differences in drinking which were found in this survey but also by collateral findings that "social" factors were predominant among the reasons given for past increases or decreases in alcohol consumption.

It is unlikely that it will be easy to bring about any rapid decrease in the prevalence of problem drinking with the United States. Not only do the old-country habits of heavy drinking of certain groups (notably the Irish and the Latin-American or Caribbeans) retain their hold, but they have become overlaid with indigenous American attitudes and values related to alcohol and other drugs. One is the attitude among the youthful that heavy use of alcohol or other drugs is daring or manly. Another is the modern American conviction (aided and abetted by advertising and press and television reportage, and to a considerable extent by the medical profession itself) that it is acceptable to try to reach nirvana or comfort or at least legitimate temporary forgetfulness through drinking or popping pills. The same society which would laugh at the naïve South Sea Islanders who used to believe in the cargo myth that some day golden galleons would sail into their harbors and give them all their hearts desired is now coming to believe implicitly in the cargo myth that one can make life supportable indefinitely on a diet heavily laced with alcohol or pills or marijuana. Hence it is understandable how it is that MacAndrew and Edgerton say (1969, p. 173): "The moral, then, is this. Since societies, like individuals, get the sort of drunken comportment that they allow, they deserve what they get."

A further handicap in coping with problem drinking in America is the backlash against our heritage of Prohibition and other forms of blue-nosed coercion of private behavior both in the past and in the present. One consequence of this heritage is to make the reasonable, scientific-minded, and civil-libertarian leaders of public health and welfare programs extremely reluctant to undertake remedial treatment or educational measures which might appear to involve compulsion or moralizing. Another possible consequence of the polarization between the blue-nosed wowsers and the liberal-minded scientists and public health authorities is the belief (often latent) in the Freudian hydraulic, or frustration-aggression, model for human behavior on the part of social scientists. In this model it is assumed that if the problem drinker is not permitted to continue in the same course, the pressure will be so tremendous that he will be bound to break out with some other (and probably worse) form of socially unacceptable or personally hurtful form of behavior.

Whatever worthwhile advances have been made in physiological studies of addiction, the behavioral sciences have exhibited an inadequate understanding of the processes of habituation and addiction, whether it be habituation and addiction to cigarettes, alcohol, or other drugs. Perhaps the main reason for inadequate understanding is the existence of conceptual conflicts and confusions created by the interplay of old-fashioned notions of free will and moral power, Freudian and behavioristic theories of determinism, the Protestant ethic of the past, and the permissive ethic of the present. Living in a culture with so many antithetical cross-currents in theories about man's nature, few behavioral scientists have come forth with a clear and objective conception of the process of addiction which could serve as a basis for programs to prevent and to treat addicts and their addictions.

I believe that the process of addiction will be best understood—and treated—through a detailed study of how alcohol and drugs work in the process of shaping drug-using behavior into cycles of increasingly greater dependence and increasingly greater difficulty of keeping the habit within bounds. The following paradigm is offered, tentatively, as one way of explaining the process of becoming a problem drinker. First: the culture must permit drinking, and heavy drinking at least occasionally, before the individual can get himself into a position to become a problem drinker. Second: given that the culture is permissive of heavy drinking under at least some circumstances, the individual may become a heavy drinker under circumstances permitted him in his sex, age, ethnic, social-class, and other roles. Third: an individual may find himself suddenly to be a problem drinker because of a change in the cultural environment; for example, he moves or marries or ages *out* of an environment permissive of heavy drinking, but still remains a heavy drinker. Fourth: given that the individual may have formed a habit of heavy drinking which he discovers to have become maladaptive in his environment, he may continue as a heavy drinker under one or more of the following circumstances: (a) if his social adaptability is hampered by a highly impulsive tendency toward resorting to short-term gratifications, he may continue to drink heavily even in the face of social disapprobation; (b) if the gradient between his usual subjective condition when he is not drinking and the way he feels when drinking is a steep one (such as might stem from either a highly alienated, neurotic, or depressive personality, or living under conditions of high subjective deprivation of the worthwhile things in life), he may continue to drink heavily because of the powerful reinforcements obtained from drinking and the lack of rewards for not drinking. Fifth: given that the individual has become a heavy drinker to the point where it has occasioned problems for him in his environment, he may continue heavy drinking if that environment is modified to be more permissive (such as by his becoming separated from such significant others as his family, his work associates, and his cultural peers). However, he may cease heavy drinking if the environment continues to exert counter-pressure through the persons who are important in his life. Thus those with severe drinking problems are more likely to eliminate such problems if they maintain social ties which support them as persons and do not reinforce the problem behavior.

At the risk of being labeled a biological reductionist, I must point out that in all cultures, man has shown that his status as a social being—enjoying the fruits of a mutually supportive relationship with other people—is a prime human value. To the extent that man resorts to broadly socially disapproved means of dealing with his problems or needs, he weakens his capabilities for coping with the challenges of his environment through employing social resources, both by becoming more asocial or antisocial himself and through his alienation of others by his behavior. Thus, continued reliance on the mood-altering properties of heavy dosages of alcohol or other drugs leads to behavior which creates problems in one's normal functioning in society. Also, the process of reliance on alcohol and other drugs tends to have a long-term adverse effect upon the individual's psychophysiological functioning, so that the individual tends to lose both the social and physical elasticity to bounce back up after being down.

PSYCHOLOGICAL FACTORS

As in other studies, this national survey failed to find conclusive evidence of any uniform alcoholic personality or problem drinker personality. Specific attitudes and values regarding the utilities and proprieties of drinking are found to be much more strongly associated with problem drinking than are general states of alienation or maladjustment. The findings clearly indicate that maladjustment does play a role in many instances; but the findings are also in keeping with the obvious fact that there are many substances and actions besides alcohol available for the reduction of anxiety, and that many people (particularly the women and the elderly, for whom heavy drinking is ordinarily seen as inappropriate in this culture) who do have a higher-than-average rate of alienation or maladjustment or deprivation do utilize means other than alcohol for relief. Women appear to use church activities and prayer, talking with friends or relatives, working harder, and tranquilizers or other medicines for tension relief more than is the case with men (Cahalan, Cisin, and Crossley, 1969, p. 150).

It may be that most problem drinkers become conditioned at a very early age to expect that alcohol will do great things for them. This possibility stems both from scattered evidence that most problem drinkers report they started drinking at a very early age and also that their very first drinking experiences are remembered very vividly, and from other studies which prove that individuals absorb the values of their subcultures at a very early age. Perhaps sometimes a process of early cathection (analogous to imprinting, as in ducklings' forming an attachment for objects to be followed) may occur in relation to alcohol; if this be true, then it follows that the right sort of training and example regarding appropriate and inappropriate use of alcohol should be applied at a very early age.

The failure to find a strong correlation between problem drinking and psychological maladjustment does not lend much confidence to the efficacy of redoubling of efforts to mitigate problem drinking primarily through reduction of anxiety. Rather, as discussed in Chapter Four, and below, the findings are congruent with the plausibility of an operant conditioning approach to etiology and treatment, when one puts together what various writers have to say about the process of developing a dependency upon alcohol or other drugs with the results obtained in this national survey on problem drinking.

In this regard, Allport's functional autonomy of motives (1964, p. 29) appears to be the cognitive concomitant of the operant conditioning process; here Allport says that attitudes which are developed out of early circumstances and needs become functional as motivants in their own right. Thus the person learns through experience that alcohol does certain pleasurable things for him, so he tends to develop attitudes and values which both demand alcohol for reinforcement and in turn tend to have an anticipatory heightening effect upon what alcohol will do for him. A corollary of the concept of the functional autonomy of motives, or of the apparently related hedonic calculus of the transactional point of view described by Orford (1970) (that the probability of change in use of drugs will depend upon the balance of incentives), is that in order to change the attitude that heavy drinking is highly functional, a systematic (and probably protracted) application of counter-conditioning activities is essential.

Proof of the potency of the operant conditioning process in learning and unlearning problem drinking cannot be obtained through quantitative surveys, but can be found only through controlled experiments or observations. However, the operant conditioning hypothesis is consistent with most of the observed facts about how problem drinking develops; this study shows that problem drinkers get much more immediate reinforcement, on the average, from drinking than do others. They also are shown to have more adverse experiences with alcohol; but, as Conger (1956), Wikler (1961), Ferster and associates (1962), and Blachly (1969) point out, the positive reinforcement is more dramatic and immediate, and the negative reinforcement tends to be more tepid and delayed or uncertain.

Operant conditioning mechanisms would appear to be central in the development of dependence on heavy amounts of alcohol, which usually takes many years to reach full-blown form, for if the tissue dependence upon alcohol were a very strong influence, the process of addiction usually would be a much shorter one. It is hypothesized that the regular drinker begins to get psychologically addicted (in the sense of being unable readily to control the amounts he drinks) when the positive reinforcement of the euphoric effect of the depressive drug, alcohol, is consistently further enhanced by contrast with the negative effect of the physiological and psychological letdown, or hangover, which ensues when the alcohol's positive effects begin to wear off; learning that the aversive effect of the hangover can be postponed by continued drinking may explain the compulsive behavior of the addictive drinker. The plausibility of the relevance of operant conditioning concepts in explaining much of the process of alcohol addiction is heightened because alcohol is a drug which tends not only to erase temporarily much anxiety and malaise and self-doubt but also to erase at the same time the memory of past resolutions to limit one's drinking and the memory of past adverse consequences of drinking.

VALUES AND ATTITUDES

Findings on the social-psychological correlates of problem drinking clearly indicate that the chief single variable is that of values and attitudes toward drinking and heavy drinking, as measured by questions on whether good things can be said for drinking, whether the person scores high on a scale on the social utilities of drinking, and whether he enjoys drinking and getting drunk once in a while. Not only did this variable contribute the lion's share in explaining the variance in current problem drinking, but the importance of values and attitudes came to light in many other ways during the study.

Given that values and attitudes are important correlates of problem drinking, the implications of this finding will be quite different for those who believe that values and attitudes favorable to heavy drinking are developed primarily prior to the development of a habit of frequent heavy drinking, as against those who believe the values and attitudes arise primarily after the person became a heavy drinker. Those who believe the favorable attitudes arise primarily prior to heavy drinking will tend to see values and attitudes as playing a causal role in the development of heavy drinking habits, and that thus the alteration of attitudes may reduce heavy drinking; while those who believe the values and attitudes primarily develop after heavy drinking (ostensibly as a means of self-justification of one's conduct) will not think that the changing of attitudes can have much effect on problem drinking.

Certainly it is only realistic to assume that the development of favorable attitudes toward heavy drinking and the development of heavy drinking itself are reciprocal phenomena in real life—that a rather favorable attitude may be followed by some heavy drinking, followed in turn by intensification of favorableness of attitude (because of reinforcement through rewards obtained by drinking, and through self-justification of one's drinking), followed in turn by more heavy drinking, and so on. However, even if attitudes and heavy drinking are reciprocal phenomena to at least some extent, the issue is whether the effects of attitudes upon drinking are strong enough that intervention to change attitudes would be likely to be an effective way of breaking the reciprocal cycle and thus contributing to diminishing the heavy drinking. While no one at this point can say for sure that attitudes do or do not have an effect on problem drinking, data from this study suggest strongly that there is at least a cyclical process involved, in which attitudes affect drinking and drinking affects attitudes. Moreover, the logic of the usual development of problem drinking provides a plausible argument that attitudes have a potent effect on drinking behavior, for it ordinarily takes many years for a person to develop into a full-blown heavy drinker: and it would appear indeed improbable that people would persist in drinking more heavily over a period of years unless they both obtained positive reinforcement (or avoided negative reinforcement) from the drinking and also developed favorable anticipatory reactions (attitudes) concerning what alcohol could do for them.

The guess is hazarded that attitudes and expectations about the value of alcohol on the part of the heavy drinker are not a matter of shallow sentiment which is readily changed, but are a matter of immediate perception, in which alcohol is seen as endowed with all manner of magical qualities, in the same way as a woman might be perceived instantly as beautiful, without there being need for a continuous intervening process of reasoning and weighing of pros and cons. The perception of the value of alcohol is probably not an intellectual matter with the heavy drinker who has built up his perception of alcohol through a period of years. Thus it may have no effect whatsoever to reason with a problem drinker until his perception of alcohol is changed by a perhaps gradual program of counter-conditioning, preferably accompanied by substituting certain other values (such as supportive social relations on the part of people who matter) for the high value he has learned to place on alcohol in his life.

It would appear to be no easy matter to change the heavy drinker's values about alcohol, particularly in a society where such a substantial minority resorts to alcohol not just as a pleasant adjunct to sociability but as a drug used to blot out tensions or anxieties or socialized inhibitions. The American society is ambivalent about alcohol: on the one hand, we preach the goal of moderation, but on the other, we are hesitant to make it our business to be our brother's keeper when it comes to dealing with the early signs of problems related to alcohol. As Plaut says:

> The continuing discrimination against most problem drinkers, the low level of interest in their care and treatment, all reflect the general American ambivalence and confusion regarding alcohol use and abuse. Although a wide range of persons are involved in alcohol problems—the problem drinker and his family, his

> employer, "helping" or "care-giving" agencies, such as mental hospitals, general hospitals, clinics, welfare and social agencies, physicians, police, and clergy—there has been surprisingly little interest and activity directed toward providing assistance for these patients. Preventive approaches, especially those relating to altered drinking patterns in the American society, have received even less attention. While many individuals are not uneasy about their own use of alcohol, there is much disagreement regarding matters of public policy. Americans prefer to avoid issues of this nature—they rarely are confronted with them. The result has been that undue prominence is often given to the views of two relatively small segments of the population—those concerned directly with the production, marketing, and sale of alcoholic beverages, and those opposed to all use of alcohol. [1967, pp. 11–12]

EDUCATIONAL AND PUBLIC HEALTH PROGRAMS

To the extent that most of us contribute in one way or another to a climate of attitudes in which the heavy drinker may continue to have the impression that his heavy drinking is socially acceptable merely because his behavior is seldom challenged, we contribute to continuance of problem drinking. If the social consequences of heavy drinking have heavy costs, then problem drinking ought to be everybody's business—always provided that the remedies adopted are not worse than the problem drinking itself. If the general public gets to accept the fact that problem drinking is too serious a business to be left passively in the hands of the medical profession and the professional alcohologists, then—and only then—will the climate of attitudes about the appropriate uses of alcohol be modified enough to result in a reduction in the present rate of various problems related to alcohol. Use of the disease concept of alcoholism should not be permitted to encourage continuance of a passive attitude on the part of the problem drinker and those close to him (family, friends, work associates) that the layman can do little to help to reduce problem drinking. Since heavy drinking first comes about (evidently) because it is encouraged or condoned by persons in the drinker's immediate environment, it would seem to follow that people in the drinkers' social orbit may be able to contribute much to a reduction in drinking problems, through example and through persuasive efforts.

Again, more research is needed in order to determine exactly how attitudes and values influence drinking behavior and how experimentally determined changes in attitudes influence changes in drinking. In the interim, even while such research is in progress, educational and treatment programs should concentrate on inculcating attitudes toward alcohol which are realistic in recognizing that the overwhelming majority of adults drink, but which drive home the adverse consequences of continued heavy drinking.

Ordinarily, those who are in charge of the educational and treatment process themselves have not been problem drinkers; and consequently they often fail to reach the actual or potential problem drinker with as effective arguments or moral support as the problem drinker might get from his peers. As discussed above, cultural influences upon drinking are very strong; and to be most effective, the changing of attitudes should be done by one's peers as well as by those in authority. This implies the need for a heavy emphasis (both in preventive efforts and in therapy to treat problem drinkers) upon the peer-group influences upon attitudes which are exerted within such auspices as Alcoholics Anonymous to be broadened to reach groups which may not be amenable to the AA regimen and to reach people at a much earlier age than do such programs as AA, which traditionally have been designed to treat those problem drinkers who already have been labeled "alcoholics."

Obviously such relatively effective peer-group mechanisms for training and moral support of adults as Alcoholics Anonymous will have to be modified drastically in order to reach the young at a time when they are first at risk of psychological overdependence upon alcohol or other drugs. In preventive efforts to reduce the incidence of problem drinking, the traditional mechanisms of formal education about alcohol and drugs (such as lectures and leaflets) may not be persuasive because they emanate from out-groups, in terms of the values of the in-group which is turned on by the merits of alcohol or other drugs. It is likely that effective means of reaching the young are to be found through formal and informal peer-group participation in both learning the appropriate perspectives regarding use of alcohol and other drugs and achieving some fairly immediate rewards in the process. Such a reciprocal process of learning, and of achieving rewards as a consequence of learning, is involved in the setting of the family and peer group in such subcultures as those of the Jews, Italians, and Chinese. The element of reinforcement of appropriate values through fairly immediate rewards (of approbation and of tangible benefits) is missing in most formal educational and informational programs regarding alcohol at present; and this essential ingredient of reinforcement or reward must be incorporated in any preventive program if it is to be successful.

As to the specifics of educational and informational campaigns to help to bring about a reduction in excessive use of alcohol and other drugs, while surveys such as this on the correlates of problem drinking cannot alone provide a basis for determining which types of campaigns might be effective, it seems only reasonable to have some confidence that effective campaigns for moderation in drinking can be devised in the light of the apparent progress of the current public information campaigns about the dangers of heavy cigarette smoking. The motivations, consequences, and mechanisms of heavy drinking and cigarette smoking are presumed to be quite different. However, if the anticigarette campaign can make inroads in diminution of a habit as deep-seated as the smoking of cigarettes, there may be some prospects of success for campaigns to promote moderation in drinking. Such campaigns should be directed at specific audiences with a high prevalence of problem drinking—such as young men and people living in large cities. Because of the importance of early formation of attitudes, any effective campaign should also be directed to parents to point out the dangers of a home atmosphere which is permissive of heavy drinking, and to emphasize the importance of parents' setting a good example for their children in their own drinking.

RESEARCH-ORIENTED THERAPY PROGRAMS

Modern mental health programs include research directed to the evaluation of treatment for problem drinking. One promising approach is that of behavior therapy, because it appears to be in tune with the findings of the current study in focusing upon ultimate change in the values and attitudes of the patient through a process of reconditioning, and because behavior therapy enlists the resources of both the patient and his significant others. In advocating more research on the operant conditioning point of view in preventive public health measures and therapy for persons involved in problem drinking, I hold no particular brief for any single specific mode of treatment. Behavior therapy methods appear to be in a process of rapid evolution and most of them are much in need of both improvement (as noted below) and validation; and in any case the treatment mix should depend upon the individual and the environment and the resources available. The operant point of view is that behavior can be shaped toward desired ends, through a slow but patient process of conditioning. Again it seems only reasonable that if it takes perhaps ten to twenty years to build up a set of unacceptable habits related to the use of alcohol, it may take a lengthy period to reverse the process and to build up a set of more acceptable behaviors.

To some, the operant conditioning process may seem like brainwashing or thought control; but if so, it is a process which involves the informed choice or consent of the individual. One way or the other, we are all subject to a continuous flow of conditioning influences; and it would seem ethically sounder and more in keeping with respect for the dignity of man to put a premium upon giving the individual a summary of the implications of the alternative choices he has regarding the use of alcohol and letting him choose that course which does a minimum of injury to the rights of others, rather than applying either a doctrine of laissez faire or demands for conformity to a rigid code of abstinence or punitively controlled drinking.

Before discussing some of the specifics of the application of operant conditioning principles to helping to clear up problems related to drinking, it should be recognized that application of these principles should involve changes in the individual's environment. As Bandura, one of the foremost exponents of behavior therapy, puts it:

> It is sometimes erroneously assumed by the critics of treatment programs aimed at the direct modification of drinking behavior that these approaches are based on the premise that alcohol is the sole problem of the alcoholic. Quite to the contrary, they assume that psychological functioning involves a reciprocal influence process in which the characteristics of behavior are important determiners of the way the environment responds to it; as a person changes, so does his environment. Sustained abstinence is therefore largely ensured not by the fact that liquor has been endowed with negative properties, but because elimination of drinking behavior removes the adverse consequences of chronic inebriation and creates new reinforcement contingencies with respect to a broad range of behavior. The restoration of physical well-being and the positive experiences derived from improved social, marital, and financial functioning can reinforce sobriety and reduce aberrant tendencies. For this reason, "neuroses" and grossly deviant behaviors often disappear after alcoholism has been brought under control. [1969, p. 547]

Operant conditioning principles to help mitigate alcohol-related problems could be applied at many levels. Within society as a whole, there needs to be continuing effort to improve the human condition so as to reduce the extent of hopelessness and inhuman environmental stresses. Also, there should be far greater effort to inculcate positive values concerning the worth of finding satisfactions through mutual understanding and help in dealing with other people rather than through seeking escape through alcohol and drugs.

On the level of preventive public health and educational activity, consistent informational campaigns should be utilized on the dangers inherent in heavy drinking or use of other drugs beyond medical requirements. If they are to be effective, such campaigns should be realistic, nonmoralistic, and constructive, and should show respect and understanding for the individual with problems. People in general also should be educated to a realization that drinking problems usually arise out of environmental conditions rather than being strictly the fault of the excessive drinker, so that constructive changes in the environment may be attempted rather than mere recrimination over someone's drinking.

Employers should remember that the job is a very important environmental influence for most employees; and they should learn that therefore whatever they do to reduce undue or demanding stresses and tensions on the job (and temptations regarding job-related drinking) will help reduce problems related to drinking. Employers also should remember that they have a responsibility for tactful yet firm assistance of the problem drinker to meet his responsibilities to coworkers and to make progress toward more enjoyable and rewarding working relationships.

The individual in society should be educated to know his own limitations and capabilities in relation to alcohol and other drugs, so that he can be alerted to the risks involved in drifting into undue reliance upon artificial props as a substitute for more constructive means of enjoying life. At present, the individual is usually exposed to a confusing barrage of temptations toward excessive drinking on the one hand from peer groups, advertising and marketing, and the general glamorizing of artificial mood-changing substances from many quarters; and on the other hand, from exposure to authoritarian or misinformed or pseudoscientific lecturings or alarums on the evils of drink or of dope. The processes of habit-formation and modification should not be such mysterious ones that the average layman should not know exactly what they are and how they work, so that he can build the kinds of habits which are effective for him in the most optimum environment he might realize.

The therapist should take a skeptical look at the utility of the hydraulic Freudian model of behavior, which implies that if one tries to get rid of unacceptable behavior it merely crops out in another form of unacceptable behavior (because of underlying frustrations and aggressions), and that thus little modification of behavior can take place before the root causes of the frustrations are eliminated or brought out into the open. The behavior therapy point of view is that problem drinking may well have started from underlying causes, but that the problem drinking, if untreated, will continue on its own self-reinforcing course because the individual has learned to derive certain satisfactions from his drinking behavior for which substitutes must be found before the behavior will be modified. The direct treatment of the symptoms of problem drinking ordinarily will at least make the patient amenable to a recovery of his own sense of worth, which is one step on his progress to an enjoyable life. The therapist's enlisting the active cooperation of the patient (a better term would be trainee) in the process of step-by-step modification of the habits involved in problem drinking should also make it easier for the therapist to clear up underlying psychological or environmental problems in the long run.

Although a behavior therapy point of view may be found to be effective as a general guide to therapy, specific kinds of therapy should depend upon the individuals concerned. In principle, it should be obvious that no one form of behavior therapy could be universally efficacious. Thus in situations in which family or other environmental considerations appear to play a prime role, there should be considerable emphasis upon family counseling and small-group therapy of all concerned—and not of just the drinker. Also, in dealing with individuals with a high level of anxiety and guilt feeling about drinking, the emphasis in therapy might be upon helping to channel the anxiety into attaining a feeling of self-respect and achievement through progress toward continued sobriety; but in dealing with an individual with little anxiety but weak ego controls, it might be necessary to use one or other of a range of negative reinforcers so as to get the individual to stay sober long enough that positive reinforcement training (involving his own active cooperation) can come into play. The mix of positive and negative reinforcements thus needs to be varied in the individual case, depending upon the insight of the therapist and findings of experimental clinical research.

With respect to the relative emphasis upon positive and negative conditioning, positive reinforcements are generally considered by psychologists to be better in the long run than negative ones, because, as Bandura says, "persons who are repeatedly subjected to unpleasant experiences without any rewarding respites and opportunities for positive relationships with the therapist administering the aversive procedures are likely to develop resentment, antipathy to the entire treatment situation, and escape behavior" (1969, pp. 551–552). For these reasons, as well as elementary regard for human rights and human dignity, a substantial amount of positive reinforcement should be incorporated into any aversive conditioning procedures which may be found necessary.

Up to the present time, negative or aversive types of treatment appear to be applied more frequently than the positive types, perhaps because the negative techniques (particularly the use of emetine, antabuse, and electric shock) are readily available from the armamentarium of the behavioral psychologists who conduct experiments on rats, dogs, pigeons, and primates, and perhaps because of a lingering on of a social expectation that somehow the drunkard must be punished out of his sinfulness. Thus for some time aversion therapy has been practiced through the use of emetine before taking a drink, so as to associate drinking with subsequent vomiting; or of antabuse before drinking, so that drinking becomes associated with violent headaches and alarming heart symptoms; or of electric shock when one takes a drink; or of autosuggestion, such as imagining eating loathsome things while one is drinking.

The positive mechanisms, while in the long run more effective, are less well formalized than are the negative reinforcements; positive reinforcements mostly involve interpersonal relations, through the continued sympathy and understanding (and approbation for progress) on the part of the therapist, the small group, and the family and work associates. What is needed is experimental testing of the effectiveness of immediate and more pervasive positive reinforcements, primarily in the form of moral support from other people, but also perhaps in the development of more effective non-habit–forming palliatives which will help the problem drinker over the initial period when he suffers from the deprivation from large amounts of alcohol but has not as yet replaced the vacuum with the enjoyment of positive experiences. Such palliatives, in order to be effective without running the risk of substitute psychological addiction, should be used temporarily as a formal part of the positive reinforcement process, to provide immediate reinforcement as a reward for sobriety, until such time as social reinforcements become adequate.

It is likely that the application of behavior therapy usually will be more successful if the individual's primary groups—wife and family, friends, work associates—still exist in supportive forms. (This is inferred from the strong correlation found between heavy drinking and the permissiveness of significant others toward heavy drinking.) If at all possible, the therapy process must involve primary groups in the process of behavior change. If the person's primary groups are not sufficiently intact to provide him with moral support on a continuing basis, then substitute primary groups must be found or created for him. The recent rapid growth of small-group therapy (for many problems in addition to alcohol-related ones) is both a testimonal to the effectiveness of the small-group therapy concept and also a reflection of the fact that in an age of evolution away from tribal and extended family social controls and toward an emphasis upon personal privacy and independence, the creation of ad hoc primary groups for therapy or sociability fills a growing need for mutual interpersonal support in a rapidly changing age of insecurity.

Given current trends, it appears there will be a fairly rapid increase in the use of operant conditioning or behavior-therapy methods of treatment of problem drinking. The general Zeitgeist of psychotherapy appears to be moving in the direction of treating maladaptive behavior directly (rather than looking for latent causal factors in the past development of the personality) and enlisting the homeostatic resources of the patient through rewarding improvements in behavior. It seems only reasonable to believe that if operant-conditioning principles appear highly relevant in the development of problem drinking, then operant-conditioning principles should be efficacious if applied in treatment; and already a number of experimental studies have begun to show significant improvements in the treatment of problem drinkers through behavior-therapy methods (Thimann, 1949; Lemere and Voegtlin, 1950; Hsu, 1965; Cautela, 1967; Anant, 1967; and McBrearty *et al.,* 1968). Future experimental studies should continue to improve on research designs to make more explicit exactly which treatment effects are being tested; and future studies need to do more to solve the always difficult problem of matching experimental and control groups so that experimental groups are not overweighted with persons highly motivated toward a change in their drinking habits.

CHANGES

Although the study here reported was not concerned with alcoholics as such, implicit in the rationale of the research is that the findings will be found to have some applicability to problems of alcoholism. One of the most encouraging series of findings concerns the variability, or turnover, of problem drinking. For example, while 9 per cent of the people interviewed were regarded as having at least fairly severe drinking problems, another 9 per cent used to have such problems but did not at the time of the second interview. It was found that people's drinking habits change, for better or worse; and their drinking problems can grow or diminish.

Such findings can lend encouragement to the growing group of physicians and others involved in the therapeutic process who believe alcoholics can be helped. In the recent past, the medical profession has tended to be rather pessimistic about the possibility of improvement in chronic alcoholics. This attitude stemmed in part from the fact that chronic alcoholics make poor patients (they smell bad, are hard to handle, are generally unreliable, and often do not pay their medical bills), and in part from the fact that most often the chronic alcoholic is not presented for medical and psychiatric care until after his drinking habits are very deep-seated and most of his social support has become worn away. One consequence of this pessimism about the chronic alcoholic has been the self-fulfilling prophecy of failure in the revolving-door practice of drying out the alcoholic and giving him other medical first aid, giving him a scolding if the physician is moralistic or the silent treatment if the physician is not, and turning him out in the street with the expectation that he will revert to the same sodden state within a few weeks.

One of the remedies for this revolving-door charade is for society to see to it that the problem drinker gets constructive help in modifying his behavior and environment when the early signs of addiction to alcohol appear. It is strongly suspected that here the human tendency toward variability over time can work to provide opportunities for intervention in nudging the problem drinker into improving his situation. In spite of the once-prevalent pessimism on the prognosis for the chronic alcoholic, the evidence continues to accumulate that remissions in problem drinking are indeed frequent enough to provide encouragement about helping most chronic problem drinkers. A number of other statistical and observational studies reviewed by Tremper (1969) (particularly the studies of Drew, 1968; Gibbins, 1968; and Malzberg, 1953) indicate that while a fair amount of the apparent maturing out of heavy drinkers as they get older is the result of early mortality rather than a change of habits, the evidence is that a large share of former heavy drinkers indeed do moderate their drinking in the long run. (The same phenomenon has been noted by Winick (1964) as regards the use of addictive drugs). This study itself furnished substantial evidence as to turnover, or change, in problem drinking, as reflected in different ways: through differences in drinking behavior among those at various age levels, in changes up and down in fairly heavy drinking or in psychological dependency on alcohol on the part of 15 per cent of the sample within the brief three-year period covered, and in respondents' reports of past changes in their drinking behavior.

The fact that a fairly large proportion of people go into and out of the heavy-drinking population at frequent intervals would appear to offer frequent opportunities to intervene so as to mobilize the resources of the individual and his environment to bring about improvement. It would appear only common sense to concentrate the intervention process at stages early enough in the development of heavy drinking so that there will still be frequent occasions when the person is sober enough for the intervention process to be effective. If the heavy drinker and the rest of society become alerted to the early signs of overdependence upon alcohol, and if all persons concerned—the heavy drinker, his family and friends, his employer, and social agencies—get to work as early as possible in the process of retraining of attitudes and behavior of all who need it, there will be a material reduction in the prevalence of problems associated with drinking.

Sampling and Field Procedures

The data from this national study of the correlates of problem drinking came from two probability samplings of the U.S. household population of adults, in which a sample of persons who were initially interviewed in 1964–1965 were reinterviewed in 1967. The details of the sampling and data-gathering are presented below.

Stage I of the national survey was carried out through personal interviews conducted between October 1964 and March 1965. The sample was designed to give each person 21 or older living in households within the United States (exclusive of Alaska and Hawaii) an equal representation in the final results. The operations followed established principles for probability sampling throughout all steps: in the selection of one hundred primary sampling units in accordance with the distribution of the population, the prelisting of all households within primary sampling units and the selection of every *n*th household on a random basis by central office personnel rather than by interviewers, and in the selection of the specific adult within the household by use of a table of random numbers specified for the preselected household. Interviews were completed with 2,746 persons, constituting 90 per cent of the eligible stipulated respondents in the occupied selected households after setting aside those ineligible because of extreme senility or illness severe enough to make interviewing impossible. This 90 per cent rate of completion was achieved through repeated visits of interviewers and supervisors, telephone calls, and letters from the home office whenever refusals were encountered. It should be noted that the sample was designed to represent the total adult *household* population. Consequently, institutions and rooming houses and transient facilities were excluded from the sample.

All interviewers were personally trained and supervised either by members of the home office staff or by one of twenty regional supervisors. All of the interviewers were non-abstainers, it having been found in prior studies (Kirsch, Newcomb, and Cisin, 1965; Mulford and Miller, 1960) that abstaining interviewers tend to get a lower proportion of drinkers and heavy drinkers than is true for non-abstainers. All initial interviewing assignments were given to male interviewers, it having been found in the earlier Richmond pilot study (Kirsch, Newcomb, and Cisin, 1965) that male respondents (who include most of the heavy drinkers) tend to be less likely to reveal the true extent of their drinking to women interviewers. In a few instances where a selected respondent (almost always a woman) refused to be interviewed when the male interviewer called, interviews were later completed by women interviewers or supervisors.

Since the primary purpose of Stage II, the 1967 follow-up survey, was to measure the correlates of problem drinking, in the interest of sampling efficiency abstainers and very infrequent drinkers (as ascertained in Stage I) were subsampled at a lesser rate than those who had reported themselves in the first survey as usually drinking at least once a month. The responses for those who were subsampled were later weighted in proportion to their numbers in the initial survey, for the purpose of projecting the Stage II findings against the total U.S. adult population. The subsampling process was carried out as follows.

First, among the abstainers (those who were drinking not at all or less than once a year at Stage I), all those who said they *used to* drink at least once a year were included in the eligibles for the Stage II interview. All of the remaining male current abstainers (113) were retained in order to maintain statistical reliability; but because there were many more women who had never drunk, only one-fifth of these (or 103) were selected for reinterview. Second, among the very infrequent drinkers at Stage I (those who drank less than once a month but at least once a year), all of the males (121) and one-half of the females (142) were selected for Stage II. Third, among the light drinkers at Stage I (typically, those drinking about once or twice a week but as many as five drinks only "once in a while"), half of the males (162) and half the females (221) were selected. Fourth, all persons above the "light" category were included in the eligibles for Survey II. This subsampling process yielded 1,810 persons eligible for the Stage II reinterview.

The field work in Stage II was carried out in accordance with the standards used in the initial survey. One hundred twenty interviewers were utilized, all of whom (as in Stage I) were non-abstainers. The 103 male interviewers conducted all the interviews except for the small number of respondents (mostly women) who refused to be interviewed by the assigned male interviewer and who were finally interviewed by a female interviewer-supervisor. Interviewers were not informed of respondents' answers on drinking questions in the earlier survey. The 1,359 interviews were completed during the period from April to October of 1967.

The outcome of the field work for Stage II is shown in Table A-1. Many special procedures were resorted to in order to achieve the completion rate of 80 per cent of those eligible for reinterviewing, including the following: personal letters to recalcitrant respondents, soliciting their cooperation; use of city directories to trace respondents who had moved; repeated visits to the old address, and checks with neighbors and relatives; inquiries made of employers or former employers and public agencies (for example, welfare offices); checks of forwarding addresses left with post offices; special delivery letters wherever there appeared to be any possibility of delivery; and Retail Credit Bureau checks for those for whom no current address could be found.

A word about *statistical significance* is in order here. This book contains many hundreds of explicit or implicit comparisons of findings for various subgroups—men as compared to women, upper socioeconomic status as compared to lower, younger persons as compared to older, and so on. Since the sample used in this national survey was a probability sample (scientifically random) of the household population, all of the findings can be subjected to tests of statistical significance. These statistical tests are not presented here, however, both be-

Table A-1. Sample Completion Rates for Stage II Interviews

	N	Unweighted Per Cent	Weighted[a] Per Cent
Reinterviewed	1,359	75	75
Excluded from the base because not part of normal household population			
Deceased since initial interview	52	3	3
Institutionalized or too ill or senile to be interviewed	29	2	1
Absent from the 48 states during time of survey	34	2	2
Total ineligibles	115	7	6
Refused or unusable partial interview	218	12	13
Unusable interview because with wrong person (was established that either the Stage I interview was not with person selected according to specifications, or that the Stage II interview was not with same individual interviewed in Stage I)	29	2	2
Not found or never home after repeated calls	89	5	5
Eligible but not interviewed	336	19	20
Total selected for reinterview	1,810	101[b]	101[b]
Base of eligible respondents (selected minus ineligibles)	1,695		
Completion rate among those eligible	80%		

[a] Weighted to give equal representation to all adults in the household, and to compensate for planned undersampling of those found to be light drinkers or abstainers at Stage I. All other tables in this book present *percentages* that are weighted accordingly, for projection against the U.S. household population. The numbers of interviews (N) are given in unweighted form, to permit computation of statistical reliabilities.

[b] Percentages add up to 101 because of rounding.

cause they would clutter up the text and because other important criteria—including independent corroboration of findings from other sources within the same survey, or replications from other surveys—have been used in commenting about the implications of discerned differences.

The following summary table, Table A-2, is provided for those who wish to perform an approximate test of the statistical significance

Table A-2. APPROXIMATE SAMPLING TOLERANCES FOR DIFFERENCES BETWEEN TWO SURVEY PERCENTAGES AT OR NEAR THESE LEVELS

Size of Samples Compared	10% or 90%	20% or 80%	30% or 70%	40% or 60%	50%
750 and 750	4%	5%	6%	6%	6%
and 500	4	6	6	7	7
and 250	5	7	8	9	9
and 100	8	10	12	13	13
500 and 500	5	6	7	8	8
and 250	5	8	8	9	9
and 100	8	11	13	14	14
250 and 250	7	8	10	11	11
and 100	9	12	13	14	14
100 and 100	10	14	16	17	17

(95 in 100 Confidence Level)

Adapted, with permission, from a table published by ORC Caravan Surveys, Inc., Princeton, N.J., May 1965. The effect of clustering (selecting respondents in groups within primary sampling units) is taken into account in the formula used.

of the difference between any two percentages presented in this book. An illustration of the use of the statistical significance table is as follows: in Table 1 in the text it was noted that 15 per cent of the 751 men had a Current Problems Score of seven or more points, as compared to 4 per cent among the 608 women in the national survey. Extrapolating among the first two columns of the significance table, it is seen that for sample sizes of approximately 500 to 750 and percentages ranging from about 10 to 20 per cent, the difference would have to be above 6 per cent to be statistically significant (applying the standard of 95 chances in 100). The observed difference of 11 percentage points thus is found to be statistically significant at the .05 level.

Two questions of concern to sampling methodologists and those who utilize data from panel or longitudinal studies are: what is an adequate completion rate for reinterviews, and what are the potential consequences of bias as a consequence of attrition after two waves of interviewing? One criterion for completion rates is a normative one—what other researchers have been able to achieve in completion rates. Another criterion is that of potential bias—how much could results be affected by attrition. These two criteria will be discussed in turn.

As for comparative completion rates: as stated above, this two-stage study resulted in a completion rate of 80 per cent of the selected persons who were eligible for reinterview. This constitutes 75 per cent of persons initially selected for reinterview (including persons later found to be deceased or otherwise ineligible), which, projected against the 90 per cent of eligible households represented in Stage I interviews, yields a net of 67.5 per cent reinterviews among those initially selected for interviews in Stage I. A study by Glock (1952) reports attritions in panel studies ranging from 5 per cent to 40 per cent. In Robins' 30-year study of children referred to St. Louis guidance clinics, interviews were conducted with subjects *or* relatives in 82 per cent of the cases (1966, p. 33); if this St. Louis recovery rate is recomputed on the basis of personal interviews (rather than interviews with relatives or a record of respondent's death), the St. Louis recovery rate would be 76 per cent. Knupfer, Clark, and associates recently conducted a follow-up study on drinking practices in San Francisco, with a completion rate of 77 per cent of those with whom reinterviews were attempted after approximately a three-year period (Clark, 1966, p. 648), and the present writer directed a three-year follow-up in Hartford with an 81 per cent completion rate (1968, p. 169). The national Stage II completion rate of 80 per cent reinterviews with eligible respondents thus is consistent with the completion rates in the St. Louis and San Francisco studies. It appears that the 80 per cent completion rate represents about the maximum which can be achieved in a three-year national follow-up study at the present state of field techniques, because many weeks were consumed in getting the last few interviews:

the field work was not drawn to a close until every available clue to missing persons' whereabouts had been pursued and until all persons who refused were sought out by supervisors and every effort made to persuade them to cooperate in the study.

Assuming that it is well-nigh impossible to achieve completion rates of better than about two-thirds to three-fourths of persons initially selected for interview in a two-stage longitudinal study with a three-year span, it is readily seen that attrition over even a short time span holds the potential for injecting a serious bias in a study of drinking behavior. Bias from attrition could affect either the aggregate findings (such as the proportion of drinkers or problem drinkers) or the interrelationship between variables (such as the correlations between attitudinal and behavioral variables and drinking behavior). The issue of bias of nonresponse could be crucial in a field of study such as drinking behavior, where a differential rate of heavy drinking might be expected between those easier or more difficult to interview, and where a differential rate of mortality among heavier and lighter drinkers might be assumed.

Fortunately, we are able to make a number of comparisons of reinterviewees and non-reinterviewees to assess some components of potential bias which might have arisen from not interviewing everyone who was selected for reinterview. Obviously, it is impossible to establish from the Stage II data whether the drinking behavior at Stage II of Stage I respondents who were not reinterviewed in Stage II differed from those who were reinterviewed. However, it is possible to estimate the probable extent of bias in non-reinterviewing by analyzing the differences at Stage I between those who were later reinterviewed and those who were not. These differences were examined for 63 items, comparing the responses of those who were reinterviewd against three groups of non-reinterviewees (those who had died, those who refused to be reinterviewed, and those unavailable for other reasons).

The two principal implications of this comparison of respondents and non-respondents to Stage II on 63 items are as follows. First, on comparison of this broad range of demographic characteristics, measures of attitudes and personality traits, and behavior and attitudes related to drinking, there is no indication that failure to reinterview 100 per cent (rather than 80 per cent) of the respondents to the initial survey injected any material bias. Second, although the net effect of the attrition appears to have been small, comparing the various groups of non-respondents points up the potential dangers of bias which might ensue *if* the rate of attrition were much greater.

In comparison to the 1,359 who were reinterviewed, the 451 who were *not* reinterviewed were slightly higher in percentages of persons whose Stage I status was as follows. Age 60 and older (27 per cent for non-respondents versus 18 per cent for respondents): much of the attrition of those 60 and older was attributable to death. Not married (71 per cent versus 81 per cent): the unmarried consisted in part of those who were single (and thus more mobile and harder to find for reinterview) and in part of widowed persons (more of whom died in the interim between the Stage I and Stage II interviews). Scoring higher on rigidity scale among the non-reinterviewed (51 per cent with a score of 3 or higher, v. 41 per cent for respondents): much of this difference is attributed to the older age of the non-reinterviewed respondents. More non-reinterviewees (16 per cent) than others (11 per cent) had been "heavy" drinkers on the quantity-frequency-variability scale used in the Stage I survey (Cahalan, Cisin, and Crossley, 1969, p. 12).

Although these few differences between those who were reinterviewed and those who were unavailable are of methodological interest because they demonstrate the need for continued vigilance in obtaining the highest possible completion rates in order to avoid bias, the differences were found not to be of any practical consequence in this particular study.

A comparison was made of reinterviewees to those lost through death between the time of the Stage I and II interviews. Fifty-two respondents died between the Stage I interview and the scheduled Stage II attempt at interview. Loss of these persons through death over the approximately three years between Stages I and II could have little practical effect on the findings of the Stage II survey, for the 52 interviews constituted only 3 per cent of the 1,810 persons selected for the Stage II reinterview sample. However, a comparison of data obtained on these 52 dead respondents (in Stage I) to Stage I data obtained on the 1,359 who were reinterviewed on Stage II is of interest for two reasons. One is that a comparison can provide us with some clues as to the short-term mortality rates for heavier as against lighter drinkers. Another utility is a general methodological interest (tangential to the purpose of the present study) in the social-psychological characteristics of those who drop out of a sample because of death: for example, Riegel, Riegel, and Meyer (1967) in a recent German longitudinal study of elderly respondents, found that those who were lost from the sample because of death tended to be more alienated, maladjusted, withdrawn from society, and depressed than were those who did not drop out because of death. Accordingly, some key comparisons were made of those who died and those who were reinterviewed, first as regards drinking behavior, and second as regards demographic and social-psychological characteristics, with results summarized below.

A higher proportion of those who died were abstainers (40 per cent versus 33 per cent); this is attributed in large part to the fact that two-thirds of those who died were sixty years of age or older. Despite the high proportion of abstainers, however, a somewhat higher proportion of those who died exhibited signs of being heavy drinkers (started drinking before the age of eighteen, scoring as "heavy" drinkers on the quantity-frequency-variability scale and as high volume and high maximum-per-sitting on the volume-variability index, and drinking for "escape" reasons).

In demographic characteristics, relative to those who were interviewed in both Stages I and II of the longitudinal study, those who died between the two stages had a larger proportion of men, older persons, big-city residents, those of lower socioeconomic status, respondent being the main earner in the family (which was partially a function of a higher rate of unmarrieds among those who died), and of characteristics correlated with higher age and lower socioeconomic status—such as lower education and lower income. As regards social-psychological characteristics, fewer of those who died had rated the year preceding the Stage I interview as being a "good" year for them or rated their own health as "excellent"; and more of them had been hospitalized within the year prior to the Stage I interview. Consistent with their greater average age, more of those who died rated high on the rigidity, alienation, and religious fundamentalism scales, and lower on an impulsivity scale. The comparisons of those who died between the two interviews as against those interviewed in both surveys thus are consistent with the Riegel, Riegel, and Myer study, even though that study was conducted on the quite different population of aged people in Germany. The German study and this national U.S. study were consistent in finding that those who died were in poorer health and spirits, were more rigid, and were more alienated and withdrawn from society than those who survived and were reinterviewed.

Again, these differences are of little practical consequence for the present short-term study of changes in drinking behavior, because such a small proportion of the total died during the approximately three years between the Stage I and Stage II interviews. However, as stated earlier, the direction of the finding is such that they have implications for future research on the possible causal connections between negative attitudes, rigidity, and alienation and subsequent mortality rates; and they point up the potential bias in a sample which is subject to mortality over a long period of years. Obviously, for longer-term longitudinal studies of drinking practices and associated behavior, provisions will need to be made for compensating for such attritional biases, through a combination of introducing fresh subsamples at intervals to replace those lost through death (or other causes) and of holding constant the factor of age and other correlates of early morbidity in the analysis of the data.

B Publications

*E*xcept as indicated below, single copies of any publication are available without charge from the Social Research Group (Western Office), 2180 Milvia Street, Berkeley, California 94704. Materials listed as out of print are available at cost of xeroxing. The samples on which the publications are based are described at the end of this section.

BOOKS, MONOGRAPHS, AND THESES

CAHALAN, D. *Correlates of Change in Drinking Behavior in an Urban Community Sample over a Three-Year Period.* Unpublished doctoral dissertation, The George Washington University, 1968. Hartford I and Hartford II data; available for purchase from University Microfilms, Ann Arbor, Michigan, 48106.

CAHALAN, D., CISIN, I. H., AND CROSSLEY, H. M. *American Drinking Practices: A National Study of Drinking Behavior and Attitudes.* New Brunswick, N.J.: Rutgers Center of Alcohol Studies, 1969. National I data; available for purchase from the Publications Division, Rutgers Center of Alcohol Studies, New Brunswick, N.J. $9.50.

PUBLISHED ARTICLES

KNUPFER, G. "Use of alcoholic beverages by society and its cultural implications," *California's Health, 18*(3) (August 1, 1960), 17–21. Theoretical discussion; presented at a conference on Planning for Alcohol Education, Asilomar, California, Feb. 17–19, 1960.

FINK, R. "A social scientist's view of drinking and driving," *California Alcoholism Review and Treatment Digest, 4*(3) (May–June 1961), pp. 32–33. Theoretical discussion; presented at the annual Northern California Safety Congress, Berkeley, California, April 1961.

CISIN, I. H. "Community studies of drinking behavior," *Annals of the New York Academy of Science, 107*(2) (May 22, 1963), pp. 607–612. Theoretical discussion; presented at a conference on Research Methodology and Potential in Community Health and Preventive Medicine, New York Academy of Sciences, December 1962.

CISIN, I. H. "Social psychological factors in drinking-driving." Pages 1–25 in Bernard H. Fox and James H. Fox, eds., *Alcohol and Traffic Safety* (PHS Publication No. 1043), Bethesda, Md., National Institutes of Health, May 1963. Berkeley 1960 preliminary data; presented at the National Conference on Alcohol and Traffic Safety, Pittsburgh, 1961. Available for purchase from the Superintendent of Documents, Washington, D.C., 20402. $1.75.

CAHALAN, D. "Motivational and educational aspects of drinking-driving." Pages 189–219 in Bernard H. Fox and James H. Fox, eds., *Alcohol and Traffic Safety* (PHS Publication No. 1043), Bethesda, Md., National Institutes of Health, May 1963. Review article; presented at the National Conference on Alcohol and Traffic Safety, Pittsburgh, 1961. Available as for preceding item.

KNUPFER, G. "Wine drinking patterns in the Bay Area," *Bulletin of the Society of Medical Friends of Wine, 6*(2) (September 1964), 4–6. San Francisco 1962 data; presented at the Society's Spring Meeting, May 1964.

KNUPFER, G., AND ROOM, R. "Age, sex, and social class as factors in amount of drinking in a metropolitan community," *Social Problems, 12*(2) (Fall 1964), 224–240. San Francisco 1962 data.

KNUPFER, G. "Female drinking patterns." Pages 140–160 in North American Association of Alcoholism Programs, *Selected Papers Presented at the 15th Annual Meeting, Sept. 27–Oct. 1, 1964.*

Washington, D.C., NAAAP. San Francisco 1964 preliminary data.

FINK, R. "Modifications of alcoholic beverage choice in social and non-social situations," *Quarterly Journal of Studies on Alcohol, 26*(1) (May 1965), 80–94. Oakland, Concord, and Berkeley 1960 data.

KNUPFER, G. "Some methodological problems in the epidemiology of alcoholic beverage usage: the definition of amount of intake," *American Journal of Public Health, 56*(2) (February 1966), 237–242. San Francisco 1962 data.

KNUPFER, G., CLARK, W., AND ROOM, R. "The mental health of the unmarried," *American Journal of Psychiatry, 122*(8) (February 1966), 841–851. San Francisco 1964 data; presented at the 121st Annual Meeting of the American Psychiatric Association, New York City, May 7, 1965.

CLARK, W. "Demographic characteristics of tavern patrons in San Francisco," *Quarterly Journal of Studies on Alcohol, 27*(2) (June 1966), 316–327. San Francisco 1962 data.

CLARK, W. "Operational definitions of drinking problems and associated prevalence rates," *Quarterly Journal of Studies on Alcohol, 27*(4) (December 1966), 648–668. San Francisco 1964 data.

CLARK, W. Appendix to "Operational definitions of drinking problems and associated prevalence rates." Unpublished paper. October 1966.

KNUPFER, G. "The epidemiology of problem drinking," *American Journal of Public Health, 57*(6) (June 1967), 973–986. San Francisco 1964 data; presented at the 94th Annual Meeting of the American Public Health Association, San Francisco, November 2, 1966.

KNUPFER, G. Appendix to "The epidemiology of problem drinking." June 1967.

KNUPFER, G., AND ROOM, R. "Drinking patterns and attitudes of Irish, Jewish, and White Protestant American men," *Quarterly Journal of Studies on Alcohol, 28*(4) (December 1967), 676–699. East Bay 1963 data.

CISIN, I., AND CAHALAN, D. "Comparison of abstainers and heavy drinkers in a national survey." Pages 10–21 in Jonathan O. Cole, ed., *Clinical Research in Alcoholism* (Psychiatric Research Report No. 24), Washington, D.C., American Psychiatric Association, March 1968. National I data; presented at a Research Conference held under the joint auspices of the American Association for the Advancement of Science and the Committee on Research of the American Psychiatric Association, Washington, D.C., December 1966.

CAHALAN, D., AND CISIN, I. H. "American drinking practices: summary of findings from a national probability sample; I. Extent of drinking by population subgroups," *Quarterly Journal of Studies on Alcohol, 29*(1) (March 1968), 130–151. National I data.

ROOM, R. "Cultural contingencies of alcoholism: Variations between and within nineteenth-century urban ethnic groups in alcohol-related death rates," *Journal of Health and Social Behavior 9*(2) (June 1968), 99–113. Mortality data from 1890 for ethnic groups by sex, marital status, and social class.

CAHALAN, D., AND CISIN, I. H. "American drinking practices: Summary of findings from a national probability sample; II. Measurement of massed vs. spaced drinking," *Quarterly Journal of Studies on Alcohol, 29*(3) (September 1968), 642–656. National I data.

KNUPFER, G., AND ROOM, R. "Abstainers in a metropolitan community," *Quarterly Journal of Studies on Alcohol, 31*(1) (March 1970), 108–131. San Francisco 1964; presented at the 28th International Congress on Alcohol and Alcoholism, Washington, D.C., September 15–20, 1968.

KNUPFER, G., AND ROOM, R. "Description of personality score construction." Appendix to "Abstainers in a metropolitan community." Unpublished paper. June 1969.

CAHALAN, D. "A multivariate analysis of the correlates of drinking-related problems in a community study." *Social Problems, 17*(2) (Fall 1969), pp. 234–247. Hartford I and II data.

SOCIAL RESEARCH GROUP PROJECT REPORTS

KIRSCH, A. D., NEWCOMB, C. H., AND CISIN, I. H. *An Experimental Study of Sensitivity of Survey Techniques in Measuring Drinking Practices* (Report No. 1), Social Research Group, The George Washington University, Washington, D.C., March 1965. Richmond data. Out of print.

CAHALAN, D., CISIN, I. H., KIRSCH, A. D., AND NEWCOMB, C. H. *Behavior and Attitudes Related to Drinking in a Medium-Sized Urban Community in New England* (Report No. 2), Social Research

Group, The George Washington University, Washington, D.C., March 1965. Hartford I data. Out of print.

CAHALAN, D., CISIN, I. H., AND CROSSLEY, H. M. *American Drinking Practices: A National Survey of Behavior and Attitudes Related to Alcoholic Beverages* (Report No. 3), Social Research Group, The George Washington University, Washington, D.C., June 1967. National I data. Out of print, superseded by Cahalan, Cisin, and Crossley; see under "Books, Monographs, and Theses."

CAHALAN, D. *Correlates of Change in Drinking Behavior in an Urban Community Sample Over a Three-Year Period* (Report No. 4), Social Research Group, The George Washington University, Washington, D.C., March 1968. Hartford I and II data. Out of print; see Cahalan, *Correlates of Change,* under "Books, Monographs, and Theses."

DRINKING PRACTICES STUDY PROJECT REPORTS

KNUPFER, G., with the assistance of E. Lurie. *Characteristics of Abstainers: A Comparison of Drinkers and Non-Drinkers in a Large California City* (Report No. 3 Revised), California Drinking Practices Study, Berkeley, California State Department of Public Health, November 1961. Oakland, Concord, and Berkeley data, 1960.

FINK, R., with the assistance of W. Clark. *Factors Related to Alcoholic Beverage Choice* (Report No. 4), California Drinking Practices Study, Berkeley, California State Department of Public Health, October 1961. Oakland, Concord, and Berkeley 1960 data. Out of print; superseded by R. Fink, "Modifications of alcoholic beverage choice," under "Published Articles."

FINK, R., with the assistance of P. Chroman and W. Clark. *Parental Drinking and Its Impact on Adult Drinkers* (Report No. 5), California Drinking Practices Study, Berkeley, California State Department of Public Health, March 1962. Berkeley 1960 data.

KNUPFER, G., FINK, R., CLARK, W. B., AND GOFFMAN, A. S. Factors Related to Amount of Drinking in an Urban Community (Report No. 6), California Drinking Practices Study, Berkeley, California State Department of Public Health, April 1963. Berkeley 1960 data. [KNUPFER, G., *et al.*] Appendix Tables: Factors Related to Amount of Drinking in an Urban Community, Supplement to Report No. 6. Berkeley 1960 data.

PAPERS

FINK, R. "Survey method in the study of drinking behavior." Methodological discussion of Oakland, Concord, and Berkeley 1960 studies. Presented at the annual meeting of the Society for the Study of Social Problems, Washington, D.C., August 1962.

CISIN, I. H., AND CAHALAN, D. "American drinking practices: some implications for our colleges." National I data. Presented at the Symposium on Alcohol and College Youth, American College Health Association, Lake Tahoe, Calif., June 10, 1965. Out of print.

MONSKY, S. F. "Special problems in interviewing married couples in longitudinal samples." San Francisco 1964 data. Presented at the annual meeting of the Pacific Coast Chapter, American Association for Public Opinion Research, Los Angeles, February 1966.

CISIN, I. H. "Implications of a survey of American drinking practices upon research on drugs." National I data. Presented at the symposium on The Drug Takers, University of California at Los Angeles, June 12, 1966. Out of print.

CISIN, I. H. "Driving after drinking as a social problem." Theoretical discussion. Presented at the Western and Midwest Conferences on Traffic Safety, Albuquerque, N.M., and Minneapolis, Minn., April 19 and 21, 1967. Out of print.

WILLIAMS, J. "Waxing and waning drinkers." San Francisco 1962 and 1964 data, correlates of changes in drinking patterns. Presented at the annual meeting of the Society for the Study of Social Problems, San Francisco, August 27, 1967.

CISIN, I. H. "Alcohol, traffic safety, and the Moebius strip." Theoretical discussion. Presented at the National Safety Congress, Chicago, October 25, 1967. Out of print.

CISIN, I. H., AND CAHALAN, D. "Regional variations in drinking practices." National I data. Presented at the annual meeting of the Southern Sociological Association, Atlanta, April 12, 1968. Out of print.

KNUPFER, G. "The use of psychosomatic symptom lists in mental health surveys." Review article, with San Francisco 1964 data. Presented at the First Annual Meeting of the Society for Epidemiological Research, Washington, D.C., May 10, 1968.

CISIN, I. H., AND CAHALAN, D. "The role alcohol fulfills in our society." National I data. Presented at the Residential Summer Course on

Alcohol and Problems of Addiction, Laurentian University, Sudbury, Ontario, June 3, 1968. Out of print.

CAHALAN, D. "Differences in subgroup drinking patterns in a U.S. national survey." National I data. Presented at the 28th International Congress on Alcohol and Alcoholism, Washington, D.C., September 15–20, 1968. Out of print; see the two published articles by Cahalan and Cisin on American drinking practices.

ROOM, R. "Amount of drinking and alcoholism." San Francisco 1962 and 1964 pilot intake study and 1880's Brooklyn Inebriates Home data; presented at the 28th International Congress on Alcohol and Alcoholism, Washington, D.C., September 15–20, 1968.

BRENNER, B., CISIN, I. H., AND NEWCOMB, C. "Drinking practices and accidental injuries." Data from National I and a telephone reinterview; presented at the annual convention of the Society for the Study of Social Problems, Miami Beach, Florida, August 27–28, 1966. Out of print.

CAHALAN, D. "Multivariate analysis of the correlates of problems related to drinking: Report of a national sample survey." National I and II data; presented at the American Psychological Association national meeting, Washington, D.C., Sept. 1, 1969.

CAHALAN, D. "A National Survey on the Attributes of Problem Drinkers." National I and II data; presented at the 29th International Congress on Alcoholism and Drug Dependence, Sydney, N.S.W., Australia, Feb. 2–14, 1970.

ROOM, R. "Assumptions and Implications of Disease Concepts of Alcoholism." Review article; presented at the 29th International Congress on Alcoholism and Drug Dependence, Sydney, N.S.W., Australia, Feb. 2–14, 1970.

WORKING PAPERS

Papers subsequently published or presented at conferences are listed above under Published Articles and Papers Presented at Conferences and Meetings.

KNUPFER, G., *et al.* "Approaches to the prediction of future problem drinking." Working Paper No. 1, 1964. A pilot study using San Francisco pretest data (Berkeley reinterviews), and conceptual materials. Out of print.

KNUPFER, G. "Reciprocal perception of personality traits by married couples." Working Paper No. 2, October 1965. San Francisco 1964 data.

CLARK, W. "Notes on anomie: 1897–1959." Working Paper No. 3, October 1965. Review article.

ROOM, R. "Data and assumptions in prior surveys of alcoholics and alcoholism." Working Paper No. 6, August 1966. Review article, data collected from studies of drinking histories of alcoholics and community surveys.

LEACH, E. "Impressions of the character of the Irish, of the Irish-Americans, and of the Jewish-Americans." Working Paper No. 7, March 1964. A survey of literary works.

FINK, R. "A report on the relationship between change on 'invariant' items and change on six measures of drinking." Working Paper No. 9, August 1966. San Francisco 1962 and 1964 data.

ROOM, R. "Notes on 'Identifying problem drinkers in a household health survey' by Harold Mulford and Ronald Wilson." Working Paper No. 10, November 1966. Methodological discussion of problem drinking indicators.

KNUPFER, G. "Abstainers." Working Paper No. 14, February 1964. Oakland, Concord, Berkeley 1960, San Francisco 1962 data. Originally prepared for Jellinek's projected Encyclopedia of Problems of Alcohol.

KNUPFER, G. "The use of longitudinal studies in alcoholism research." Working Paper No. 15, November 1963. Review article. Originally prepared for Jellinek's projected Encyclopedia of Problems of Alcohol.

CLARK, W. "Sex roles and alcoholic beverage usage." Working Paper No. 16, June 1964. San Francisco 1962 data.

KNUPFER, G., AND KANTOR, R. E. "Personality traits and life styles in three American ethnic groups: Irish, Jews, and White Protestants." Working Paper No. 19, January 1968. East Bay 1963 data.

ROOM, R., AND HALL, A. "Do San Franciscans drink more?" Working Paper No. 20, January 1968. San Francisco 1962 data, compared with urban data from National I.

The following data were collected by the Social Research Group and Drinking Practices Study. All of this research has been supported by grants from the National Institute of Mental Health. All questionnaires can be purchased from Research Reference Files, Committee on Drinking Behavior, SSSP, c/o Dept. of Sociology, Eastern Washington State College, Cheney, Washington.

PRELIMINARY STUDIES

Oakland 1960. 173 interviews with men from a selection of middle-class neighborhoods in Oakland, California. The form and order of questionnaire items were varied experimentally. (RRF #907B)

Concord 1960. 249 interviews with men from a selection of middle-class tracts around Concord, California. The form and order of questionnaire items were varied experimentally. (RRF #907B)

East Bay 1963. 755 mail questionnaires returned from East Bay Irish, Jewish, and white Protestant respondents; conducted summer 1963. (RRF #909B, $1.05)

Richmond 1963. 162 interviews with criterion respondents (registrants at an alcoholic clinic) and a matching control group, in Richmond, Virginia. Experimental study; conducted February–March 1963.

COMMUNITY STUDIES

Berkeley 1960. 560 interviews forming a probability sample of the adult population of Berkeley, California; conducted in late 1960. (RRF #907A, $1.50)

San Francisco 1962. 1268 interviews forming a probability sample of the adult population of San Francisco, California; conducted in early 1962. (RRF #909A, $2.55)

San Francisco 1964. 970 interviews with a selected sample of San Francisco 1962 respondents and their spouses; conducted in late 1963 and early 1964. (RRF #909B, $3.30)

San Francisco 1967. 786 interviews with a new sample of San Francisco men ages twenty-one to fifty-nine; conducted in late 1967 and early 1968. (RRF #923, $32.20)

Hartford I. 433 interviews with probability sample of adults in Hartford and West Hartford, Connecticut. Conducted January through April 1964.

Hartford II. 325 reinterviews with respondents initially interviewed in 1964. Conducted fall 1966 and spring 1967.

NATIONAL STUDIES

National I. 2,746 interviews with probability sample of adults representative of adult household population of the U.S., exclusive of Hawaii and Alaska. Conducted in late 1964 and early 1965. (RRF #918, $1.65)

National II. 1,359 reinterviews with subsample of respondents initially interviewed in 1964–1965 national survey. Conducted March through October 1967.

National III. 978 interviews within a new probability sample of U.S. men ages twenty-one to fifty-nine; completed late 1969.

Bibliography

ABU-LABAN, B., AND LARSEN, D. E. "The Qualities and Sources of Norms and Definitions of Alcohol." *Sociology and Social Research,* 1968, *53,* 34–43.

ALLPORT, G. W. Review of *The American Soldier. Journal of Abnormal and Social Psychology,* 1950, *45,* 172. Cited by H. Hyman, *Survey Design and Analysis.* New York: Free Press, 1955. Pp. 257–258.

ALLPORT, G. W. *Personality and Social Encounter.* Boston: Beacon, 1960.

ANANT, S. "A Note on the Treatment of Alcoholics by a Verbal Aversion Technique." *Canadian Psychologist,* 1967, *8,* 19–22.

ARMSTRONG, J. D. "The Search for the Alcoholic Personality." *The Annals of the American Academy of Political and Social Science,* 1958, *315,* 40–47.

ARMSTRONG, J. D. "Psychiatric Theories of Alcoholism." *Canadian Psychiatric Association Journal,* 1961, *6,* 140–148.

AUSUBEL, D. P. *Drug Addiction: Physiological, Psychological, and Sociological Aspects.* New York: Random House, 1958.

BACON, S. D. "Social Settings Conducive to Alcoholism." *Journal of the American Medical Association,* 1957, *164,* 177–186.

BAILEY, M. B. "Some Issues in Epidemiologic Surveys of Alcoholism." Paper presented at the annual meeting, American Public Health Association, Epidemiology Section, San Francisco, November 1966.

BAILEY, M. B., HABERMAN, P. W., AND ALKSNE, H. "The epidemiology of alcoholism in an urban residential area." *Quarterly Journal of Studies on Alcohol,* 1965, *26,* 19–40.

BALES, R. F. The 'fixation factor' in alcohol addiction: An hypothesis derived from a comparative study of Irish and Jewish social norms. Unpublished dissertation, Harvard University, 1944.

BANDURA, A. *Principles of Behavior Modification.* New York: Holt, Rinehart and Winston, 1969.

BELSON, W. A. "Measuring the effects of television: A description of Method." *Public Opinion Quarterly,* 1958, *22,* 11–18.

BELSON, W. A. "Matching and prediction on the principle of biological classification." *Applied Statistics,* 1959, *8,* 65–75.

BLACHLY, P. H. Seduction as a conceptual model in the drug dependencies. Paper presented in part at the 31st annual meeting of the Committee on Problems of Drug Dependence, Division of Medical Sciences, National Academy of Sciences and National Research Council, Palo Alto, California, February 26, 1969.

BLANE, H. T. "Attitudes, treatment, and prevention." In Mendelson, J. H. (Ed.). *Alcoholism.* Boston: Little, Brown & Co., 1966. Pp. 103–126. (International Psychiatry Clinics, V. 3, No. 2, Summer 1966).

BLANE, H. T., OVERTON, W. F., AND CHAFETZ, M. E. "Social factors in the diagnosis of alcoholism. I. Characteristics of the patient." *Quarterly Journal of Studies on Alcohol,* 1963, *24,* 640–663.

BLOCK, J. *The Challenge of Response Sets: Unconfounding Meaning, Acquiescence, and Social Desirability in the MMPI.* New York: Appleton Century Crofts, 1965.

BLUM, R. H. (assisted by Lauraine Braunstein). "Mind altering drugs and dangerous behavior: Alcohol." In Appendix B, *Task force report: Drunkenness.* The President's Commission on Law Enforcement and Administration of Justice. Washington, D.C.: Government Printing Office, 1967, pp. 29–49.

BOALT, G., JONSSON, E., AND SNYDER, C. Alcohol and alienation. Paper presented at the 28th International Congress on Alcohol and Alcoholism, Washington, D.C., September 15–20, 1968.

BOWMAN, K. M., AND JELLINEK, E. M. "Alcohol addiction and its treatment." *Quarterly Journal of Studies on Alcohol,* 1941, *2,* 98–172. Cited by H. M. Trice, "Alcoholism: group factors in etiology and therapy," *Human Organization,* 1956, *15,* 34.

CAHALAN, D. Correlates of change in drinking behavior in an urban community sample over a three-year period. Unpublished dissertation, The George Washington University, 1968.

CAHALAN, D., AND CISIN, I. H. "American drinking practices: summary of findings from a national probability sample: II. Measurement of massed vs. spaced drinking." *Quarterly Journal of Studies on Alcohol,* 1968, *29,* 642–656.

CAHALAN, D., CISIN, I. H., AND CROSSLEY, H. M. *American Drinking Practices: A National Survey of Behavior and Attitudes.* Monograph No. 6. New Brunswick, N.J.: Rutgers Center of Alcohol Studies, 1969.

CAHALAN, D., CISIN, I. H., KIRSCH, A. D., AND NEWCOMB, C. *Behavior and Attitudes Related to Drinking in a Medium-sized Urban Community in New England.* Social Research Group, Report No. 2. Washington, D.C.: The George Washington University, 1965.

CAMPBELL, D. T., AND STANLEY, J. C. *Experimental and Quasi-experimental Designs for Research.* Chicago: Rand McNally, 1966. Reprinted from N. L. Gage (Ed.), *Handbook of Research on Teaching.* Chicago: Rand McNally, 1963.

CATANZARO, R. J. "The disease: alcoholism." In R. J. Catanzaro (Ed.), *Alcoholism: The Total Treatment Approach.* Springfield, Ill.: Charles C. Thomas, 1968, pp. 5–25.

CAUTELA, R. R. "Covert sensitization." *Psychological Reports,* 1967, *20,* 459–468.

CHAFETZ, M. E. "Alcohol excess." *Annals of the New York Academy of Sciences,* 1966, *133,* Art. 3, 808–813.

CISIN, I. H. "Community studies of drinking behavior." *Annals of the New York Academy of Sciences,* 1963, *107,* Art. 2, 607–612.

CISIN, I. H., AND CAHALAN, D. "Comparison of abstainers and heavy drinkers in a national survey." In J. O. Cole (Ed.), *Clinical Research in Alcoholism.* Psychiatric Research Report No. 24. Washington, D.C.: American Psychiatric Association, 1968, pp. 10–21.

CLARK, W. Sex roles and alcoholic beverage usage. Drinking Practices Study, Working Paper No. 16. Berkeley: Mental Research Institute, June 1964.

CLARK, W. Operational definitions of drinking problems and associated prevalence rates. *Quarterly Journal of Studies on Alcohol,* 1966, *27,* 648–668.

CLOWARD, R., AND OHLIN, L. E. *Delinquency and opportunity.* New York: Free Press, 1960.

CONGER, J. J. "Reinforcement theory and the dynamics of alcoholism." *Quarterly Journal of Studies on Alcohol,* 1956, *17,* 296–305.

DE LINT, J. E. E. "The position of early parental loss in the etiology of alcoholism." *Alcoholism: Journal on Alcohol and Alcoholism* (Zagreb), 1966, *2,* 56–64.

DREW, L. R. H. "Alcoholism as a self-limiting disease." *Quarterly Journal of Studies on Alcohol,* 1968, *29,* 956–967.

EKHOLM, A. A study of the drinking rhythm of Finnish males. Paper presented at the 28th International Congress on Alcohol and Alcoholism, Washington, D.C., September 15–20, 1968.

FERGUSON, F. N. "Navaho drinking: some tentative hypotheses." *Human Organization,* 1968, *27,* 159–167.

FERSTER, C. B., NURNBERGER, J. I., AND LEVITT, E. B. "The control of eating." *The Journal of Mathetics,* 1962, *1,* 87–109.

FIELD, P. B. "A new cross-cultural study of drunkenness." In D. J. Pittman and C. R. Snyder (Eds.), *Society, Culture, and Drinking Patterns.* New York: Wiley, 1962, pp. 48–74.

FINK, R. "Modification of alcoholic beverage choice in social and nonsocial situations." *Quarterly Journal of Studies on Alcohol,* 1965, *26,* 80–94.

FLANAGAN, J. C. "The critical incident technique." *Psychological Bulletin,* 1954, *51,* 327–358.

GIBBINS, R. J. The fate of a natural alcoholic population over a ten year period. Paper presented at the 28th International Congress on Alcohol and Alcoholism, Washington, D.C., September 15–20, 1968.

GLAD, D. D. "Attitudes and experiences of American-Jewish and American-Irish male youth as related to differences in adult rates of inebriety." *Quarterly Journal of Studies on Alcohol,* 1947, *8,* 406–472.

GLATT, M. M., AND HILLS, D. R. "Alcohol abuse and alcoholism in the young." *British Journal of Addiction,* 1968, *63,* 183–191.

GLOCK, C. Y. Participation bias and reinterview effect in panel studies. Unpublished dissertation, Columbia University, 1952.

GRAVES, THEODORE D. "Acculturation, access, and alcohol in a tri-ethnic community." *American Anthropologist,* 1967, *69,* 306–321.

GUILFORD, J. P., AND ZIMMERMAN, W. S. *Guilford-Zimmerman Temperament Survey.* Beverly Hills, Calif.: Sheridan Supply Co., 1949.

GUSFIELD, J. R. "Status conflicts and the changing ideologies of the American temperance movement." In D. J. Pittman and C. R. Snyder (Eds.), *Society, Culture, and Drinking Patterns.* New York: Wiley, 1962, pp. 101–120.

HABERMAN, P. W. "Psychophysiological symptoms in alcoholics and matched comparison persons." *Community Mental Health Journal,* 1965, *1,* 361–364.

HABERMAN, P. W. "Drinking and other self-indulgences: complements or counter-attractions?" *The International Journal of Addictions,* 1969, *4,* 157–167.

HABERMAN, P. W., AND SHEINBERG, J. "Implicative drinking reported in a household survey." *Quarterly Journal of Studies on Alcohol,* 1967, *28,* 538–543.

HABERMAN, P. W., AND SHEINBERG, J. "Public attitudes toward alcoholism as an illness." *American Journal of Public Health,* 1969, *59,* 1209–1216.

HATHAWAY, S. R., AND MC KINLEY, J. C. *Minnesota Multiphasic Personality Inventory Manual* (revised 1951). New York: The Psychological Corporation, 1951.

HOFF, E. C. The alcoholisms. Paper presented at the 28th International Congress on Alcohol and Alcoholism, Washington, D.C., September 15–20, 1968.

HOLLINGSHEAD, A. B. Two factor index of social position. New Haven: 1957. Mimeographed.

HOLMES, T. H., AND RAHE, R. H. "The social readjustment rating scale." *Journal of Psychosomatic Research,* 1967, *11,* 213–218.

HSU, J. J. "Electroconditioning therapy of alcoholics: a preliminary report." *Quarterly Journal of Studies on Alcohol,* 1965, *26,* 449–459.

JACKSON, J. Social stratification, social norms, and roles. In I. A. Steiner and M. Fishbein (Eds.), *Current Studies in Social Psychology.* New York: Holt, Rinehart, and Winston, 1965, pp. 301–309.

JELLINEK, E. M. "Phases of alcohol addiction." *Quarterly Journal of Studies on Alcohol,* 1952, *13,* 673–684.

JELLINEK, E. M. *The Disease Concept of Alcoholism.* New Brunswick, N.J.: Hillhouse, 1960a.

JELLINEK, E. M. "The problems of alcohol." *Quarterly Journal of Studies on Alcohol,* 1960b, *21,* 187–202. Reprinted from *Alcohol, Science, and Society.* New Haven: *Quarterly Journal of Studies on Alcohol,* 1945, pp. 13–28.

JESSOR, R., GRAVES, T. D., HANSON, R. C., AND JESSOR, S. L. *Society, Personality and Deviant Behavior: A Study of a Tri-ethnic Community.* New York: Holt, Rinehart, and Winston, 1968.

JONES, M. C. "Personality correlates and antecedents of drinking patterns in adult males." *Journal of Consulting and Clinical Psychology,* 1968, *32,* 2–12.

KELLER, M. Documentation of an interdisciplinary field of study: alcohol problems. Paper presented at the 28th International Congress on Alcohol and Alcoholism, Washington, D.C., September 19, 1968.

KELLER, M. "The definition of alcoholism and the estimation of its prevalence." In D. J. Pittman and C. R. Snyder (Eds.), *Society, Culture, and Drinking Patterns.* New York: Wiley, 1962, pp. 310–329.

KILPATRICK, F. P., AND CANTRIL, H. "Self-anchoring scaling, a measure of individuals' unique reality worlds." *Journal of Individual Psychology,* 1960, *16,* 158–173. The Brookings Institution, Reprint No. 47, 1960.

KINSEY, A. C., POMEROY, W. B., AND MARTIN, C. C. *Sexual Behavior in the Human Male.* Philadelphia: Saunders, 1948.

KIRSCH, A. D., NEWCOMB, C. H., AND CISIN, I. H. An experimental study of sensitivity of survey techniques in measuring drinking practices. Social Research Group, Report No. 1. Washington, D.C.: The George Washington University, 1965.

KNIGHT, R. P. "The dynamics and treatment of chronic alcohol addiction." *Bulletin of the Menninger Clinic,* 1937, *1,* 233–250 (a).

KNIGHT, R. P. "The psychodynamics of chronic alcoholism." *Journal of Nervous and Mental Disease,* 1937, *86,* 538–548 (b).

KNUPFER, G. "The epidemiology of problem drinking." *American Journal of Public Health,* 1967, *57,* 973–986.

KNUPFER, G. "Psychosomatic complaints and problem drinking." April 1968. Unpublished paper.

KNUPFER, G. The use of longitudinal studies in alcoholism research. Drinking Practices Study, Working Paper No. 15. Berkeley: State of California, Department of Public Health, November 1963.

KNUPFER, G., AND MONSKY, S. F. The contribution of police and hospital records to the measurement of problem drinking. 1966. Unpublished paper.

KNUPFER, G., AND ROOM, R. "Abstainers in a metropolitan community." *Quarterly Journal of Studies on Alcohol,* 1970, *31,* 108–131.

KNUPFER, G., AND ROOM, R. "Age, sex, and social class as factors in amount of drinking in a metropolitan community." *Social Problems,* 1964, *12,* 224–240.

KNUPFER, G., AND ROOM, R. "Drinking patterns of Irish, Jewish, and white Protestant American men." *Quarterly Journal of Studies on Alcohol,* 1967, *28,* 676–699.

KNUPFER, G., FINK, R., CLARK, W. B., AND GOFFMAN, A. S. *Factors Related to Amount of Drinking in an Urban Community.* Drinking Practices Study, Report No. 6. Berkeley: State of California, Department of Public Health, 1963.

KVARACEUS, W. C., AND MILLER, W. B. *Delinquent Behavior: Culture and the Individual.* Washington, D.C.: National Education Association, 1959.

LANGNER, T. S. "A twenty-two item screening score of psychiatric symptoms indicating impairment." *Journal of Health and Human Behavior,* 1962, *3,* 269–276.

LARSEN, D. E., AND ABU-LABAN, B. "Norm qualities and deviant drinking behavior." *Social Problems,* 1968, *15,* 441–450.

LEMERE, F., AND VOEGTLIN, W. L. "An evaluation of aversion treatment of alcoholism." *Quarterly Journal of Studies on Alcohol,* 1950, *11,* 199–204.

LEVY, R. I. The psychodynamic functions of alcohol. *Quarterly Journal of Studies on Alcohol,* 1958, *19,* 649–659.

LEWIN, K. *A Dynamic Theory of Personality.* New York: McGraw-Hill, 1936.

LINDESMITH, A. R. *Addiction and Opiates.* Chicago: Aldine, 1968.

LIPSCOMB, W. R. Alcoholism—an epidemiological viewpoint. *Excerpta Medica International Congress Series No. 150,* 1415–1417. Proceedings of the Fourth World Congress of Psychiatry, Madrid, September 5–11, 1966.

LOLLI, G., SERIANNI, E., GOLDER, G. M., AND FEGIZ, P. *Alcohol in Italian Culture.* New Brunswick, N.J.: Rutgers Center of Alcohol Studies, 1958.

MAC ANDREW, C., AND EDGERTON, R. B. *Drunken Comportment: a Social Explanation.* Chicago: Aldine, 1969.

MAC ANDREW, C., AND GARFINKEL, H. "A consideration of changes attributed to intoxication as common-sense reasons for getting drunk." *Quarterly Journal of Studies on Alcohol,* 1962, *23,* 252–266.

MADDOX, G. L., AND BORINSKI, E. "Drinking behavior of Negro collegians; a study of selected men." *Quarterly Journal of Studies in Alcohol,* 1964, *25,* 651–668.

MALZBERG, B. *The Alcoholic Psychoses: Demographic Aspects at Midcentury in New York State.* New Haven: Yale Center of Alcohol Studies, 1960.

MALZBERG, B. "Rates of discharge and rates of mortality among first admissions to the New York State civil state hospitals." *Mental Hygiene,* 1953, *38,* 619–654. Cited by Mel Tremper, What happens to alcoholics? Unpublished paper, 1969.

MC BREARTY, J. F., DICHTER, M., GARFIELD, Z., AND HEATH, G. "A behaviorally oriented treatment program for alcoholism." *Psychological Reports,* 1968, *22,* 287–298.

MC CORD, W., AND MC CORD, J. "A longitudinal study of the personality of alcoholics." In D. J. Pittman and C. R. Snyder (Eds.), *Society, Culture, and Drinking Patterns.* New York: Wiley, 1962, pp. 413–430.

MC NEMAR, Q. *Psychological statistics.* 2nd ed. New York: Wiley, 1955.

MENDELSON, J. H., AND STEIN, S. "The definition of alcoholism." In J. H. Mendelson (Ed.), *Alcoholism.* Boston: Little, Brown & Co., 1966, pp. 3–16. International Psychiatry Clinics, V. 3, No. 2, Summer 1966.

MERTON, R. K. *Social Theory and Social Structure.* Glencoe, Ill.: Free Press, 1957.

MIZRUCHI, E. H. Norms, interaction, and drinking behavior. Paper presented at the 62nd annual meeting of the American Sociological Association, San Francisco, August 30, 1967.

MIZRUCHI, E. H., AND PERRUCCI, R. Norm qualities and differential effects of deviant behavior: an exploratory analysis. *American Sociological Review,* 1962, *27,* 391–399.

MULFORD, H. A. "Drinking and deviant drinking, U.S.A., 1963." *Quarterly Journal of Studies on Alcohol,* 1964, *25,* 634–650.

MULFORD, H. A. Meeting the problems of alcohol abuse: a testable action plan for Iowa. Cedar Rapids, Iowa: Iowa Alcoholism Foundation, 1970.

MULFORD, H. A., AND MILLER, D. E. "Drinking in Iowa. II. The extent of drinking and selected sociocultural categories." *Quarterly Journal of Studies on Alcohol,* 1960, *21,* 26–39 (a).

MULFORD, H. A., AND MILLER, D. E. "Drinking in Iowa. IV. Preoccupation with alcohol, heavy drinking, and trouble due to drinking." *Quarterly Journal of Studies on Alcohol,* 1960, *21,* 279–291 (b).

MULFORD, H. A., AND MILLER, D. E. "Public definitions of the alcoholic." *Quarterly Journal of Studies on Alcohol,* 1961, *22,* 312–320.

ORFORD, J. Aspects of the relationship between alcohol and drug abuse. Paper presented at the 29th International Congress on Alcoholism and Drug Dependence, Sydney, February, 1970.

PELZ, D. C., AND ANDREWS, F. M. "Detecting causal priorities in panel study data." *American Sociological Review,* 1964, *29,* 836–848.

PITTMAN, D. J., AND SNYDER, C. R. (Eds.), *Society, Culture, and Drinking Patterns.* New York: Wiley, 1962.

PLAUT, T. F. *Alcohol Problems: A Report to the Nation by the Cooperative Commission on the Study of Alcoholism.* New York: Oxford University Press, 1967.

PLAUT, T. F. "Psycho-social forces and public health problems." *International Journal of Health Education,* 1966, *9,* 3–11.

RAHE, R. H., AND ARTHUR, R. J. "Life-change patterns surrounding illness experience." *Journal of Psychosomatic Research,* 1968, *11,* 341–345.

REINERT, R. E. "The concept of alcoholism as a disease." *Bulletin of the Menninger Clinic,* 1968, *32,* 21–25 (a).

REINERT, R. E. "The concept of alcoholism as a bad habit." *Bulletin of the Menninger Clinic,* 1968, *32,* 25–46 (b).

RIEGEL, K. F., RIEGEL, R. M., AND MEYER, G. "A study of the dropout rates in longitudinal research on aging and the prediction of death." *Journal of Personality and Social Psychology,* 1967, *5,* 342–348.

RILEY, J. W., MARDEN, C. F., AND LIFSHITZ, M. "The motivational pattern of drinking." *Quarterly Journal of Studies on Alcohol,* 1948, *9,* 353–362.

ROBINS, L. N. *Deviant Children Grown Up.* Baltimore: Williams and Wilkins, 1966.

ROMAN, P. M. Constructive coercion and the "alcoholic": A critique of assumptions. Paper presented at the 28th International Congress on Alcohol and Alcoholism, Washington, D.C., September 15–20, 1968.

ROMAN, P. M., AND TRICE, H. M. "Alcoholism and problem drinking as social roles: the effects of constructive coercion." Paper presented at the 17th annual meeting of the Society for the Study of Social Problems, San Francisco, August 27, 1967.

ROOM, R. Assumptions and implications of disease concepts of alcoholism. Paper presented at the 29th International Congress on Alcoholism and Drug Dependence, Sydney, February, 1970.

ROSE, A. M. "A social-psychological theory of neurosis." In A. M. Rose (Ed.), *Human Behavior and Social Processes.* Boston: Houghton Mifflin, 1962, pp. 537–549.

ROSEN, A. C. "A comparative study of alcoholic and psychiatric patients with the MMPI." *Quarterly Journal of Studies on Alcohol,* 1960, *21,* 253–266.

ROTTER, J. B. *Social Learning and Clinical Psychology.* New York: Prentice-Hall, 1954.

ROZELLE, R. M., AND CAMPBELL, D. T. "More plausible rival hypotheses in the cross-lagged panel correlation technique." *Psychological Bulletin,* 1969, *71,* 74–80.

RUDIE, R. R., AND MC GAUGHRAN, L. S. "Differences in developmental experience, defensiveness, and personality organization between two classes of problem drinkers." *Journal of Abnormal and Social Psychology,* 1961, *62,* 659–665.

SCOTT, P. D. "Offenders, drunkenness, and murder." *The British Journal of Addiction,* 1968, *63,* 221–226.

SEELEY, J. R. "Alcoholism is a disease: implications for social policy." In D. J. Pittman and C. R. Snyder (Eds.), *Society, Culture, and Drinking Patterns.* New York: Wiley, 1962, pp. 586–593.

SEELEY, J. R. "The W.H.O. definition of alcoholism." *Quarterly Journal of Studies on Alcohol,* 1959, *20,* 352–356.

SEEVERS, M. H. "Pharmacological elements of drug dependence." *Journal of the American Medical Association,* 1968, *206,* 1263–1266.

SKINNER, B. F. *Science and Human Behavior.* New York: Free Press, 1953.

SNYDER, C. R. *Alcohol and the Jews: A Cultural Study of Drinking and Sobriety.* New Brunswick, N.J.: Rutgers Center of Alcohol Studies, 1958.

SNYDER, C. R. "Culture and Jewish sobriety: the ingroup-outgroup factor." In D. J. Pittman and C. R. Snyder (Eds.), *Society, Culture, and Drinking Patterns.* New York: Wiley, 1962, pp. 188–225.

SNYDER, C. R. "Inebriety, alcoholism, and anomie." In M. B. Clinard (Ed.), *Anomie and Deviant Behavior.* New York: Free Press, 1964, pp. 189–212 (a).

SNYDER, C. R. "A sociological view of the etiology of alcoholism." In S. N. Eisenstadt (Ed.), *Comparative Social Problems.* New York: Free Press, 1964, pp. 16–19 (b).

SONQUIST, J. A., AND MORGAN, J. N. *The Detection of Interaction Effects.* Monograph No. 35. Ann Arbor: University of Michigan, Survey Research Center, 1964.

STAR, S. A. "The screening of psychoneurotics in the army: technical development of tests." In S. A. Stouffer, *et al., Measurement and Prediction.* Princeton University Press, 1950, pp. 486–567.

STORM, T., AND SMART, R. G. "Dissociation: a possible explanation of some features of alcoholism and implication for its treatment." *Quarterly Journal of Studies on Alcohol,* 1965, *26,* 111–115.

SUTHERLAND, E. H., AND CRESSEY, D. R. *Principles of Criminology* (5th ed.). New York: Lippincott, 1955.

SWIECICKI, A. The adult adjustment of children from alcoholic and nonalcoholic families. Ten years follow-up study. Paper presented at the 28th International Congress on Alcohol and Alcoholism, Washington, D.C., September 15–20, 1968.

SYME, L. "Personality characteristics of the alcoholic." *Quarterly Journal of Studies on Alcohol,* 1957, *18,* 288–301.

SZASZ, T. S. "Alcoholism: a socio-medical perspective." *Washburn Law Journal,* 1967, *6,* 255–268.

THIMANN, J. "Conditioned reflex treatment of alcoholism. I. Its rationale and technique." *New England Journal of Medicine,* 1949, *241,* 368–370.

TREMPER, M. What happens to alcoholics? Unpublished paper, 1969.

TRICE, H. M. "Alcoholism: group factors in etiology and therapy." *Human Organization,* 1956, *15,* 33–40.

TRICE, H. M. "The job behavior of problem drinkers." In D. J. Pittman and C. R. Snyder (Eds.), *Society, Culture, and Drinking Patterns.* New York: Wiley, 1962, pp. 493–510.

U.S. Supreme Court, *Powell* v. *Texas.* U.S. Supreme Court Reports, Lawyers' Edition, Second Series, October Term, 1967, Volume 20 L Ed. 2d, No. 7, July 25, 1968, pp. 1254–1288.

WEXBERG, L. E. "Alcoholism as a sickness." *Quarterly Journal of Studies on Alcohol,* 1951, *12,* 217–230.

WIKLER, A. "On the nature of addiction and habituation." *British Journal of Addiction,* 1961, *57,* 73–79.

WILLIAMS, A. F. "Epidemiology and ecology of alcoholism." In J. H. Mendelson (Ed.), *Alcoholism.* Boston: Little, Brown & Co., 1966, pp. 17–49. International Psychiatry Clinics, V. 3, No. 2, Summer 1966.

WILLIAMS, A. F. "Self-concepts of college problem drinkers. 1. A comparison with alcoholics." *Quarterly Journal of Studies on Alcohol,* 1965, *26,* 586–594 (a).

WILLIAMS, A. F. "Social drinking, anxiety, and depression." *Journal of Personality and Social Psychology,* 1965, *3,* 689–693 (b).

WILLIAMS, J. Waxing and waning drinkers. Paper presented at the annual meeting of the Society for the Study of Social Problems, San Francisco, August 27, 1967.

WINICK, C. "The life cycle of the narcotic addict and of addiction." United Nations, Department of Economic and Social Affairs, *Bulletin on Narcotics,* 1964, *16,* 1–11.

World Health Organization. Expert Committee on Mental Health, Alcoholism Subcommittee. *Second Report.* W.H.O. Technical Report Series, No. 48, August 1952.

Index

A